GW01017879

ENGLISH FOR NURSING AND HEALTH CAF

A course in general and professional English

ENGLISH FOR NURSING AND HEALTH CARE

A course in general and professional English

Robin A. Bradley

Cartoon Illustrations by
Claudio Bez

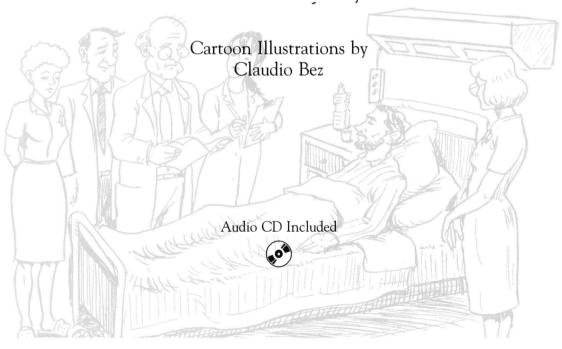

Audio CD Included

McGraw-Hill

Milano • New York • St. Louis • San Francisco • Auckland • Bogotá • Caracas • Lisbon • London •
Madrid • Mexico City • Montreal • New Delhi • San Juan • Singapore • Sydney • Tokyo • Toronto

Copyright © 2004 The McGraw-Hill Companies, srl
Publishing Group Italia
Via Ripamonti, 89 – 20139 Milano
Tel. 02/535718.1 – 02/5397527

McGraw-Hill

A Division of The **McGraw·Hill** Companies

All rights reserved. No part of this pubblication may be reproduced,
stored in a retrieval system, or transmitted in any form or by any means,
electronic, mechanical, photocopying, recording, or otherwise
without the prior permission of McGraw-Hill Companies S.r.l.

Editor: Teresa Massara
Production: Donatella Giuliani
Copyediting and composition: Fotocompos, Gussago (BS)
Printing: Vincenzo Bona, Torino

ISBN 88-386-1647-7
123456789VBNVBN087654

1st Edition: April 2004

CONTENTS

UNIT 1
ENGLISH, THE HOSPITAL AND THE PEOPLE

UNIT 2
THE PATIENT AND THE WARD

VII

Contents

APPENDICES

FOREWORD

Several years ago, as a response to the recent changes in education for trainee nurses and students of other health care professions in Italy, the subject of Scientific English was introduced. Consequently, the nursing school at the "Claudiana College" in Bolzano/Bozen (which is affiliated with the Faculty of Medicine at the University of Verona) was required to include a 50 hour English course in the nursing syllabus.

When it became apparent that there was very little material available for teaching English to students of health care professions, we launched a project to create an English course with contents that would be of use to our students in their future working fields. In collaboration with Robin Bradley, a specialised health care professional herself, and a local school of English in Bolzano/Bozen, material for a module system was compiled and then introduced into the nursing curriculum. Robin Bradley, who has been doing scientific English courses for all the health professionals at our school for more than 15 years, arranged for ten different English teachers (without any prior medical knowledge) to use the modules she had prepared. These modules have now been used to teach Scientific English to more than 650 nursing students over a four year period. During this time, constant feed–back from the students and the teachers, has allowed Ms. Bradley to continually improve the material. The modules have now been completely revised and have become the sections of this book.

Since research and science will become even more important to the nursing profession in the future, greater emphasis will have to be placed on English related to the nurses' training. We hope that this book will be helpful in preparing dedicated young people for their future professional career in other schools as well as at the "Claudiana".

Dr. med. Lukas Lochner   Dr. med. Werner Wallnöfer
(Scientific Tutor)   (Course Director – Nursing)

CLAUDIANA – Provincial Tertiary Training College for Health Care Professions, Bolzano / Bozen , Italy

ABOUT THE AUTHOR

Having done my general nursing training at the Royal North Shore Hospital in Sydney, Australia, and then midwifery at the Royal Women's Hospital in association with the Melbourne University, I had more than 20 years experience working in different medically related environments – general and private hospitals, nursing homes and a medical laboratory before coming to Italy to live. My nursing training was entirely carried out at the hospital at that time – it was a four–year course followed by another year to specialise in midwifery. We worked 'broken shifts' and attended lectures in our 'time off'! – living in the nurses' quarters at the hospital made this possible.

I started teaching general English at English schools in South Tyrol and medical and scientific English to health care professionals at the local hospital in Bolzano/Bozen in Italy in 1989. I am proud of the many students who have followed a medically–related career and are now successfully and happily employed in their chosen field. I have continued to learn from my students and thanks to them, my family, my colleagues and friends – and the librarians and staff at the "Claudiana College", this book, the recordings for the listening exercises and a teachers' manual have become a reality. It has been a challenge from the beginning and after four years, I feel I have produced an interesting and comprehensive course for nurses who want to improve their English language skills both in social situations and at work.

All medically–related professions have become more specialised over the years and methods and equipment used for teaching and working have changed dramatically in the last few decades. The priority in all areas was and is still, the well–being of the patients in our care. We must all take time to discover the 'person behind the patient' and to develop a positive rapport with each and every one. All humans are individuals with specific needs. Illness, disability or disease puts any person at a disadvantage. Hospitalisation can be an intimidating and frightening experience and it is important that all staff personalise their attention to patients to ensure the best possible outcome. Being well–informed and well–prepared for all situations bring multiple benefits to all concerned.

Robin Bradley
SN (Double Cert.) TOEFL (Cambridge)

UNIT

1

ENGLISH
THE HOSPITAL AND THE PEOPLE

WHY IS ENGLISH INCLUDED IN THE NURSING SYLLABUS?

📖 🎧 **Listening 1 – An introduction to a nursing career** *Read the text and listen to the recording*

Nursing is a profession which involves caring and sharing with people from all walks of life.

Care and Empathy are illustrated, by each one of us, through communication and actions.

A good basic education and professional nursing training are tools for an exciting, interesting and rewarding career.

English can widen your horizons tremendously, help to deepen your scientific knowledge and create many other work–related opportunities:

♦ **Internationally.** Most scientific conferences and congresses are now held in English and visiting lecturers, colleagues and tutors often prefer to use English.

♦ **Work Experience.** There is a demand for nurses in every country in the world. Nurses can gain valuable experience by working overseas and also obtain higher qualifications in specialised fields.
Aid–workers are required in war–torn countries and areas of natural disasters.
Work is available for nurses in tourist resorts and health care clinics and even on cruise ships!

♦ **Education.** Surfing the Internet for information and research updates.
Using American and English Medical, Nursing and Scientific Journals – which often take months to be translated.
English documentaries and science programmes on satellite TV.

♦ **Manuals.** Instruction manuals for various machines and instruments are frequently written in English.

♦ **Patient Care.** Patients who cannot communicate their needs to hospital staff are at a distinct disadvantage and very often have a slower recovery rate.
Patients may present case histories or medication details in English.

The services offered by all professions are improved when its members are willing to work together to help each other and when they share their individual knowledge. The amount of study and the depth of knowledge required for health care professions, is steadily increasing and all health care professionals are being given more responsibility for the patients in their care.

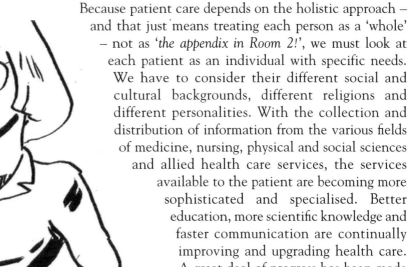

Because patient care depends on the holistic approach – and that just means treating each person as a 'whole' – not as 'the appendix in Room 2!', we must look at each patient as an individual with specific needs. We have to consider their different social and cultural backgrounds, different religions and different personalities. With the collection and distribution of information from the various fields of medicine, nursing, physical and social sciences and allied health care services, the services available to the patient are becoming more sophisticated and specialised. Better education, more scientific knowledge and faster communication are continually improving and upgrading health care. A great deal of progress has been made in surgical, endoscopic, sonographic, radiographic, laser and computer techniques, reducing both the time and cost of surgery and treatment to the general public. The speed at which information can now be transmitted, enables all health care workers to have endless resources 'at their fingertips', and gives everyone the opportunity to 'stay abreast of ' (or 'keep up with') new trends and treatments.

The purpose of this book is to give all those people working in health care systems, enough useful English language to read professional literature, to do research and to communicate successfully in English in their everyday lives. Basic grammar exercises, reading practice and dialogues use relevant vocabulary – and there are exercises to help you increase your knowledge of medical terminology too.

EXPRESSION and WORD LIST   1A

To help you learn the following expressions, they are listed in alphabetical order in groups of nouns (n.), adjectives (adj.) and verbs (v.). All of the words on this page are nouns. A noun followed by (n.) is a countable noun and has a plural form and those that are uncountable (n. uncountable) do not have a plural form and use verbs in the singular form only.

aid [eid] (*n. uncountable*) is money, equipment or services that are provided for people or countries who need it.

an aid worker [eid wɜːkə] (*n.*) is a person, usually working for a charity organisation, who offers his services in other countries.

care [keə] (*n. uncountable*) Looking after somebody or something and keep them in a good state or condition.

health care [heiθ keə] (*n. uncountable*) refers to all the areas related to medicine and the attention to individual well–being.

patient [peiʃ'ənt] **care** (*n. uncountable*) refers to all areas involved – mental, physical and psychological – in looking after a patient.

career [kə'riə] (*n.*) A career is the job or profession that someone does for a long period of their life.

A **rewarding** [ri'wɔːdiŋ] **career** is stimulating and brings job satisfaction and/or benefits.

clinic [klinik] (n.) A clinic is a building where people go to receive medical advice or treatment.

empathy [empəθi] (n. uncountable) The ability to share another person's feelings and emotions as if they were yours.

environment [en'vairən'mənt] (n. uncountable) the physical world in which people, animals and plants live.

health [helθ] (n. uncountable) is the condition of the human body and the extent to which it is free from illness or can resist illness.

lecturer [lek'tʃə'rə] (n.) A teacher at a university or college.

   visiting lecturers (adj. + n.) Teachers who come from other universities or colleges on a temporary basis.

opportunity [ɒpə'tjuːnə'ti] (n.) An opportunity is a situation in which it is possible for you to do something that you want to do.

   work related opportunities (adj. + n.) Different situations or areas where you can work in your chosen field.

personnel [pɜsə'nel] (n.pl.) The people who work for an organisation (or the armed forces).

professional [prə'feʃə'nl] (n.) A Professional is a person who has a job that requires advanced education or training.

rate [reit] (n.) The rate, is the speed or the amount of time it takes for something to happen.

recovery [ri'kʌvri] (n. uncountable) If a sick person makes a recovery, he or she gets well (returns to good health).

relationship [rə'leiʃən'ʃip] (n.) The way in which two people, groups or countries behave towards each other.

skill [skil] (n.) A skill is a type of work or activity which requires special training and knowledge.

staff [staːf] (n.pl.) The staff of an organisation are the people who work for it.

   hospital staff/personnel (n. pl.) are the people who work for that hospital.

surgery ['sɜːdʒəri] (n.) Medical treatment that involves cutting open the body and often removing or replacing parts.

syllabus [silə'bəs] (n.) The subjects studied in a particular course.

   nursing syllabus The subjects included in the nursing degree (university) course.

tool [tuːl] (n.) A tool is any hand–held instrument or simple piece of equipment you need to do your job properly.

   the tools of your trade are the skills or abilities, instruments or equipment you need to be able to do your job properly.

training [treiniŋ] (n. uncountable) Training is learning the skills for a particular profession or activity.

   Nursing training is the course you do while learning the skills and theory to become a professional nurse.

workers [wɜːkəz] (n. pl.) Particular people who do the kind of work mentioned.

☺ *With all the students in the class, read this list of new words out loud, paying attention to your pronunciation. Now, work with a partner: say a word and ask your partner for a suitable definition.*

INTRODUCING YOURSELF AND HOSPITAL STAFF

Hello Annie! We were expecting you to join us today. I'm a Staff Nurse here in the Surgical Ward at the Royal General Hospital. I finished my training 2 years ago in Australia and love working here. My name is Rosie and I'd like to introduce you to a few of my colleagues…

In this ward, Sister Pat is the Ward Charge Nurse and Mr. James is our Head Consultant and surgeon. Dr. Singh is the Senior House Officer and I'll introduce you to some of the others soon. We work with all the other health care workers in the hospital, that is, the physiotherapists, the occupational therapists, the dieticians and many others. Firstly, this is Sandra…

She has been here longer than me… Hi Sandra! I'd like to introduce you to Anna Kennedy, she is starting her work experience today….

How can I remember who everyone is?
I hope I say the right things...
This is Rosie – she's a Senior Staff Nurse,

Dr. Singh is...............................
What is the Consultant's name?

....
I'm going to meet the Charge Nurse soon, her name's............... Oh! This is Sandra, she's a staff nurse too.

Introducing Yourself, Friends and Colleagues

Formal:	How do you do?		*How do you do?*
	May I introduce you to........?	..........this is..............	*It's a pleasure to meet you.*
	I'd like to introduce you to...........		*It's a pleasure to meet you.*
	Have you met......................?		*No, I haven't … It's a pleasure …*
	Good morning. My name is............		
	Excuse me. Are you...............?		
	I'm sorry, I didn't hear your name.		
Less Formal:	Hello (or Hi!)		
	Do you know ....?	..........this is................	*Nice to meet you.*
	I don't think we've met. I'm...............		
	Hello. Are you........................?		

PRONUNCIATION AND PHONETICS

Medical and technical words are similar in most languages, but the pronunciation is very different!

Correct pronunciation will make a big difference in the understanding of spoken English.

Understanding the phonetic symbols helps the student learn new words and the English pronunciation from dictionaries and to gradually build up a good general and medical vocabulary. More importantly these new words can be readily understood.

Phonetic symbols in English are divided into Consonant sounds, Vowel sounds and Diphthongs (which are two vowel sounds together). *Study the Phonetics Reference in Appendix 6.*

It isn't necessary to memorise all the symbols but reference to the table and practice, will help you recognise them in dictionaries and work easily through this book.

"SCHWA": [ə] 'Schwa' (number 12 on the reference chart) is the most important vowel sound in English (but it is very different because it often replaces any of the other vowel sounds in the English language). It is used in syllables of words where there is no emphasis. The following exercises will help you to understand this.

☺ **1. Look at the following words and decide on the correct pronunciation with a partner. Where is the main emphasis – Is it on the first or the second syllable of the word?**

about   pocket   pupil   apron   circus

🖉 *Mark the strong syllable with a dot (ˈ) on the top. Now, practice saying the words and put a circle around the other vowel(s) in the word. Which letters are <u>not</u> emphasised?*

2. Look at the same words written in phonetics below and check that the vowels you circled are written as 'schwa'! Can you recognise them?

[sɜːkəs]   [əbaut]   [eiprən]   [pjuːpəl]   [pɒkət]

This exercise demonstrates that any vowel in English can have a weak pronunciation, i.e. [ə]

🖉 **3. Which vowel(s)/syllables in the following words have weak pronunciation, i.e. 'Schwa'?**

America	manager	cleaner	urgent
patient	important	foreign	pharmacy
recovery	other	practise	computer
doctor	technician		

4. Check your answers with the same words written using phonetic symbols.

[dɒktə]...................... [peiʃənt]..........................

[ɜːdʒənt] .... [mænədʒə].......................

[tekˈniʃən].................. [kəmˈpjuːtə].....................

[imˈpɔːtənt]................ [kliːnə]..........................

[əˈmerikə] .... [rikʌvri]..........................

[præktis] .... [ʌðə]............................

[fɒrən] .... [faːməsi].......................

5. Look at these words in phonetic transcription – write the words next to them. They all appear in the text on pages 2 and 3.

[mænˈjuːəl] .... [əksˈpiːriəns] ....

[prəˈfeʃən] .... [helθ].............................

[kəˈmjuːniˈkeit] .... [disədˈvæntidʒ]...............

[inˈstrʌkʃən] .... [wɜːk]...........................

🎧 **Listening 2 – Phonetics** *Listen to the recording and check your answers – then check the spelling in the text on pages 2 and 3.*

ACCEPTED ABBREVIATIONS (1)

A lot of words and expressions used in hospitals and other fields of medicine are abbreviated to letters only. Using the alphabet pronunciation reference section at the back of the book – practice saying the following accepted abbreviations with a partner, using the letters of the alphabet with the correct pronunciation.

International Organisations:	UN	WHO	CDC
Personal Details:	DOB	M/F	M/W/D
Hospital Charts:	Ca – 2 meanings:	1 (*an element*)	2 (*a disease*)
	BP	TPR	Hb (*a blood test*)
	XR or X/R	IV	IM
	GA/LA	EDD (*Obstetrics*)	NAD
	OT (*a person/job*)	Dr.	FBE (*a blood test*)
General Use:	ASAP	VIP	NB
	e.g.	i.e.	c̄
	TLC	etc.	O.K.
Qualifications:	RN	BSc	PhD

✎ **Check if your partner knows what they stand for. Write as many as you can in full.**
e.g. UN [juː en] *stands for 'The United Nations'.*

Do you know what the letters UN stand for?

Yes, I do. They stand for 'the United Nations'.

✎ **Here are some more commonly used abbreviations. Write them in full below.**

Pt.		K	(*an element – periodic table*)
gm.	(*a measure of weight*)	ht & wt	
fl. oz.	(*an Imperial liquid measure*)	RBC	(*cytology*)
M.S.	(*an illness*)	AIDS	(*an illness*)
HIV		SID(S)	(*neonatology*)
R.	(*location*)	L.	(*location*)
IQ		OD	(*diagnosis*)
ENT	(*medical*)	BBC	
A & E	(*hospital department*)	EDD	(*obstetrics*)
TB	(*an illness*)	PMT/PM(S)	(*a gynaecological problem*)
OT/OR	(*hospital department*)	RC	(*religion*)
H_2O		(*n.*)	
(*adj.*)		(*v.*)	
(*adv.*)		(*coll.*)	
(*irreg.*)		(*reg.*)	
BC		AD	

☺ **Where would you see these abbreviations?**

1. in a doctor's notes
2. in a patient's case history
3. in a history textbook
4. in a cooking book
5. in an English student's book (or a dictionary)

DIFFERENT COUNTRIES, NATIONALITIES AND LANGUAGES

Good morning Rosie.
Hello Annie! It's nice to meet you… welcome to the best and busiest ward in the hospital! There are four new nurses starting here this week – you're the first!
Most of our staff are from different countries. I'm English – I was born in York – Rosie is Australian and Pat is Irish! Dr. Singh is Indian, Mr. James was born in Germany, and where do you come from? ….Oh, South Africa, really!…..It's beautiful there! Where exactly in South Africa?

🎧 **Listening 3a – Countries and Nationalities** **Listen to the recording, practise the conversation.**

Look at these examples:	I come from England / I'm from England	I'm English.
	Dr. Singh comes from India / He's from India	He's Indian
	Sister Rosie comes from Australia / Rosie's from Australia	She's Australian

✎ *Now, write the nationality (which is very often the same as the name of the language).*

Country		Nationality, Adjective AND Language(s)
Albania	[ælˈbeinˈɪə]	....
Argentina	[aːdʒənˈtiːnə]	....
China	[tʃainə]	....
England	[iŋglənd]	....
France	[fraːns/fræns]	....
Germany	[dʒɜːməni]	....
Greece	[griːs]	....
Holland (The Netherlands)	[hɒlənd – ðə neðəˈləndz]	....
Ireland	[eilənd]	....
Italy	[itəli]	....
Japan	[dʒəˈpæn]	....
Korea	[kəriːə]	....
Portugal	[pɔːtˈjuːgəl]	....
Scotland	[skɒtlənd]	....
Spain	[spein]	....
Switzerland	[switzələnd]	....
The United States	[ðəˈjuːneitidˈsteits]	....
Turkey	[tɜːki]	....
Wales	[weilz]	....

🎧 **Listening 3b – Exercise** *Check your answers then correct the spelling of the nationalities in the tape–script at the back of the book.*

☺ *Practise saying the names of the countries and the nationalities. Can you add more countries and nationalities to the list? With your partner discuss the languages people speak in the different countries.*

✏ *Complete the following sentences with the correct adjectives. (Remember they always start with a capital letter).*

1. Swiss people usually speak at least 3 or 4 languages, i.e. they can speak ...., ..., ... and very often their very own 'Romantic' language ....

2. Chianti is a well–known .... wine, Champagne is ...., and Calvados is ....

3. What language(s) do people speak (a) in Holland, (b) in Greece, (c) in Tunisia, (d) in Palestine? ....

4. "The Lancet" is an .... Medical Journal, "L'Infermiere" is an .... Nursing Newsletter and "La Recherche" is a .... magazine.

☺ *Look at the pictures. What do you think the people are saying?*

1

2

3

Listening 4 – Exercise **Read and listen to these conversations. Match a conversation with one of the pictures.**

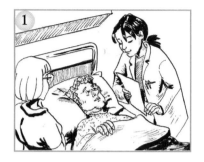

A. Dr. Singh: Good afternoon Mr. James. May I introduce you to Professor Bertolli from Italy?

Prof. Bertolli: How do you do?

Mr. James: How do you do? Welcome to this beautiful country. It's a pleasure to meet you. I'm looking forward to working with you.

Prof. Bertolli: And you. I know you do a lot of research here and I would really like to…

B. John: Hello Rosie! Do you know Steve? He's Irish and works in Intensive Care.

Rosie: No, I don't. Hello Steve, it's nice to meet you.

Steve: And you, Rosie. Where are you working Rosie?

Rosie: I'm in Surgical A1 – we're very busy at present but probably not as busy as Intensive Care. Four new nurses are starting this week and I have to show them around the hospital and teach them some procedures. Where are you working now John?

John: I'm in Orthopaedics – it's very interesting and the ward is full at the moment… I'm on night shift this week and it's getting late, so I'll say goodbye and see you tomorrow evening. Look after Rosie, Steve!

C. Sandra: Good morning Rosie. This is Mrs Green who was admitted last night. Mrs Green, this is Rosie, my Australian colleague and she is going to get you ready for your operation.

Rosie: Good morning, Mrs Green. I'm Rosie Kemp and I will be looking after you this morning.

Mrs Green: Hello nurse. Thank you. Do you know if doctor will see me before I have the operation?

Rosie: Yes, he's coming very soon. He's talking to another patient at the moment.
Now, first I'd like to take your blood pressure and then you can change into a hospital gown. You mustn't eat or drink anything at all this morning and your pre–med (the little injection that makes you sleepy) is due at eleven o'clock.

Listen to the recording again, then in groups of 3 students, practice the conversations.

☺ **Can you add more sentences to the dialogues?**

📖 **When you introduce yourself, it is often important to say what your position is and what you do.**

> Good afternoon, Professor Bertolli.
> I'm Rosie Kemp and I'm *in charge of* the ward today.
> I'm *responsible for* the staff, admissions and discharges and general ward organisation.
> Would you like me to show you around?

ENGLISH FOR WORK AND PLAY

Role play

☺ *Work in groups of 3. Read your role–card and decide what you are going to say.*

STUDENT A	STUDENT B	STUDENT C
You are Terry Smith, staff nurse, responsible for the medical ward. A new student nurse has just started. Introduce yourself to him/her and welcome him/her to the ward. Then introduce the student nurse to the consultant, Dr. Orchard, who has just come in.	You are Sammy Lewis, a student nurse on your first day in the medical ward. You are meeting the staff nurse for the first time. Then the consultant comes in and the staff nurse will introduce you to him/her.	You are Dr. Orchard, the Head Consultant in the medical ward. You enter the ward and the staff nurse will greet you (you know him/her) and he/she will introduce you to a new student nurse. Make him/her feel welcome.

Useful Every Day Expressions (1)

🖉 *We use certain expressions in different social and work situations. Match the following expressions and the responses.*

Hello, Jan.	Same to you!
Cheers!	Yes, that's very kind of you. Thank you.
Goodnight everyone!	Not at all, don't mention it.
Can I get you another pillow or a cushion?	Hi, Andrew. What a nice surprise to see you here.
Good morning, I'm Barbara Scott.	Cheers!
How do you do?	Goodbye, see you tomorrow.
Thank you so much.	Pleased to meet you, Barbara.
Have a good weekend.	How do you do?
Excuse me!	Yes, of course. Come with me.
Do you mind if I sit here?	Yes. Can I help you?
Could you please tell me where the outpatients' department is?	No, not at all, please do.

☺ *Check your answers then practise saying them. Work in pairs – choose an expression and test your partner for the correct response.*

HOSPITAL PERSONNEL – HEALTH CARE WORKERS

Throughout the world, communities rely on the numerous people trained to take care of their health, from birth to death: doctors, nurses, technicians, therapists, pharmacists, dentists and many other specialists within these groups. There are many different personnel in hospitals, clinics and in the community with different roles to play.

Who are they?

Can you recognise these professions from the phonetic symbols in column A? Use the phonetic symbol reference section to help translate them and then match them with a job title in column B.

	Column A:	Column B:
1.	[nɜːs]	doctor
2.	[daiəˈtiʃən]	nurse
3.	[teknikl əsistənt]	dentist
4.	[dentəst]	surgeon
5.	[spiːtʃ ˈθerəpist]	dietician
6.	[sɜːdʒən]	health inspector
7.	[fisiaʊˈθerəpist]	speech therapist
8.	[dɒktə]	laboratory technician
9.	[enˈiːsθətist]	physiotherapist
10.	[reidiˈɒɡrəfə]	technical assistant
11.	[pəˈdaiətrist] [kirˈɒpəˈdist]	podiatrist (US) = chiropodist (GB)
12.	[ləˈbɒrətri tekniʃən]	occupational therapist
13.	[okjuːˈpeiʃənəl θerəpist]	anaesthetist
14.	[helθ inspektə]	radiographer
15.	[faːməsist]	pharmacist

What do they do?

☺ *Put the professional name next to the correct job description using the correct article 'a' or 'an'. Using the expressions list on pages 20–21, work with a partner to match a profession with a job description.*

a. .... takes X/Rays
b. .... operates on patients
c. .... tests specimens [spesəmənz] of urine [juːrən], blood [blʌd], sputum [spjuːtəm] etc. for abnormalities
d. .... exercises injured limbs [limz] – arms and legs
e. .... puts patients to sleep before an operation
f. .... looks after the daily needs of patients in hospital
g. .... teaches patients to live as normally as possible with a disability
h. .... diagnoses a patient's problems and prescribes treatment
i. .... decides what food a patient can eat
j. .... cares for teeth, gums and oral diseases [diziːziz]
k. .... assists people of all ages who have problems communicating
l. .... looks after injured or diseased [diziːzd] feet [fiːt]
m. .... prepares and dispenses medications
n. .... works in the hospital, in the community and outdoors in all areas regarding health [helθ], safety [seifti] and sanitation [ˈsænəˈteiʃən]
o. .... assists [əˈsists] staff to regulate [regˈjuːleit] or repair [ripˈeə] machinery [məˈʃiːnri]

Now, look at the following phrases and add one to each of the sentences on the previous page.

(i)   ...and looks at different tissues under a microscope.

(ii)   ...and acts as an intermediary between doctors and relatives.

(iii) ...or gives a local or spinal ['spainəl] anaesthetic ['ænəs'θetik] before an operation.

(iv)   ...and replaces light bulbs when necessary.

(v)   ...and/or hearing difficulties ['difikəltiz].

(vi)   ...MRI's [em'a:r'aiz] (Magnetic Resonance Imagining) and CAT [kæt] scans (Computerised Axial Tomography).

(vii) ...and organises different diets for ill patients.

(viii) ...and works with orthopaedic prosthetists to find the most comfortable walking shoes.

(ix)   ...and prepares moulds for technicians to make dentures ['dentʃəz] or other dental prostheses [prɒsθi:si:z].

(x)   ...he/she may be a junior or senior or a specialist in any ward [wɔːd] in the hospital.

(xi)   ...and helps patients with post–operative breathing exercises.

(xii) ...and adapts different every–day utensils, for example knives, forks and spoons, to make them easy to use for patients with limited or impaired motor function.

(xiii) ...and visits patients daily post–operatively to order any change in treatment.

(xiv) ...tests the purity of drinking water and is able to detect excess radiation ['reidɪˌeiʃən] in the environment [en'vai'rən'mənt].

(xv)   ...and can give advice about the quantity of a drug to give (dosages).

Job Titles are nouns and are formed by adding endings (suffixes) such as:
-ian, -ist, -er, -r, -or, -ant

Can you think of more than your partner?   How many different job titles can you think of?

Who works 'indoors' and who works 'outdoors'?

Which jobs are 'sedentary'?

What is the difference between   a radiographer and a radiologist?
a doctor and a specialist?

INTRODUCTION TO MEDICAL TERMINOLOGY (1)

Medical Terminology is easy to understand if words are broken down into components. The basic medical part of the word is the **'root'** and can be changed by adding letters before **(a prefix)** or after **(a suffix)** the root.

Often the root is derived from Latin or Ancient Greek but its origin can also be English, German or Arabic. The root(s) can be understood and the meaning of the whole word can change with the addition of other roots, a prefix or a suffix.

Look at the following examples:

"radi" is a 'root' meaning radiation or radioactivity
"graph" is also a 'root' meaning a picture or recording
"olog-" is a suffix and refers to the scientific study or science of something
"-ist" and *"-er"* are both suffixes used for job or professional titles

The most frequently used vowel to join the root and the prefix and/or the suffix is 'o' (the combining vowel)

radi + 'o' + graph + er	can be literally 'translated' as a person who takes pictures using radiation [reidiˈɒgrəfə].
and	
radi + olog + ist	can be literally translated as a person who is a specialist in the area of radiation, i.e. has studied the science of radiation [reidiˈɒlədʒəst].
and	
radi + olog + y	becomes a noun describing the study of radiation [reidiˈɒlədʒi].

Can you make similar words using the following 'roots' and then explain the meaning?

bi-	[bai]	which is the root referring to *life* [laif]
ur-	[juː]	refers to *urine* [juːrən] or the *urinary* [juːrənri] system
psych-	[saik]	refers to the mental state or *psych* [saik] of a person
cardi-	[kaːdi]	means *heart* [haːt]
onc-	[ɒnk]	is the root referring to *cancer* [kænsə]

D

WARDS AND DEPARTMENTS IN A HOSPITAL

Where do Health Care Professionals work?

Health care professionals are needed all over the world in health care centres, hospitals, clinics and in the community, to work with governments, individuals or groups interested in public health, disease prevention, health education or rehabilitation.

☺ *Look at the different Wards and Departments using the phonetic symbols to practise saying them*

Department or Unit		
Accident & Emergency (A&E)	[æksi'dənt n im'ɜːdʒənsi]
Intensive Care	[in'tensiv keə]
Operating Theatre	[ɒpə'reitiŋ θiːətə]
Radiology or X–Ray	[reidi'ɒlədʒi]
Laboratory	[ləbɒrətri]
Outpatients'	[aut'peiʃənts]
Kitchen	[kitʃən]
Pharmacy	[faːməsi]
Technical Services	[tek'nikl 'sɜːvəsəz]
Blood Bank	[blʌd bæŋk]
Administration	[əd'minə'streiʃən]
Central Sterilisation Dept. (CSD)	[sentrəl sterə'laiˈzeiʃən di'paːtmənt – siː es diː]

Ward		
Children's ("kids")	[tʃildrənz]
Neurology	[njuː'rɒlədʒi]
Neurosurgery	[njuːrəu sɜːdʒəri]
Urology	[juː'rɒlədʒi]
Gynaecology	[gainə'kɒlə'dʒi]
Obstetric/Labour	[əb'stet'rik] [leibə]
Surgery/Surgical	[sɜːdʒəri] [sɜːdʒikl]
Medicine/Medical	[medə'sin] [medikl]
Neonatal Nursery	[niːəu'neitl nɜːsəri]
Thoracic	[θə'ræsik]
Geriatric	[dʒeri'ætrik]
Cardiology	[kaːdi'ɒlədʒi]
Dermatology	[dɜːmə'tɒlədʒi]
Psychiatric	[saiki'ætrik]
Orthopaedic	[ɔːθə'piːdik]

MEDICAL TERMINOLOGY (2)

NB The names of the wards are the same as listed on the previous page but when used as an adjective (words that describe nouns), the suffix sometimes changes:

surgery   becomes   the *surgical* ward
medicine (a noun)   becomes   the *medical* ward
gynaecology   becomes   the *gynaecological* [ˈgainəˌkəlˈɒdʒikl] *ward*

The word "obstetrical" is not used for the ward – use **labour ward** instead.

Adjective suffixes that occur frequently in Medical English are:

-ac   e.g. when used with *cardi-* describes something 'pertaining to' or 'to do with' the heart. e.g. (*cardiac arrest*)
-al   e.g. when used with *or(o)-* describes something 'relating to' or to do with the mouth. e.g. (*oral hygiene*)
-ary e.g. when used with *pulmon-* means pertaining to the lungs. e.g. (*pulmonary embolus*)
-ous e.g. *mucous membrane*
-ic   e.g. *peptic = (relating to digestion) peptic ulcer; optic nerve*
-id   e.g. *morbid = (relating to disease) morbid anatomy*
-ose e.g. *adipose tissue*
-ical e.g. *medical ward*

Make an adjective from these words by removing the letters in blue **and adding a suffix.**

1. Neurology	....	7. Psychology	....
2. Cardiology	....	8. Diabetes	....
3. Gastrology	....	9. Neonate	....
4. Cranium	....	10. Medicine	....
5. Pharmacology	....	11. Centre	....
6. Urology	....	12. Physician	....

GRAMMAR NOTES – Prepositions (1)

Look at the prepositions used in the following examples:

A paediatric nurse works **in** the nursery or **in** the children's ward.
Which floor is the children's ward **on**? It's **on** the 6th floor.
My friend works **in** the Operating Theatre.

The Children's Ward is **next to** the Orthopaedic Ward, **on** the same floor.
The baby is due **in** 3 weeks' time.
The Laundry is **in** the basement.

We use different expressions depending on the situation:
we go to a ward or department
we work in a ward, but at the hospital
we take/send a patient to a department|theatre| but he is in the ward, hospital or theatre.

Complete the following sentences with the correct preposition from the box.

to
with
for
for
for
at
about
in
in
on
on
on
under

1. I don't agree .... you. I think you're wrong.

2. I'm not interested .... sport at all.

3. We can take the patients into the garden, but it depends .... the weather.

4. What did they talk .... at the meeting?

5. What did you do that ....? Don't do anything like that again.

6. Mr. Richardson is going .... theatre .... 1 o'clock.

7. His wife can wait .... him in the lounge room

8. Your pen is .... the floor, ... the bed.

9. Please write all the details .... this form.

10. I'm working .... Emergency every Saturday .... the next four weeks.

☺ *Ask your partner the following questions, checking the use of correct prepositions in the answers.*

1. Where can a mother go to visit her premature baby?

2. Where do ambulances take victims of road accidents?

3. Where do I go to donate blood?

4. Where can I get help with a machine that doesn't work properly?

5. Where do you ring to order a patient's medications?

6. Where can I find a dermatologist to look at my son's moles (small dark spots on his skin)?

7. Where do patients usually go if they have a heart attack?

8. Where do you want to work? What is your favourite ward?

9. Is there a ward that you don't really want to work in?

10. Where do you take an urgent specimen of urine for microscopic examination?

Add the following wards or departments to the diagram below.

the Staff cafeteria   the Radiology Department   the Post–natal Ward and Neonatal Unit

the Children's Ward   the Operating theatres

HOSPITAL

-7th floor	Medical Wards	E. N. T.
-6th floor	Orthopaedic Ward	
-5th floor		Recovery Room
-4th floor	Surgical Wards	Intensive Care Unit
-3rd floor	Urology	Endoscopy Department
-2nd floor	Labour Ward	Sonography & E.C.G. / Central Sterilising Department
-1st floor	Outpatients' Department	Hospital Administration Offices / Nursing Administration
Ground floor	Reception Coffee shop / Technical Services Department / Blood Bank	Pharmacy / Laboratory / Dental Services
Lower Ground floor	Kitchen	Emergency
Basement	Laundry	Stores / Mortuary

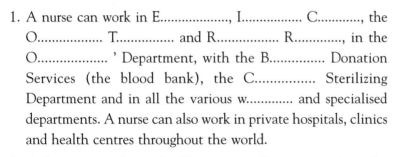

Can you complete the words to name some of the various wards and departments where health care workers can be found?

1. A nurse can work in E................., I................. C............, the O................. T................ and R................ R............, in the O................. ' Department, with the B............... Donation Services (the blood bank), the C................ Sterilizing Department and in all the various w............. and specialised departments. A nurse can also work in private hospitals, clinics and health centres throughout the world.

2. A dietician works in the K................, O...................', in the wards as a consultant and can also work privately.

3. An anaesthetist works in both public and private hospitals and clinics in the O................. T................ . He checks the general health of patients in the w............. prior to (before) surgery.

4. A dentist can work in a private ...., in the Outpatients' Department of public hospitals and in the O................. T................ .

5. Speech Therapists work in both public and private clinics, in the Outpatients' Department and in the wards – frequently in the C.................'s Ward, in the G................. unit, the M............... ward, N.................... or the Ps................... ward.

6. Surgeons work in the Operating Theatres, in private C................'s rooms and in the w............ .

7. Physiotherapists work in the O...................' Department, Private clinics and surgeries and in most of the wards in the hospital. They can also treat patients in a s................. p...............!!!! (Can you guess what?)

8. List the places where a doctor could work: ....

9. A radiographer usually works in R................... and in other 'scanning' departments and sometimes in the other wards and departments or private clinics.

10. A paediatric nurse works in the N................. nursery, the C...................'s ward, in kindergartens and in communal health centres.

Mm.....

11. A Laboratory Technician works in both public and private M............... laboratories.

12. An Occupational Therapist may work in all the .... of the hospital including the G................... ward, N...................... ward, the C...................'s ward and Rh.................... and can also have a private practice.

13. A Pharmacist can work independently from the hospital in a Chemist's shop or in the P...................... or Dispensary at the hospital.

14. A Health Inspector mainly works out in the community but may also work in a L................... or the CSD, i.e. the C................. S................... D................... .

19

✐ *Fill in the gaps with the appropriate preposition and/or one of the following words.*

Pharmacy
Post–natal
to (×3)
the operating theatre
Emergency Department
Surgical
hospital
on (×2)
with
into
kitchen
Administration
X/Ray
theatre
at
in (×6)

1. Can you please take Mrs. Jones .... to have a CAT scan – .... the ground floor?

2. Come .... me, I'll show you where to go.

3. Mrs. Rossi is ...., she's having a hip replacement operation.

4. There are two ambulances parked outside the ....

5. Send this prescription [prəˈskripˌʃən] .... the .... now, we don't have any morphine on the ward.

6. There are not enough beds .... the adult .... ward for this 16–year old boy, who is going to theatre tomorrow, so admit him .... the Children's Ward.

7. Both my parents work .... the local .... My mother works .... the .... (she's a cook) and my father works .... (he's in the Accounts Department).

8. My best friend had a baby girl yesterday, she is still .... hospital, ... the second floor.

9. I'm going to send her some flowers .... the .... ward.

10. Mr Bailey's operating at the moment, he's .... Number 3.

THE BOSS

Check your answers with another student or with your teacher.

EXPRESSION and WORD LIST   1B/C/D

admissions [ədˈmiʃəns] (*n.*) Admissions are the new patients accepted into the hospital.

Community Health Centres [kəˈmjuːnəti helθ sentəz] (*adj.* + *n.*) Buildings in the city and suburbs where medical services are available to the general public.

Consultant [kənˈsʌltənt] (*n.*) An experienced doctor who specialises in one area of medicine.

Head/Chief Consultant [hed / tʃiːf kənˈsʌltənt] (*n.*) The experienced specialised doctor in charge of a particular ward or department.

discharges [dis'tʃɑːdʒəz] (n.) Discharges are those patients who are permitted to go home or are being transferred to another hospital.

Intensive Care [in'tensiv keə] (n. or adj.) The specialised unit or department where extremely ill patients can be cared for individually and monitored on a 'one–to–one' basis by specially trained staff.

microscopic examination [maik'rəʊ'skɒpik eks'æmineiʃən] (adj. + n.) The analysis of a specimen under a microscope to analyse or identify it.

prescription [prə'skripʃən] (n.) An official piece of paper on which a doctor writes the types of medicine you should have and which allows you to buy it from a pharmacy or chemist's.

procedures [prə'siːdjəz] (n.) The usual or correct way of doing something. *e.g. the procedure for setting up an intravenous line.*

senior house officer [siːnjə haus ɒfəsə] (adj. + n.) An experienced doctor on the staff of a particular ward or department.

shift [ʃift] (n.) (**to be on night shift**) Shifts are the irregular hours worked by staff on a rotating roster.

>**morning/afternoon or evening/night shift** refers to the hours worked at that time on a regular basis.

specimen [spesəmən] (n.) A small amount (or sample) of tissue, blood, urine etc. taken for analysis.

staff nurse [staːf nɜːs] (n.) A staff nurse is a hospital nurse who is trained and has a rank just below that of a sister or charge nurse.

surgeon [sɜːdʒən] (n.) A doctor who is specially trained **to *perform surgery* i.e. to *do an operation***.

ward [wɔːd] (n.) A room in a hospital which has beds for many people. A **surgical ward** [sɜːdʒikl wɔːd] (n.) is the department or rooms in a hospital for patients who will have or have had surgical operations.

ward charge nurse [wɔːd 'tʃɑːdʒ 'nɜːs] (n.) A senior nurse who is in charge and has the responsibility of a ward or department.

to donate blood [dəʊ'neit blʌd] (v. + n.) To have blood taken to give freely to another person.

to help/relieve pain [help/riliːv pein] (v. + n.) To alleviate or reduce any discomfort.

to prescribe/order treatment/medications [prə'skreib/ɔːdə medə'keiʃənz] (v. + n.) When a doctor prescribes or orders something, he tells you what to do or what to take.

to take drugs, tablets or medication [teik drʌgz, tæblətz medə'keiʃən] (v. + n.) To inject or ingest these substances (regularly).

to teach procedures [tiːʃ prə'siːdjəz] (v. + n.) [tiːtʃ prə'siːdjəz] To show or teach someone the usual and correct way or method of doing something.

to test a specimen [test ə 'spesəmən] (v. + n.) To analyse or examine a sample of body tissue to identify it or make a diagnosis.

Read the following sentences and write the appropriate words in the gaps from the "Expression and word list" above.

1. New mothers can take their babies to .... for advice and consultation.

2. More than one .... operates for hours to do 'open heart surgery'.

3. All the patients in this .... are going to be transferred to the new building.

4. Trainee nurses have to learn a lot of different ....

5. .... of blood must be put into different test–tubes for different examinations.

6. When a patient is ready for ...., the staff must be sure he has understood the doctor's directions.

7. Urine is inspected visually and also taken to the laboratory for ....

8. Medications to .... are called analgesics.

9. Before you ...., you have to sign a form saying that you have no diseases or infections that could be transmitted to someone else.

10. Some people need to .... to help them to sleep.

THE PRESENT SIMPLE TENSE (1)

USE

A.	PERMANENT STATES	e.g. It snows here in winter. My father is a doctor.
B.	THINGS THAT STAY THE SAME FOR A LONG TIME	e.g. I live in a city. He doesn't speak Spanish.
C.	ROUTINES AND HABITS	e.g. He drives to work. I usually work at weekends.

The Present Simple is often used with frequency adverbs, such as 'always', 'usually', 'generally', 'often', 'sometimes', 'occasionally', 'never' and 'hardly ever'.

REMEMBER

1. In positive statements there is an 's' added to the main verb in the 3rd person singular (he/she/it): e.g. I/you/we/they live here but he/she/it lives here.

2. All verbs, *except the verb 'to be' (and modal auxiliary verbs)* must have the auxiliary verb (helping verb) do/does in questions and negative statements.

3. Add 'not' to the auxiliary verb to form negative sentences: *e.g. I don't know the new students very well. He doesn't work in the surgical ward.*

4. The auxiliary verb tells us the tense and the 'person' and the main verb stays in the base infinitive form when used with the auxiliary verb.

QUESTIONS

In English, questions are nearly always in the same order (in all tenses):

± Question word(s)	Auxiliary verb	Subject	Main Verb	(all the rest!)
What	do	you/we/they	want	for breakfast?
Which department	does	he/she	work	in?

There may or may not be a question word or question words.
When the question starts with the auxiliary verb we have a 'yes/no' question with only a 'short answer' necessary.

Short answer questions:	Do	I/you/we/they			
	Does	he/she		have	tutorials today?

Short Answers: Yes, they do. / No they don't.   Yes, he does. / No, he doesn't.

✎ *Fill in the gaps with the correct form of the verb or an auxiliary verb.*

1. John .... (work) in the orthopaedic ward, he .... (not work) in theatre.
2. A general surgeon .... (do) all types of operations.
3. What .... a radiologist .... (do)?
4. How long .... you have to .... (wait) for a knee operation?
5. An orthopaedic surgeon .... (operate) on knees.
6. .... you .... (know) a good surgeon? No, I'm sorry, ...
7. How long .... the operation .... (take)?
8. Where .... you .... (have) your lectures?
9. .... he .... (drive) to work? Yes, he ....
10. What .... you .... (do) in the evenings after work?
11. How often .... you .... (go) swimming?
12. .... you ever .... (go) to the gym? No, ... I prefer to go swimming.
13. What time .... Rosie .... (start) work?
14. Where .... she .... (come) from?
15. .... they .... (want) to come to the cinema tonight? Yes, ...
16. Why .... you all .... (not finish) this exercise for homework?

THE VERB 'TO BE' AS A MAIN VERB **is different from other verbs:**
'not' can be added to the verb, and questions are made by **inverting** the subject and the verb i.e. putting the verb *before* the subject.

+ S. V. O.
I am a nurse.	*You are a nurse too.*	*He/She is a nurse.*	*We/You/They are nurses.*

– S. V.+ not O.
I'm not a nurse.	*You aren't a nurse.*	*He/She isn't a nurse*	*We/You/They aren't nurses.*

? V. S. O
Am I late?	*Are you a nurse?*	*Is he/she a doctor?*	*Are we/you/they in the right ward?*

Short answer questions

Only the subject and the positive or negative form of the verb 'be' are used in the short answer. The words 'yes' or 'no' used by themselves sound rude, abrupt and impolite.

✎ *Complete these 'short answer questions' with both 'yes' and 'no' and the correct auxiliary verb.*

e.g.	*Are you a student?*	Yes, I am. (*not I'm)	No, I'm not.
(a)	*Do you work here?*	....	....
(b)	*Is he a doctor?*	....	....
(c)	*Does he have a stethoscope?*	....	....
(d)	*Are we on duty today?*	....	....
(e)	*Do we/they need more money?*	....	....
(f)	*Am I late?*	............*you*............	............*you*............

MODAL AUXILIARY VERBS

Modal verbs are used to express different things: ability, requests and offers and willingness to do something etc.

The same modal verb is used in all persons, singular and plural, and <u>All Modal Auxiliary verbs</u> (**Can, Could, Shall, Should, Will, Would**) are always followed by the main verb in the base infinitive.

Inversion is used when asking questions (a second auxiliary verb is **never** used).

Can/Can't are <u>used to talk about the ability or inability to do something</u> ('Could/Couldn't' are used in the past tense)

e.g. I/you/he/she/it/we/they can [kn kæn]/can't [ka:nt] swim.
    Can [kn] I/you/he/she/it/we/they swim?
<u>or to make an offer or a request</u> ('Could' is used to make a formal request)

Short answer questions   Can [kn] I/you/he/she/we/they come to the party?
                    Can [kn] I/you/he/she/we/they please open the window?

                    Yes, I/you/he/she/we/they can [kæn].
                    No, I/you/he/she/we/they can't [ka:nt].

🖉 **Fill in the gaps with 'can' or 'can't'.**

🎧 Listening 5 – Can/can't
Listen and check your answers, then practise the sentences with a partner.

1. I .... use a computer, but I .... programme them.

2. He .... do this exercise so .... you help him?

3. When the children .... swim very well, I want to take them to the seaside.

4. If he .... come to the party, I'll have to ask someone else.

5. The new patient .... walk unaided – we ...... put him in a wheelchair to go to X/Ray.

6. .... you read this? No, I ...., the writing's too small.

7. .... you open the door a little bit? I like watching the people in the corridor.

8. Jane .... speak German but her brother ....

9. The doctor's really busy at the moment, but he .... see you in about 45 minutes. .... you wait here? You .... have a cup of tea from the machine, if you like.

10. Where .... Steven find some information about that? He looked for a book in the library but *........n't (*past tense*) find anything.

> *John arrives at work, talks to the staff on evening shift ("hand–over") and checks his patients' case histories. Next he visits each of his patients.*

 Put the following conversation in the correct order.

John:	I can help you turn over on your side, but your leg stays on the pillow, O.K.? Your leg will hurt more without it. Hold on to me and I'll help you turn. There you are. Lift up your leg and I'll move the pillow, that's better. Are you comfortable, now?
Cathy:	That's much better, thank you – now I can sleep!
John:	This tablet is to help the pain and then I'm sure you'll sleep.
Cathy:	Oh, hello John. Yes, I'm a little better, but my leg still hurts a lot.
John:	Good then. I'm going to check on the other patients now, but you can call me if you need anything – just ring the bell!
Cathy:	Thank you. Can I move my leg off the pillow? I want to lie on my side.
John:	Good evening young lady! I'm looking after you again tonight. Are you feeling a bit better? You don't look very happy!

....
....
....
....

....
....
1
....

🎧 **Listening 6 – In the ward** **Listen to the recording and check your answers.**

 Now, number the pictures in order and match one with part of the dialogue.

☺ **Practise the dialogue with a partner.**

THE PRESENT CONTINUOUS TENSE

All the continuous tenses in English are used to talk about some activity which is relatively short in duration – that is, there is a start and a finish within a certain time.

Form: In all tenses the continuous form uses **'be'** as the auxiliary verb and the main verb ends with **'–ing'** in positive and negative sentences *and* questions.

The *present continuous* uses the verb 'be' in the *present* form, i.e. am/is/are + the main verb with the 'ing' ending.

USE

There are 3 different uses for the present continuous tense:

1. To talk about activity <u>now</u>: e.g. *We **are having** English lessons (right now).*

2. To talk about an activity <u>around now</u>, in this period of time: *e.g. I**'m training** to be a nurse. (I won't always be training – eventually I will be qualified and will have permanent work.)*

3. To talk about planned arrangements for <u>the future</u>: *e.g. She**'s starting** her work experience next week in the children's ward.* Although it is called the 'present' continuous tense, this is an example of using the <u>form</u> of the tense for a different time period.

QUESTIONS AND NEGATIVE SENTENCES

'be' as an auxiliary verb is used in the same way as the full verb 'be' and questions use inversion of the auxiliary verb and the subject:

e.g.	+	–	?
	I'm working hard.	*I'm not working hard.*	*Am I working…?*
	You're working hard.	*You aren't working hard.*	*Are you working…?*
	He's working hard.	*He isn't working hard.*	*Is he working…?*
	We're working hard.	*We aren't working hard.*	*Are we working…?*

✏️ **Look at the following sentences and number them according to the use of the present continuous tense:**

Is the reference to 'now' (1), 'in this period of time' (2) or to 'the future' (3)?

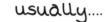

.... 1. She can't come now, <u>she's doing</u> the rounds with the doctors.

.... 2. <u>Dr. Singh is taking</u> Professor Bertolli to the laboratory on Monday.

.... 3. <u>John's working</u> night shift.

.... 4. <u>I'm studying</u> anatomy and physiology at the moment.

.... 5. Which exercise <u>are you doing</u>?

.... 6. What <u>is he wearing</u> on his feet?

.... 7. <u>Mrs Johnson is coming</u> in to see her husband this evening.

.... 8. <u>I'm renovating</u> the kitchen at the moment so things are really disorganised at home.

.... 9. <u>He's having</u> an arthroscopy, he's still in theatre.

.... 10. <u>Rosie's writing</u> the reports, so I'll go and see who's buzzing – I think Mrs Green wants another pan!

.... 11. When <u>is the doctor coming</u> to see me?

.... 12. When <u>is Mrs. Green having</u> surgery?

.... 13. <u>I'm looking after</u> all the patients in rooms 4, 5 and 6.

..... but......

..... this week....

☺ **Compare sentences (a), (b) and (c) and answer this question:**

What is the difference between 'the present simple' and 'the present continuous' tenses?

(a) I <u>always have lunch</u> at home but I'm working morning shift for a month, so <u>I'm having lunch</u> in the staff cafeteria.

(b) He <u>usually drives</u> to work, but he had an accident last week so <u>he's riding</u> his bicycle to work until the car is repaired.

(c) George <u>works</u> in theatre – his friend <u>is working</u> there too.

Discuss the differences with a partner.

THE NEW TRAINEE

📖 *Annie is a trainee nurse. Read about her experiences.*

> *Hello! My name's Anna Kennedy (my friends call me Annie) and I'm nearly 20. I started my nursing training 6 months ago. We've done quite a lot of theory so far and next week we're going to work at the hospital for 6 weeks. I'm going to work in the Surgical ward and my friend Margaret (Maggie) is starting in the Orthopaedic ward. I'm a bit nervous – there is so much to learn. I'll feel better when I start in the ward and know a few people. I'm looking forward to meeting a lot of different people and doing some of the things we've practiced at school.. Making beds isn't difficult and I'm sure I can help patients be comfortable in bed – I looked after my grandmother when she was ill, a couple of years ago, and she said I'd be a wonderful nurse – I hope so anyway. I'll do my best!*

☺ *Now, make some questions using the following words then ask your partner to answer them.*

e.g. name?   *What's her full name?*   age?
     doing now?   doing next week?
     where/work?   how/feel?
     what/easy for her?   what/do?
     why/feel (or think) she will be a good nurse?

GRAMMAR NOTES

Talking about the future

<u>Underline</u> *the different tenses in the dialogue which refer to the future. How many did you find? Why do we use these different tenses? When is the present tense used with a future meaning? When do we use 'going to do something' and when do we use 'will do something'?*

✏ <u>Underline</u> *the correct verb form in the following sentences to give the sentence a future meaning:*

e.g. She works / <u>is going to work</u> in the Orthopaedic Ward.

1. She *finished / will finish* her training in about 2 years.
2. Nurses *learned / will learn* a lot during their training.
3. All health care professionals *have to pass / are passing* exams before they can work.
4. Mr. Brown *isn't going to have / doesn't have* the operation this week.
5. I'll *take / take* his temperature before he has lunch.
6. She *'s going / goes* to the cinema after work tonight.
7. We *stay / 're staying* with her during visiting hours today and tomorrow.
8. Mrs Green *has / will have* a shower.

THE ANATOMICAL POSITION AND BODY PARTS

When looking at the human body for purposes of study, parts are referred to using the anatomical position, unless stated otherwise. Look at the way Cathy is standing on the left – facing the front with her legs slightly apart and the palms of her hands turned to the front – this is the anatomical position. Note that when looking at a diagram or a patient in the anatomical position, the left side is actually on your right and vice versa.

☺ ***How many parts of the body do you know in English? Can you pronounce them properly?***

Cathy is standing in the 'anatomical position' – you have both an anterior and a posterior view.

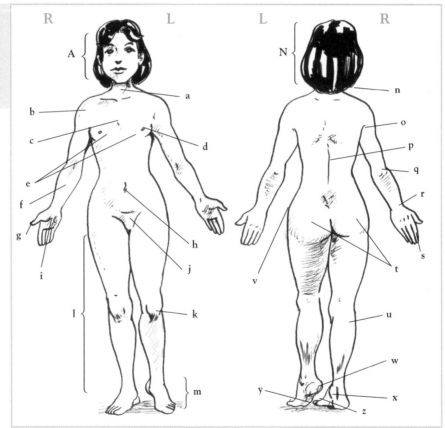

🖉 ***Can you label the diagrams with her body parts using the following words?***

1. breasts [brests]
2. knee [ni:]
3. face [feis]
4. pubes [pju:bi:z] or pubic area [pju:bikˈeriə]
5. chest [tʃest]
6. nipple [nipl]
7. leg [leg]
8. neck [nek]
9. shoulder [ʃəʊldə]
10. navel [neivl] or umbilicus [ʌmbəˈlaikəs]
11. waist [weist] (*mark this with a broken line – – –*)
12. palm [pa:m]
13. foot [fʊt]
14. thumb [θʌm]
15. arm [a:m]

16. sole of the foot [səʊləv θəˈfʊt]
17. buttocks [bʌtəks] or bottom [bɒtəm]
18. axilla [əkˈsilə] or arm–pit [a:mpit]
19. hair [heə]
20. ankle [æŋkl]

21. back [bæk]
22. toes [təʊz]
23. wrist [rist]
24. elbow [elˈbəʊ]
25. heel [hi:əl]
26. fingers [fiŋgəz]
27. head [hed]
28. calf [ka:f]

29. shin [ʃin] (*mark the front of the lower leg*)
30. hip (bone) [hip bəʊn]
31. thighs [θaiz] (*mark both anterior upper legs*)

29

Possessive adjectives

Remember that when we talk about parts of the body we use possessive adjectives: my, your, his/her, our, your, their.

e.g. She broke <u>her tibia</u> while she was skiing – <u>her leg</u> is now in a full Plaster Of Paris (POP)
<u>His ankles</u> are very swollen, <u>his foot</u> and <u>his toes</u> are too.
<u>Her fingernails</u> need cutting!

✎ *Using parts of the body or a possessive adjective, complete the following sentences:*

1. The new baby's got a very pretty ...., large blue eyes, a sweet little nose and a cute mouth. She's gorgeous!

2. Anna's got such a long ...., ... head seems a long way from ...... shoulders! She looks like a top model!

3. Mr. Gladstone has the injections in his bottom, in the gluteus maximum muscle – in ....! (You have to alternate sides).

4. My son has very big .... (*pl.*) and has trouble finding comfortable shoes, he prefers to wear trainers or gym shoes.

5. Mrs. Mills has rheumatoid arthritis in ...., she can't do up the buttons on her dressing gown. Can you help her?

6. A pulse or heart beat can be felt on the patient's ...., over the carotid artery and over the temporal artery in front of the ear.

7. Physiotherapists encourage people to have good posture and to keep .... straight whenever possible. Most people suffer from back–ache – and nurses more than others.

8. We all have 4 .... on each hand and 1 .... but the digits on the feet are called .... and we number them from the big toe to the little toe.

9. A footprint in the sand shows the .... including the toes and the .... If someone has 'flat feet', you can see the 'fallen arches' in the footprint!

10. A newborn baby's .... (or navel) doesn't form until the remaining umbilical cord atrophies [ˈætrəˌfiz] (dies) and falls off. This doesn't happen for a couple of weeks and it is better to keep the area clean and dry.

 Listening 7 – Exercise *Check your answers.*

 On Charlie's smiley face, add the following features:

- his eyebrows
- his hair
- his eyelashes
- his nose and his cheeks
- a moustache
- his chin and a beard
- his lips
- his tongue and his teeth
- his ears

☺ *Do you know what the following things are? Look these words up in your dictionary.*

- freckles [freklz]
- olive/fair complexion
  [ɒliv/feə kəmˈplekʃən]
- a birthmark [bɜ:θˈma:k]
- a bruise [bru:z]

- pimples [pimplz]
  ('spots' or 'zits')
- a suntan [sʌnˈtæn]
- a lump [lʌmp]
- a mole [məʊl]

- a scar [ska:]
- wrinkles [riŋklz]
- tattoos [tætu:z]
- a whisker [wiskə]
- a rash [ræʃ]

Describe somebody you know

⟹ *What do they look like?* **Describe their appearance.**

Are they tall or short, fat or thin? Do they wear glasses?
Is their hair long, medium–length or short? Is it straight, wavy or curly?

What sort of person are they?

⟹ *What are they like?* **Describe their personality.**

Are they shy or self–assured (self–confident), sociable or unsociable, generous or mean?

What are their preferences?

⟹ *What do they like (doing)? (in sport, free time activity or to eat)*

ADJECTIVES AND THEIR OPPOSITES

☺ *How do adjectives change to make comparative or superlative adjectives?*

Can you think of some rules to help you remember?

Which adjectives are irregular?

✏ *Look at the following adjectives. Underline the adjectives that can be used to describe people.*

fast	reliable	punctual	possible	organised
timid	healthy	polluted	late	fat	stupid
thin	comfortable	vivacious	withdrawn
tidy	polite	pure	slow	bad	intelligent	good

Antonyms
1. *Can you match some of the adjectives in the above group that have opposite meanings?*
   Often a prefix can be used to make the opposite of the adjective:
   *e.g. **un**reliable, **im**possible, **dis**organised*
2. *Find 3 other words that use a prefix to make a word with the opposite meaning and compare your answers with a partner.*

Synonyms
We often use synonyms in conversation because we don't want to repeat words:
e.g. "I think her family is very <u>rich</u>." "Yes, they are. Her father is very <u>wealthy</u>."

31

✏️ *Complete the following conversations using adjectives of similar meaning from the list:*

1. "The ward is so <u>untidy</u>." "Yes, it's really .... his morning.
2. "The operation <u>went very well</u>." "I'm glad it was so ...."
3. "Betty's boyfriend is <u>really good–looking</u>." "I know you think he's the most .... man in town!"
4. "He doesn't have a lot of money but he's very <u>thoughtful</u>." "I think he's very ...."
5. "I was really <u>angry</u> that they lied about the situation." "I can understand that you were most ...."
6. "This machine is the most <u>modern</u> available – it's brand .... on the market."
7. "The pyramids in Egypt are <u>ancient</u>, do you know how .... they are exactly?"
8. "All the staff must be <u>punctual</u>. Everyone must arrive ...."
9. "The water in the fountain is very <u>dirty</u>." "I'd say it was very ...."
10. "You can always <u>depend on</u> me!" "Thank you, you're so ....!"
11. "The baby is very <u>well</u> at the moment." "He's normally a .... boy, isn't he?"
12. "Yes, but he had a bad cold for a few days and his sister is so <u>lively</u>, she exhausts me!" "She's a gorgeous, happy, ... child, you should be glad!"
13. "Matthew's exam results were so <u>poor</u>." "They were ....! What a pity he didn't make an effort."

List: generous, old, annoyed, on time, messy, new, successful, handsome, healthy, reliable, polluted, vivacious, terrible

☺ *Check the answers with your teacher.*
Practice the conversations and test your partner.
Read half and see if your partner can match it. Test each other.
Can you list the opposites (Antonyms) of all the adjectives in this section?
You may find more than one.

☺ **CLASS DISCUSSION**
What makes a good nurse or a good doctor?

✏️ **When do we use 'so' before an adjective and when do we use 'such'?**
Write some examples to help you remember.

COLLOQUIAL LANGUAGE USING PARTS OF THE BODY

Have you got any idea what the literal translation of the following phrases is?
It's this use of the language that can often be confusing, but it's fun and can make your language much more colourful and interesting!

☺ *Work with a partner and write what you think each sentence means.*
Replace the underlined word(s) in each sentence, then make another phrase using the idiom.

1. She's got a green thumb – her balcony is a mass of flowers! ....

2. A mobile phone is very handy. I don't know how we lived without them! ....

3. It was a bit cheeky to come without being invited. ....

4. She will be very successful, she's got her head screwed on. ....

5. Everything came to a head at the meeting. ....

6. I like a good head on my beer! ....

7. He has never learnt to read music but plays wonderfully by ear. ....

8. The ball broke the window so the boys took to their heels. ....

9. I'm not sticking my neck out – I don't want to take any responsibility. ....

10. He's from my neck of the woods but I don't know him very well. ....

11. He's probably up to his neck in debt. ....

12. I always have butterflies in my stomach when I go to see a doctor. ....

13. Her ex–boyfriend has a chip on his shoulder. ....

14. She gives everybody the cold shoulder, including me ... and we used to be really good friends! ....

15. He is head and shoulders above all the others in the class, the lowest mark he had was a '9'! ....

16. "Butterfingers! That's the second time you've dropped something today" ....

17. He put his foot in it. He is so thoughtless and never considers how others might feel. ....

18. I had itchy feet for ages after travelling to Australia for my holidays. ....

19. Elbow your way onto the bus or we won't fit. ....

20. Use a bit of elbow grease [gri:s], it needs more than a gentle wipe [waip] to clean it! ....

accident [ˈæksidənt] (n.) **1.** An accident happens when a vehicle hits another vehicle, a person or an object. **2.** Something that happens by chance and is not deliberately intended.

disease [diˈziːz] (n.) An illness that affects the health of a person, animal or plant.

injury [ˈindʒəri] (n.) An injury is physical damage to the body as a result of an accident or fighting

rheumatoid arthritis [ruːməˈtɔid ˈaːθˈraitis] (n.) a long–lasting disease that causes joints (articulations) and muscles to become stiff, swollen and painful.

trainee [treiˈniː] (n.) A trainee is someone who is employed at a junior level in a particular job in order to learn the skills needed for that job.

umbilical cord [ˈʌmbilikəl ˈkɔːd] (n.) The tube [tjuːb] connecting an unborn baby to its mother, through which it receives oxygen [ˈɒksidʒən] and nourishment [ˈnʌriʃmənt].

visiting hours [ˈvizəˈtiŋ auəz] (n.) The times when friends or relatives are permitted to come into the hospital to visit patients.

swollen [ˈswəulən] (adj.) When swollen, part of the body becomes larger and rounder than normal, usually as the result of injury or disease.

to be admitted [ədˈmitid] (v.) To be formally permitted to stay in hospital for treatment.

to be discharged [disˈtʃaːdʒd] (v.) To be formally allowed to go home from hospital – appropriate documents and records are compiled in the patient's history.

to change [tʃeindʒ] **into a hospital gown** [gaun] (v. + n.) To remove personal day or night clothes and wear a gown (a cotton body cover) supplied by the hospital.

to do the rounds [raundz] (v. + n.) To visit patients individually one by one. *e.g. Ward staff do regular rounds of all the patients and doctors do a daily round with the full medical team.*

to give an injection [inˈdʒekʃən] (*or a 'pre–med'*) (v.+ n.) The use of a syringe and needle to introduce medication into the body – (into a muscle: **intramuscular** [intrəˈmʌskjuːlə]; into a vein: **intravenous** [intrəˈviːnəs]; under the skin: **hypodermic** [ˈhaipəuˈdɜːmik]).

to hang clothes [hæŋ kləuðz] (v. + n.) To put clothes on a hook, coat–hanger or clothes–line. (The clothes are attached in a high place without touching the ground.)

to have a heart attack [hævə haːt ˈətæk] (v. + n.) / **a myocardial infarction.** To have severe pain or collapse due to the sudden death of part of the heart muscle because of a blockage in the blood supply to the heart.

to have an operation [hæv ən ˈɒpəˈreiʃən] (v. + n.) To undergo major or minor surgical intervention.

to have moles (on your skin) (v. + n.) To have black spots of pigmentation (a naevus) on the skin.

to lie (on your side, on your back etc.) (v.) To be in a horizontal position (on your back etc), not sitting or standing.

to make a bed [meik ə ˈbed] (v. + n.) To tidy or change the bed–clothes so that the bed can be slept in.

to recover [rikʌvə] (v.) to return to good health following an illness or injury.

to see a doctor (v. + n.) To go to a doctor for a visit or to have the doctor come and speak to a patient.

to take a pulse [pʌls] (v. + n.) To measure [meʒə] heartbeats [haːtˈbiːts]: the rhythmic beating of the heart pumping blood around the body, felt manually at the wrist [rist], over the temporal bone [tempral'bəun], the carotid artery [kəˈrɒtidˈaːtri] in the neck or over the femoral artery [ˈfemrəl ˈaːtri] in the groin [grɔin] (inguinal [inˈgwənəl] area).

to take blood pressure [teik ˈblʌd ˈpreʃə] (v. + n.) To measure the systolic and diastolic pressure of the blood circulating in the body, using a machine called a sphygmomanometer [ˈsfigˌməuˈmanɒmətə].

✎ *Look at the noun in Column A and choose the most suitable verb(s) from Column B (on the same line) which can go with it.*

Column A – nouns	Column B – verbs
blood	take grow make
a pain	become do have
an operation	produce have recover from
a bed	make do get up
an injection	do give take
a pulse	listen to hear take
a disease	start develop seek
an injury	sustain fight change
the rounds	go walk do
the umbilical cord	produce slice cut
ill	feel have measure

Now put a different noun with the remaining verbs on each line.

34

TOILETRIES

🖉 *When you go on holidays (or into hospital), you need to pack.*
What toiletries do you need to take?

The following things are put into a toilet bag.
Can you draw them?

A comb [kəʊm]	A hairbrush [heə'brʌʃ]

A toothbrush [tʊθ'brʌʃ]	Toothpaste [tʊθ'peist]	A nail–file [neiəl'fɑiəl]	Nail–clippers [neiəl'klipəz]

Scissors [sizəz]	Shampoo [ʃæm'pu:]	Conditioner [kən'diʃənə]	Soap [səʊp]

A flannel [flænəl] (or face–washer)	Deodorant [di:'əʊdərənt]	Perfume [pɜ:'fju:m]	A shaving brush [ʃəiviŋ'brʌʃ]

Shaving cream [ʃəiviŋ'kri:m]	A razor [reizə]	Spare blades [speə'bleidz]	Talcum powder [tælkəm'paʊdə]

CLOTHES AND ACCESSORIES

☺ *Do you feel like a game of tennis? With your partner play 'word tennis': choose an article of clothing or an accessory and see if your partner knows the part of the body where it is worn.*

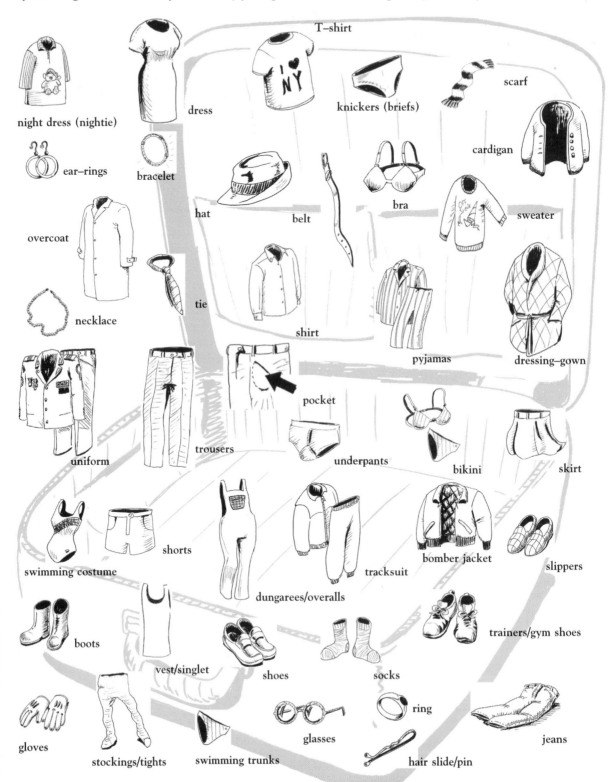

night dress (nightie)

dress

T–shirt

knickers (briefs)

scarf

cardigan

ear–rings

bracelet

hat

belt

bra

sweater

overcoat

tie

shirt

pyjamas

dressing–gown

necklace

uniform

trousers

pocket

underpants

bikini

skirt

swimming costume

shorts

dungarees/overalls

tracksuit

bomber jacket

slippers

boots

vest/singlet

shoes

socks

trainers/gym shoes

gloves

stockings/tights

swimming trunks

glasses

ring

hair slide/pin

jeans

Fasteners

Fasteners are used to close or join a piece of clothing.

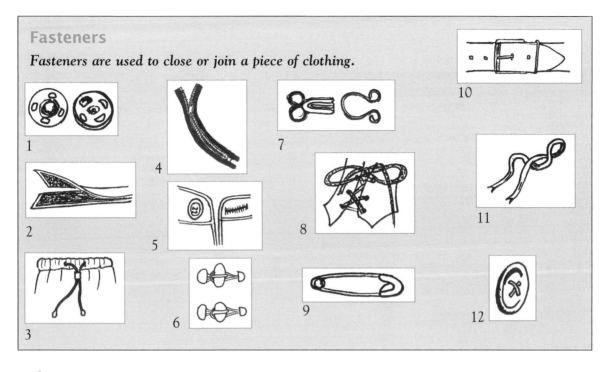

🖉 *In the box below you will find some more vocabulary used to talk about clothes. You will find all these on pages 36 or shown on this page. How quickly can you label them.*

> • suit coat • the hem of a pair of trousers • trouser pocket • bra strap and cup
> • a hairpin • a safety pin • a belt loop • a T–shirt shirt • trouser or shirt cuffs
> • a (man's) cardigan • a pullover/jumper • a coat/an overcoat • laces
> • Velcro fastener • a (hair) ribbon • sleeve(s) • a knot (in a tie or shoelaces)
> • a bow • a buckle • a dressing gown cord/belt • a button–hole
> • the heel and toe of a sock or a shoe • a toggle • hook and eye • a drawstring
> • press–studs or 'poppers'/studs (American English) • a zip (zipper – US) and the 'teeth of a zip'

☺ *Discuss with your partner the clothes and accessories that Cathy would pack to take to hospital.*

1. What different things would a man need to take?
2. What things are classed as 'valuables'?
3. Tell your partner everything you wore yesterday.
4. What do you wear to classes, to work, to the gym or to the swimming pool?
5. Name the different 'underclothes' worn by (a) men (b) women.
6. Can you think of some more clothes that have different names for men and women?
7. What is the difference between
   • a jacket, a coat and an overcoat?
   • tights, stockings and pantyhose?
   • a blouse and a shirt?

🖉 *What materials are clothes made from? Give some examples. e.g. 'wool' – a woollen vest*

CLASS DISCUSSION

Look at these verbs and phrases and make sentences using them with the appropriate clothes and different accessories.

e.g. <u>Put on</u> some warm <u>clothes</u>, it's cold outside.
My little boy can't <u>tie his shoelaces</u> yet.

put on • take off • change into • try (on) fit • suit • pull on • pull off "pop into" • "slip into" • "slip off" do (*sth.*) up • undo (*sth.*) • tie • untie knot • unbutton • zip up • unzip put (*sth.*) into • wear • "throw on" button up • get dressed • get undressed

---

Cathy is sitting up beside the bed in her nightdress, dressing–gown and slippers. She is feeling a little nervous. Her mother is putting her toiletries in the drawer of the bedside table. Sister Joanna comes back into the room with another nurse.

🎧 **Listening 8a – In the ward**

Read and Listen to the first part of the dialogue to answer the following questions.

Who is Mrs Manson?

Who is in charge – Sister Joanna or Nurse Margaret?

Where is Cathy?

Where does Sister Joanna write Cathy's home address and telephone numbers?

What other things does she write on the chart?

Why do Cathy and Nurse Margaret leave the room?

Sister Joanna:	Hello again Cathy, Mrs Manson. This's Nurse Margaret, she is helping me today and would like to stay while I ask you a few questions – is that all right?
Mrs Manson:	Good morning nurse. Yes of course – (1) <u>you don't mind, do you</u> Cathy?
Cathy:	No, of course not. Hello nurse Margaret. Are you new here?
Nurse Margaret:	Yes, I'm still doing my nursing training –(2) <u>You can call me Maggie, everyone else does</u>!
Sister Joanna:	So, now we have a few things to write down here. First, (3) <u>I'd like to check</u> that I have your full name and address – is this all correct Mrs Manson? (*Sister shows the admission chart to Mrs Manson*)
Mrs Manson:	Yes, that's fine. Perhaps I should write my husband's work telephone number too.
Sister Joanna:	That's a good idea, thank you. Now, (4) <u>I'll take</u> Cathy's blood pressure and temperature. (5) <u>Let's</u> put the thermometer under your arm ... that's it. Now give me your other arm and I'll wrap this cuff around it to take your blood pressure. Don't talk while I'm taking it, I won't be able to hear you! It might feel tight, but it won't hurt and I'll be quick! ... That's fine. Do you know how much you weigh and how tall you are, Cathy?
Cathy:	Not really – about 46 kilograms, I think. Mum says I've grown recently!
Sister Joanna:	Doctor will want to know exactly, so Maggie will take you to the scales and we can see how much you weigh – and measure your height at the same time. Thank you Maggie ... see you shortly ... (*Maggie takes Cathy out of the room*) Mrs Manson, does Cathy wear glasses, or contact lenses?
Mrs Manson:	No, her eyesight's very good – She's a healthy girl and rarely gets sick. She has never had an operation before, so she's a bit nervous about it.
Sister Joanna:	The anaesthetist will come round and talk to her soon. He's an excellent doctor and very good with young people. She won't be nervous for long! ... Here they are!

✎ *Can you explain the <u>underlined</u> words and phrases (1–5) in listening exercise 8a? Find a sentence underneath (a–l) with a similar meaning. Write your answer next to the correct expression in the box below.*

1. <u>you don't mind, do you?</u>
2. <u>You can call me Maggie, everyone else does</u>!
3. <u>I'd like to check</u>...(your temperature, pulse or BP)
4. <u>I'll take</u> (your blood pressure, temperature etc.)
5. <u>Let's</u>....
6. <u>You mustn't have</u> anything to eat...
7. <u>Your tummy has to be quite empty</u> –
8. a <u>hospital gown</u> .... <u>put on</u>
9. <u>get undressed</u>
10. <u>I'm allergic to</u>....
11. <u>My skin gets itchy</u> ... my eyes <u>get</u> all <u>puffy</u>..........
12. <u>I eat like a horse</u>!

a. That's all right, isn't it?

b. I can't eat some foods – I have a reaction to them.

c. I have a good appetite – I love food!

d. Change your clothes – get dressed into a hospital night dress (gown).

e. My friends have a short name they use for me, it's friendly.

f. I want to measure (your body temperature, pulse etc.).

g I am ready now to take these measurements.

h. It is very important NOT to eat anything.

i. Take your clothes off – (or) take off your clothes.

j. Your stomach must be empty

k. Shall we...?

l. Pruritis [pru:'raitis] develops, I scratch and my eyes swell up (get swollen).

✎ *Now match phrases 6–12 with a sentence with a similar meaning (a–l). Read the text for listening 8b on the next page, then write phrases 6–12 in the spaces provided in the written text.*

Listening 8b   *(Maggie and Cathy come back into the room)*

Sister Joanna:	Thank you Maggie ... I'll write those here ... OK. *(She writes Cathy's weight and height on the chart)* Did you have breakfast this morning, Cathy?
Cathy:	No, I haven't eaten anything since last night. I'm not really hungry though.
Sister Joanna:	Do you eat well, Cathy? Can you eat everything?
Cathy:	Yes, ask Mum! ....! I love rice and vegetables and ... chocolate, and ice cream. I don't like tropical fruit very much, paw–paws and mangoes, but I love pineapple! I think .... nuts.
Sister Joanna:	Oh! That's important. What happens when you eat them? What sort of a reaction do you have?
Cathy:	.... and sometimes ....
Sister Joanna:	That's no good! I'll write down that you have this reaction to nuts. Tomorrow we can look at the diet cards and choose something nice for you (without nuts!) – I'm sure you'll be hungry by then. Y... until we tell you – and that means no chewing gum or sweets either! (... when you have an anaesthetic.) Do you have any valuables – jewellery or money that you would like me to put in the safe until after the operation?
Cathy:	Yes, I have this necklace and my purse is in the drawer ... oh, and there's my watch too.
Sister Joanna:	OK. I'll put them away now and when I come back I'll bring a .... for you to .... You will have to .... and change into a rather inelegant hospital gown! First, because I'm taking your precious things away, I'll get you to sign this form. Here, that's right ... I can see you have a Walkman too, maybe that should be put away ... mm., we'll take that later. That's all for now. The doctor will call in very soon and I'll be back in about an hour or so. If you need anything, this is the call bell – press this button and a nurse will come. You can use that bathroom – make yourselves comfortable.
Cathy:	Thank you. Do you need anything Mum?
Mrs Manson:	No, love. Thank you Sister ... and Maggie. We will just chat until the doctor comes ...

 Listen to the recording and check your answers. Listen to both 8a and 8b again.

☺   *Practise saying the new phrases with your partner, then practice both parts of the dialogues in groups of four.*

Look up unknown words in your dictionary and add them to your vocabulary lists.
Learn the words and expressions on page 43.

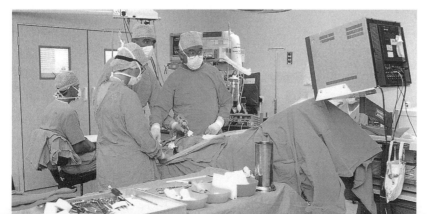

Who wears hospital gowns?

What do the staff in the operating theatres wear on their heads, over their day clothes, over their faces, over their shoes, on their hands?

MACHINES, INSTRUMENTS AND OTHER GADGETS

> **What is a machine?** (*n. countable*)
> A machine is a piece of equipment which does a particular type of work and which usually uses electricity or power from an engine (or motor).

List some machines you would find

in the laboratory:

....

....

at the hospital:

....

....

in an office:

....

....

at home:

....

....

Other words

Is it possible to use all these words to describe every machine?

appliance (*n.c.*)
device (*n.c.*)
instrument (*n.c.*)
contraption (*n.c.*)
gadget (*n.c.*)
tool (*n.c.*)
apparatus (*n.u.*)

Parts of a machine

power socket	switches
plug	levers
cables, cords or leads	control panel
main power switch	LED – Light Emitting Diode(s)
on/off switch	display
dial	flashing light(s)
buttons	VDU – Visual Display Unit
keys	

☺ *Talk about the differences with your teacher.*

INSTRUMENTS AND OTHER THINGS USED
FOR PHYSICAL EXAMINATIONS

The things shown are all used for different physical examinations of patients and other procedures. Identify them and then label them using the names in the box under the pictures.

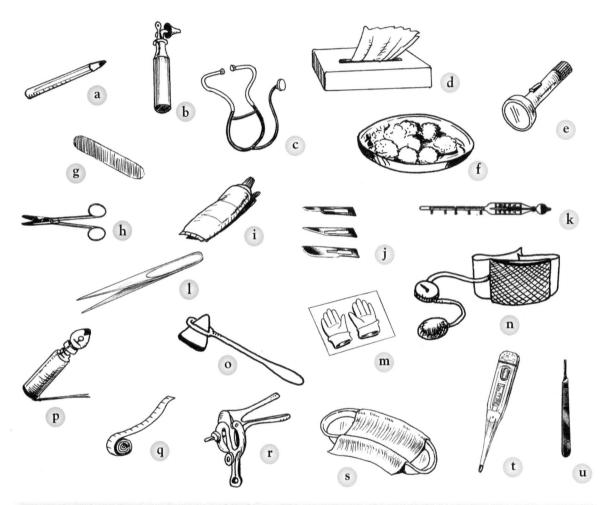

1. box of tissues [ˈbɒks əv ˈtiʃuːz]
2. vaginal speculum [vədʒˈainəl spekjuləm]
3. stethoscope [steθəskəup]
4. an otoscope [ənˈəutəskəup]
5. an ophthalmoscope [ənˈɒfθælməˈskəup]
6. scissors [sizəz]
7. sterile [sterˈail] gloves [glʌvz]
8. thermometer [θəˈmɒmətə]
9. small bowl [smɔːlˈbəul]
10. tape measure [teipˈmeʒə]
11. percussion hammer [pəkʌʃənˈhæmə]
12. cotton balls [kɒtənˈbɔːlz]
13. scalpel handle [skælpl hændl]
14. tube of lubricant [tjuːbəvˈluːbrikənt]
15. scalpel blades [skælpl bleidz]
16. torch (flashlight) [tɔːtʃ] ([flæʃˈlait])
17. skin marking pencil [ˈskinˈmaːkiŋˈpensəl]
18. paper towel [peipəˈtauəl]
19. urinometer [juːrənˈɒmətə]
20. kidney dish (vomit bowl) [kidniˈdiʃ] ([vɒmətˈbəul])
21. sphygmomanometer ('sphygmo') [sfigməuˈmənˈɒmətə]
22. plain dissecting forceps [plein dəˈsektiŋ fɔːsəps]
23. tongue depressor (spatula) [tʌŋˈdipresə] ([spætˈjulə])

What is each thing used for?

e.g. The pencil is used for marking skin.

> **When you don't know what it's called you can describe its use**
> *e.g.* This is a gadget used **for** testing reflexes.
> It's an instrument used **for** measuring blood pressure.

☺ *Describe something to your partner and ask him/her to guess what it is.*

EXPRESSION and WORD LIST   1G/H

accessories [əkˈsesəˈriz] (*n. pl.*) Items or articles that you wear but are not essential clothing. *e.g. a belt, jewellery, a handbag.*

allergy [ælədʒi] (*n.*) A particular allergy causes a person to become ill or have a reaction to something that does not normally make people ill.
allergic [əˈlɜːdʒik] (*adj.*)

appetite [æpəˈtait] (*n.*) The desire to eat. *e.g. The baby has a healthy appetite.*

apparatus [æpəˈreitəs] (*n. uncountable*) Apparatus is the equipment needed to do a particular job or activity and may include tools, machines and other instruments.

appliance [əplaiˈəns] (*n.*) is a machine or device used at home, usually electrical. *e.g. a toaster and a washing machine are household appliances.*

bathroom [baˈθruːm] (*n.*) A room in a house that contains a bath or a shower, a washbasin and sometimes a toilet.

clothes [kləʊðz] (*n. pl.*) Clothes are things that people wear, such as shirts, trousers, dresses etc. *e.g. I like casual clothes.*

contraption [kənˈtræpʃən] (*n.*) The word contraption can be used for any machine or device when it looks unusual and you don't know what it is used for.

device [dəˈvais] (*n.*) A device is something that was invented for a specific purpose. *e.g. an electronic device.*

drawer [drɔːə] (*n.*) A drawer is part of a desk, chest or box–shaped piece of furniture to put things in. To open the drawer you pull it out towards yourself.

eyesight [aiˈsait] (*n.*) The ability to see. *e.g. I have good eyesight, I don't need to wear glasses.*

fastener [faˈsəˈnə] (*n.*) Something such as a clasp, button, zip or small hook that fastens sth. especially clothing.

gadget [gædʒət] (*n.*) A small machine or device that does something useful. *e.g. a corkscrew, a potato peeler etc.*

gym [dʒim] (*n.*) **1.** A club, building or large room, usually containing special equipment for people to do physical exercise. **2.** The activity of doing physical exercise in a gym.

height [hait] (*n.*) The height of a person or a thing is their size or length from the bottom to the top.

horse [hɔːs] (*n.*) A large animal that people can ride.

instrument [inˈstrəmənt] (*n.*) **1.** A tool or device used to do a specific scientific task or for measuring speed, altitude, pressure, density etc. **2.** A musical instrument such as a guitar, piano or violin.

jewellery [dʒuːəlri] (*n.*) Various ornaments that people wear. *e.g. bracelets, brooches necklaces and rings.*

locker [lɒkə] (*n.*) A small metal or wooden cupboard (usually with a lock and key) where you can keep personal belongings.

machine [məˈʃiːn] (*n.*) A piece of equipment which does a particular type of work and which usually uses electricity or power from an engine.

material [məˈtiːriəl] (*n.*) **1.** a solid substance, **2.** a type of cloth or **3.** things you need for a particular activity.

measurement [meʒə ˈmənt] (*n.*) The result, usually expressed in numbers, that you obtain by measuring something.

operation [ɒpəˈreiʃən] (*n.*) Cutting open the human body under anaesthetic by a surgeon, in order to repair, replace or remove a damaged or diseased part.

purse [pɜːs] (*n.*) A small bag, usually for coins but may refer to a woman's handbag.

reaction to sth. [ri:ˈækʃən] (*n.*) An unpleasant affect or illness, possibly caused by chemicals or food substances.

scales [skeilz] (*n. pl.*) A piece of equipment used for weighing things or people.

stomach [stʌmək] (*n.*) The main digestive organ of the human body where food is mixed to a liquid before passing into the intestines.

toiletries [tɔilətˈriz] (*n. pl*) Toiletries are things you use when washing or taking care of your body.

valuables [vælˈjubəlz] (*n. pl*) Small objects you own that are usually worth a lot of money. *e.g. mobile phone, jewellery etc.*

weight [weit] (*n.*) The weight of a person or thing is how heavy they are, measured in grams, ounces, kilos, pounds, tons or tonnes.

to chat [tʃæt] (*v.*) To talk in an informal and friendly way.

to get undressed [get ʌndˈdrest] (*v.*) Take off the clothes that you are wearing.

to measure [meˈʒə] (*v.*) You measure a quantity that can be expressed in numbers. *e.g. The length of a baby or the height of a person, using a ruler or tape measure.*

to shave [ʃeiv] (*v.*) To remove hair from the body, using a razor or shaver.

    a close [kləus] **shave** (*coll. phrase*) A close shave is an event that was almost an accident or disaster but was luckily avoided.

to weigh (so. or sth.) [wei] (*v.*) To measure how heavy something is.

to wrap [ræp] (*v.*) To fold something around a thing to cover or protect it. *e.g. You wrap a gift, you 'wrap up' to keep warm and you can wrap the cuff of a sphygmomanometer (a blood–pressure measuring device) around a person's arm.*

empty [emˈti] (*adj.*) Something that is empty, has nothing in it. *e.g. an empty bag, an empty room, an empty box.*

hungry [hʌŋˈgri] (*adj.*) When you are hungry you want some food because you haven't eaten for a long time.

tall [tɔːl] (*adj.*) Someone or something that is tall, has a greater height than normal or average.

sick [sik] (*adj.*) Ill, not well. Sick usually means physically ill but it can be used to mean mentally ill.

itchy [iˈtʃi] (*adj.*) An unpleasant feeling on your skin that makes you scratch.

rarely [reəˈli] (*adv.*) If something rarely happens, it doesn't happen very often. *e.g. I rarely wear a hat.*

Is your vocabulary growing, like the trees on these pages?

 Choose ten words from this list and the lists on the preceding 'expression and word list' pages and write a story.
Share your story with the class.

DAYS OF THE WEEK, MONTHS AND SEASONS

There are 7 days in a week

Monday **Tuesday** **Wednesday** **Thursday** and **Friday**	are week–days
Saturday and **Sunday**	are the weekend

MONTHS OF THE YEAR

January [dʒænjəri]

February [febˈruːri]

March [maːtʃ]

April [eipril]

May [mei]

June [dʒuːn]

July [dʒəˈlai]

August [ɔːgəst]

September [sepˈtembə]

October [ɒkˈtəubə]

November [nəʊˈvembə]

December [disˈembə]

☺ SEASONS

Can you name the seasons?

Which season do you like best?

Describe the different seasons where you live.

What are some illnesses that appear more in one season than another? What are the reasons for this?

Compare: **hot and humid** and **cold and damp** *weather.*

Under the weather?

The way we feel can be influenced by the weather. 'Seasonal Affective Disorder' (SAD) is a recognised condition which occurs during the winter months when there is little sunlight and long nights. These people are diagnosed as being *weather sensitive* and suffer from depression, tiredness and lethargy.

Other illnesses which are influenced by the weather are: migraine headaches [maiˈgrein hedeiks], skin cancer [kænsə], rheumatism [ruːmətism] and asthma [æsmə].

"ORDINAL" NUMBERS

🖉 *Match the numbers with a word and rewrite them in order*

1st
2nd
3rd
4th
5th
9th
10th
12th
13th
15th
20th
23rd
31st
50th

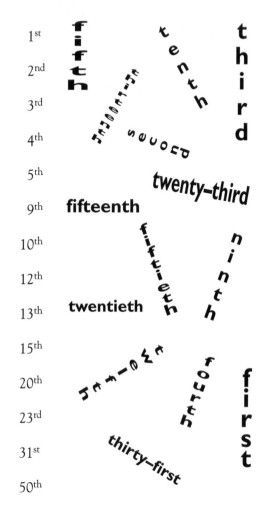

fifth
tenth
third
twenty-third
fifteenth
fiftieth
ninth
twentieth
fourth
first
thirty-first

☺ DATES

What's the date today?

It's (the) ....(of).........20....

When is your birthday?

What year were you born?

Do you have any special days to remember during the year?

Can you remember dates easily?

How do you remember dates?

GRAMMAR NOTES – Prepositions (2)

Do you need a preposition or not?

🖉 1. **Look at the pictures and answer the questions:**

1. A. Where is the nurse going?
....
  B. Where is she now?
....

2. Where's Susan?
....
  What's she waiting for?
....

3. Where's Mr. Brown going?
....

4. Where is he now?
....

5. Where is this patient going?
....

6. A. Where's the stethoscope?
....
  B. Where is it now?
....

7. Where is the stethoscope now?
....

8. Where is the visitor going?
....

9. Where is he now?
....

10. Where's the mop?
....

11. Where's Jamie?
....

12. Where is his friend?
....

13. Where are John and Judy?
....

14. Where's the Children's Ward?
....

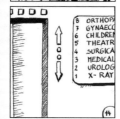

 2. Use one of the following prepositions to fill the gaps:

of (x2)	by (x1)	on (x7)
from (x2)	with (x2)	in (x5)
to (x4)	at (x4)	for (x4)

1. He works .... the General City Hospital, he starts .... 8 a.m.

2. At the moment Chris is working ...... the Neurosurgical Ward.

3. The consultant responsible .... this ward is Mr. Fitzsimmons.

4. Accident victims are usually taken to hospital ..... ambulance.

5. Mrs. Fields was complaining .... pain in her lower abdomen.

6. She was transferred ...... the ward ...... A&E (the Accident and Emergency Unit).

7. Doctors operated ...... a child for over 6 hours yesterday ..... the new theatre .... the 6th floor.

8. Neonates can generally stay in the room .... their mothers.

9. Take this specimen .... urine .... pathology. ('path' [pæθ]), ... the written order form.

10. He was admitted .... surgery, the operation will be .... the morning .... Wednesday.

11. The cause of the baby's temperature was found just ..... time.

12. They are going downstairs .... therapy, ... 10 o'clock ..... ten thirty.

13. There is a staff change–room .... the first floor, it's ..... the medical staff only.

14. Mr. Singh wants to look .... the MRI scans before he sees the patient, they are .... the desk .... the office.

15. Mr Bailey doesn't come into the hospital ... weekends, not ... Saturdays unless it's urgent and not ... Sundays unless he's 'on call'.

☺ **Check your answers with a partner then with your teacher.**

SHIFT WORKERS, TIME AND NUMBERS

📖 *Read the text and then look at the sentences on the right.*

Most nurses work in shifts – each day is usually divided into 3 equal 8–hour shifts. 'Day Shift' (or 'a.m. shift') can be from 6, 7 or 8 a.m. until 2, 3 or 4 p.m., 'Afternoon/Evening Shift' can start from 2, 3 or 4 p.m. and finish **at** 10 or 11 p.m. or 12 midnight. The 'Night Shift' may start as early as 8 pm or as late as midnight.

Sometimes the night shift can be a 12–hour shift.

The word 'duty' [dju:ti] (= moral or legal obligations or tasks that need to be done) can also be used to describe shift work.

*e.g. I'm working **night duty** for a month*
*I'm **on duty** tomorrow afternoon*
*He's **off duty** for 2 days. (He has 2 free days.)*

To talk about time in hospitals (and for public transport timetables and in the armed forces), the 24–hour clock is used. Using the 24–hour clock prevents confusion and errors in giving medications and in keeping records.

The nurses' timetable is called a **roster** and this word can also be used as a verb, *e.g.* **I'm rostered on** *morning shift.* John is working night shift – he works from 2000 (twenty hundred hours) to 0630 ('oh' six thirty hours).

Rosie is working morning shift at the moment from 0600 (oh six hundred) to 1500 (fifteen hundred). Sandra is the charge nurse and works from 0800 to 1700 Monday to Friday.

✏️ **Look at the clocks and write the time in 2 or 3 different ways:**

e.g. 0900 or 2100 = Nine o' clock in the morning (9am) or in the evening (9pm) 'o' nine hundred or twenty–one hundred hours.

✏️ *Are the following sentences true (T) or false (F)? Correct the false statements.*

1. 'Shift work' involves starting and finishing work at different times.

....

2. A 'roster' is a 12–hour shift.

....

3. Different hospitals have different shifts.

....

4. If you are 'on duty', you can stay at home.

....

5. Eight o'clock in the morning is the same as '2000 hours' (twenty hundred hours).

....

6. Soldiers in the army, sailors, pilots, doctors and other medical staff use the 24–hour clock.

....

7. English–speaking people always use the 24–hour clock.

....

8. Some hospital staff work regular 'day shifts'.

....

9. 'I'm on duty' means 'I am working'.

....

10. Using the 24–hour clock prevents misunderstandings.

....

GETTING TO WORK (OR DOING A PROCEDURE)
HOW LONG DOES IT TAKE?

🖉 *Look at the information below and write sentences in the space provided.*

	Transport	Leaves home/ Arrives at work	starts/finishes
Example			
Sandra	*bus*	0800–0845	0900–1730
goes to work by		It takes forty–five minutes	She's on duty from 9 until 5.30
Rosie	train	0515–0615	0630–1530
Steve	car and train	0615–0715	0730–1630
Pat	bicycle	1315–1345	1400–2300
Mr. Singh	car	0710–0720	0730–1800
Mr. James	nil! (he walks)	0715–0745	0800–1400
John & Judy	motorbike	0900–0935	2200–0700

VERBALISING NUMBERS

0	'o' [əʊ], nought [nɔːt], nil [nil] or zero [ziːrəʊ]
100	one/a hundred [wʌn/ə'hʌndrəd]
1,000	one/a thousand [wʌn/ə 'θaʊzənd]
1,000,000	one/a million [wʌn /ə'miljən]
* 1.075	one **point** 'oh', seven, five.
420	four hundred **and** twenty
4,220	four thousand, two hundred **and** twenty
'units'	one, two, three, four, five, six, seven, eight, nine
'tens'	ten, twenty, thirty, forty, fifty, sixty, seventy, eighty, ninety
'teens'	thirteen, fourteen, fifteen, sixteen, seventeen, eighteen, nineteen

N.B. A 'COMMA' (,) SEPARATES MILLIONS AND THOUSANDS WRITTEN IN NUMBERS.
   *A 'POINT' (or full stop) IS ALWAYS A DECIMAL POINT
   – THE NUMBERS AFTER THE DECIMAL POINT ARE ALWAYS READ SEPARATELY:
   e.g. 7.255 = *seven point two, five, five.*

When writing numbers in words: always use a 'hyphen' between the tens and units, and the word 'and' always follows the word 'hundred' in British English.
e.g. **235 =** *two hundred and thirty–five.*
   16,833 = *sixteen thousand, eight hundred and thirty–three.*

49

🖊 *Write the following numbers, fractions and symbols in words and practice saying them.*

| 2,300,000 | 699 | 4,621 | 12,042 | 1m | 9.25% | 98 | 0.003 | 34.321 | 87 | 204 | 902 |

Fractions: [frækʃənz]

$^1/_2$ [ha:f] $^1/_4$ [kwɔ:tə]

(use ordinal nos. for the following)

$^1/_3$ $^1/_6$ $^3/_4$ $^1/_8$ $^3/_{20}$ $^{11}/_{13}$ $^2/_3$ $^9/_{10}$

Powers and mathematical symbols

10^3 5^2 10^{-6} e^2 π

$A=\pi r^2$ $C=2\pi r$ $V=^4/_3\pi r^3$

(A=area   C=circumference   V=volume)

😊 *Make the questions and then ask your partner to answer them. E.g. what is $^3/_4$ of 4?*

1. $^3/_4$ of 4?
2. $^1/_2$ of 90?
3. $^1/_2$ of 0.05?
4. $^1/_4$ of 200?
5. $^3/_4$ of 1 litre? .... mls. [milz] – millilitres
6. 1/10 of 5 kg? .... gms. [græmz] – grams
7. How many cents in a dollar (or in one Euro)?
8. $^1/_2$ of 1?
9. days in 'a fortnight'?
10. 'x' mean?
11. 33 x 11 =?
12. (10 to the power of 3)?
13. patients in the medical ward at your hospital?
14. floors in the main part of your hospital?
15. wards on each floor?

Abbreviations used for Time (1)

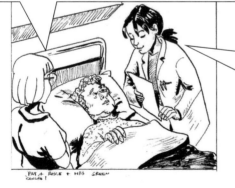

When are Mrs Green's medications due?

The doctor has prescribed antibiotics [ænti'bai'ɒtiks] *every eight hours, i.e. eight hourly (usually given at 6am, 2pm and 10pm).*

'every eight hours' can be written like this: 8/24
'every four hours' can be written like this: 4/24   (24 hours in a day)

'in' or 'for three days' can be written like this: 3/7
'in' or 'for five days' can be written like this: 5/7   (7 days in a week)

'in' or 'for three weeks' can be written like this: 3/52
'in' or 'for five weeks' can be written like this: 5/52   (52 weeks in a year)

'in' or 'for six months' can be written like this: 6/12
'in' or 'for two months' can be written like this: 2/12   (12 months in a year)

Write the following sentences and abbreviations in full (don't forget the prepositions!).

Example: Mrs Green: antibiotics 8/24. Review 4/7
Mrs Green is to take antibiotics every eight hours for 4 days.
Her doctor will review the situation in 4 days.

1. This patient can go home 3/7...
....

2. This patient has been in a coma 6/12 ....
....

3. Her baby is due 5/52 ....
....

4. He has an appointment in 'outpatients' 10/7..
....

5. PUO (Pyrexia of Unknown Origin) ca. 1/52...
....

6. Run IV (Intravenous infusion) over 6/24 ....
....

7. 2/24 Gastric Tube feed, 4/24 aspiration...
....

8. 2/24 turns and PAC (Pressure Area Care)..
....

9. NBM (Nil by mouth = fast) 6/24 prior to surgery ....
....

10. Baby Marks (Joseph) aged 2/12 admitted 3/7 ago...
....

Listening 9 – Time expressions **Listen to the recording and check your answers.**

Accepted Abbreviations used for Time and Frequency (2)

b.d. = ×2 per day	p.r.n. = when necessary
= twice a day	a.s.a.p. = as soon as possible
t.i.d./t.d.s. = ×3 per day	stat. = immediately
= three times a day	a.m. = morning
q.i.d. = ×4 per day = four times (daily)	p.m. = afternoon or evening
nocte = at night	a.c. = before (prior to) a meal (eating)
×1 = once	p.c. = after (following) a meal (eating)
×2 = twice	hr = hour
×3 = three times	hrly = every hour

The following words are not abbreviated in medical records

every	monthly	not (very) often
daily	annually (yearly)	frequently
weekly	fortnightly (every 2 weeks)	every now and again (periodically)

DAILY ROUTINES – HABITS
[PRESENT SIMPLE TENSE (2)]

Activities of a Daily Routine	*Jamie's Routine*	*Time*
wake up [weik ʌp]		6.45 am
get up		7.00 am
have | a shower, a bath or a wash – get dressed | breakfast, a cup of coffee, and listen [lisən] to the radio		7.05 am 7.15 am
leave [li:v] home – lock [lɒk] the door		7.30 am
catch | the bus | the train ride [raid] the bicycle		7.35 am
arrive [əraiv] at work		7.45 am
start work		8.00 am
have lunch | at home | in a restaurant		12.30–1.45 pm
finish work | go home | go shopping		5.30 pm
prepare | dinner have |		7.00 pm
read, do homework or watch TV go to the gym, go to the cinema, meet friends or go to the pub get undressed, have a wash and clean (your) teeth go to bed		*In the evening* About 11 pm

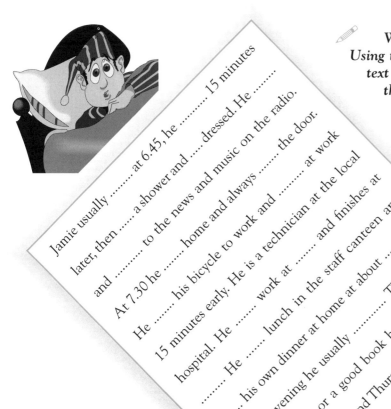

✎ *What does Jamie do almost every day? Using the table on page 52, complete the text with the correct form of the verb or the time.*

Jamie usually .... at 6.45, he .... 15 minutes later, then ...... a shower and ..... dressed. He ...... and .... to the news and music on the radio.

At 7.30 he .... home and always .... the door. He .... his bicycle to work and .... at work 15 minutes early. He is a technician at the local hospital. He .... work at .... and finishes at .... He ...... lunch in the staff canteen and .... his own dinner at home at about ....

In the evening he usually .... TV or .... a newspaper or a good book before he goes to bed. On Tuesday and Thursday evenings, he ...... to the gym and .... his friends. They ..... to the pub together on Saturday evenings or they sometimes go to the cinema or to a concert to .... to live music.

☺ **Ask your partner questions about Jamie's activities. Listen carefully for the correct answer!**

e.g. *Question: What does Jamie do at 7.15 am? Answer: He gets up and then he has a shower*

Discuss with your partner:

What do you do each day, what is your usual daily routine?
What do you do at the weekend?
How often do you go out with friends / go to the cinema / go to live concerts?

EXAMPLE OF THE ROUTINE MORNING SHIFT IN A SURGICAL WARD

There is a set routine in hospitals for each shift that nurses work, ensuring all the daily needs of the patients are met, i.e. all the patients are correctly looked after and nothing is forgotten.

It is Annie's first day of work experience in the wards. She has been introduced to the staff in the surgical ward and Rosie is explaining the normal ward routine for the day shift, starting at 0700 and finishing at 1430. (Routines, observations and procedures change slightly in the different wards in different hospitals.)

Listening 10 – Handover *First, read the text then listen to Rosie explaining the ward routine to Annie.*

0700–0715	Handover. *This is the time when the night staff tell us about the patients and report any changes. We are given a computer printout containing all the basic information about the patient: their name, admission date, doctor and diagnosis.*

We have to write down any changes in the diagnosis, observations, treatment, IV's, drainage tubes or indwelling catheters (IDC) and whether they are pre–operative patients or post–operative.

All of this is recorded on the patient's history and care plan and with practice you will know what is important and relevant.

0715	Round/Sight check. *As soon as the handover is finished, greet and check all of the patients in your care.*
0715–0800	Observations and medications. *Check that pre–operative patients are ready: Check that they are fasting, the area for surgery is free from hair (shaved), that the ladies are not wearing nail polish (the anaesthetist will want to check the natural colour of the fingers and toes). Ask if the patient has any false teeth, contact lenses or other prostheses that should be kept safely in the ward and recorded on the patient's chart. Any jewellery or valuables should be put in the safe and the chart signed by the patient.*

General observations include: temperature, pulse, respirations and blood pressure. Intravenous lines, wound drainage tubes and urinary catheter tubes should also be checked at this time.

Do everything for each patient while in the room and set each patient up for breakfast – put the table near the bed and position the patient so he/she can reach it.

0800	Help patients with breakfast where necessary and feed patients who are unable to feed themselves.

If some patients are fasting, attend to their personal hygiene and bed–making while the others are having breakfast. Check what time patients are going to theatre, what time their 'pre–meds' are due and give clear instructions to the patient. Patients who can sit out of bed or are going to the operating theatre can have their beds made later.

0930	Doctors' rounds. 15 minute break for staff when possible. We have to organise our breaks so that there are enough graduate staff in the ward at all times.

1000	Check any new orders on the patient's charts. Do the observations, give out medications and fill–in the Fluid Balance Charts (FBCs) of all the patients in your care. Empty catheter drainage bags or flasks and record amounts accurately on the FBC. Try to do your 'nursing notes' and updates whenever you have a spare moment – you can always add to them during the day.

1215	The patients' midday meals arrive. Check that patients are prepared to eat and check their BSLs (blood sugar levels) if necessary and give insulin or other medications that should be taken with food.

Staff meal break (30 minutes). All the patients must be fed prior to the staff having their lunch.

1400	Recheck all your patients' charts and notes. Hand over to the evening staff. If there is time, check all pathology and X/Ray reports and update discharge and nursing plan charts.

Make sure that the evening staff have the keys to the locked cupboards for the Dangerous Drugs (DD's) and valuables.

✎ **Listen again and write the words Annie uses to show Rosie that she is listening carefully.**

☺ **What differences can you think of between morning shift, afternoon/evening shift and night shift? What are some of the things that have to be done on all shifts?**

What are some of the differences between routines:

In a medical ward and in a surgical ward?
In a surgical ward and in the labour ward?
In a ward for adults and in a children's ward?
In an intensive care unit and a medical ward?

Read this 'professional profile'.

PROFILE OF A NURSE

1

Hello, my name is Nicole Sirianni. I'm 25 years old and I live at home with my parents in Melbourne, Australia. I am a registered nurse and I work in the Paediatric ward at the Northern General Hospital which is about 25 km. from the centre of Melbourne.

2

I have always wanted to be a nurse and when I finished high school, I applied at one of the universities here that do nursing. The Bachelor of Nursing course takes three years to complete and is very difficult. We did a lot of theory and also worked in hospitals. During the first year most of our time was spent at lectures, learning the theory, but we were able to spend a few weeks in the hospital 'observing' – just seeing how things were done! In the second year, equal time was given to lectures and work experience. We were expected to be able to care for two or three patients, with supervision by the permanent trained staff. In the final year most of our days were spent working at the hospital but we continued with some lectures. By the end of the third year we were able to care for a 'full patient load' of four or five patients – still with supervision.

3

After graduating from university with a Bachelor of Nursing Degree, it is necessary to register with the Nurses' Board so that you can work in a hospital as a Registered Nurse. The first year of working as a registered nurse is called the graduate year and I started at the Northern General and worked in three different wards: Orthopaedic, Medical and Paediatric. This is the time when most nurses really decide which area of nursing they like. I really loved working in the Children's ward and in Orthopaedic but stayed in the medical/palliative ward for 18 months before applying for a position in the Paediatric ward – it was a really good experience. I have worked in Paediatrics since then and I adore working with children – they recover from illness so quickly and it's wonderful to help them get better and to see them go home.

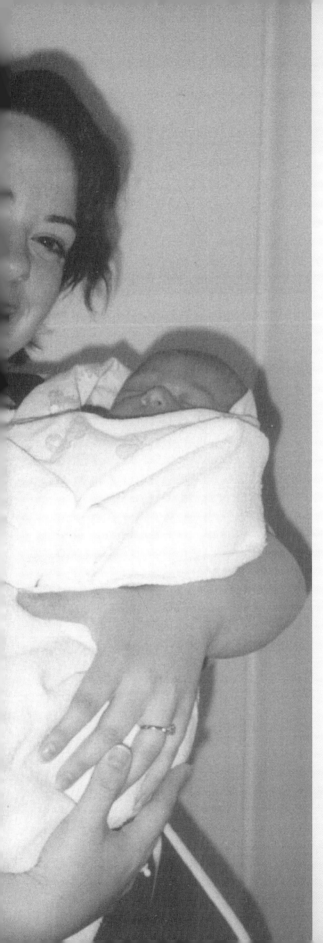

4

Nursing, overall, is a very rewarding profession and by doing your job well, it brings immense self–satisfaction and the respect of both the patients and the medical staff. The natural holistic approach to nursing means listening carefully to the patient, assisting with personal hygiene and mobilisation, giving sound advice, understanding each individual's concerns and family and medical history and developing a very special and personal relationship.

5

At the moment I am hoping to be accepted back at university to study Paediatric Oncology – a 'post graduate' Diploma Course. I have applied and if I am accepted, I will go the Royal Children's Hospital to do it. "The Royal Children's" is one of the most prestigious children's hospitals in Australia and I would be really delighted to have this opportunity. There are so many facets of nursing to choose from – it's a wonderful profession.

✎ **Label each paragraph using one of the following headings.**

a. My future plans.
b. Working professionally.
c. Nursing education.
d. An introduction.
e. My personal views about nursing

Answer these questions:
What did she want to do before finishing school?
What did she do after leaving school?
What did the nurses do during their first year?
What does she want to do in the future?

How many time clauses or expressions can you find in the text? <u>Underline them.</u>
Sequence the events in Nicole's nursing career using the following words in sentences: First, then, next, by the end of..., since (that time), until (now), finally. In the future...

L

ACTIVITIES OF DAILY LIVING (ADLs)

Working with people of all ages, social levels and nationalities is both rewarding and satisfying. Patients are first and most importantly, individuals with specific needs. The 'holistic approach' to health care recognises that good health results from a balance between physical, spiritual, psychological and social needs, relationships and environment.

Activities of daily living refer to the things we do in the course of our daily routines – often they are almost 'automatic' i.e. we do them without having to think about them. It is only when we are disabled in some way or when we are in a situation which is abnormal, that conscious effort has to be made. All therapy must include consideration of the following factors for each individual patient.

Occupation, Activity, Tasks, Skills and Sequencing

Occupation   refers to a habitual, balanced 'state of being' and the ways each individual person maintains his/her health throughout life [laif].

Activity   refers to 'doing specific things' and productive action. Activity is necessary for Man's survival and existence.

Task   A 'task' is one element or component of an activity.

Skill   A skill is having the ability to do something well, i.e. having expertise. A skill can be acquired or learned.

Sequencing   is being able to link (join together) specific tasks in a logical order to complete an activity.

Roles

Roles *(the parts people play in their lives [laivz]) are a combination of attitudes and strategies that are used to maintain status and self–esteem throughout life. Roles change depending on the age and developmental stage of the individual and his/her responsibilities as related to their environment, culture, beliefs, family, interests, skills and behaviour* [bi'heivjə].

Life skills

Life skills *are the abilities individuals acquire and develop in order to perform every day tasks successfully. These vary from person to person and throughout a person's life. Life skills can be categorised in various ways but 3 broad categories are quite useful. Look at the table on the opposite page which illustrates these. The 3 broad categories of self maintenance, role duties and leisure activities are broken down further into sub–groups. All the elements in each sub–group must be considered when assessing a patient's needs and abilities.*

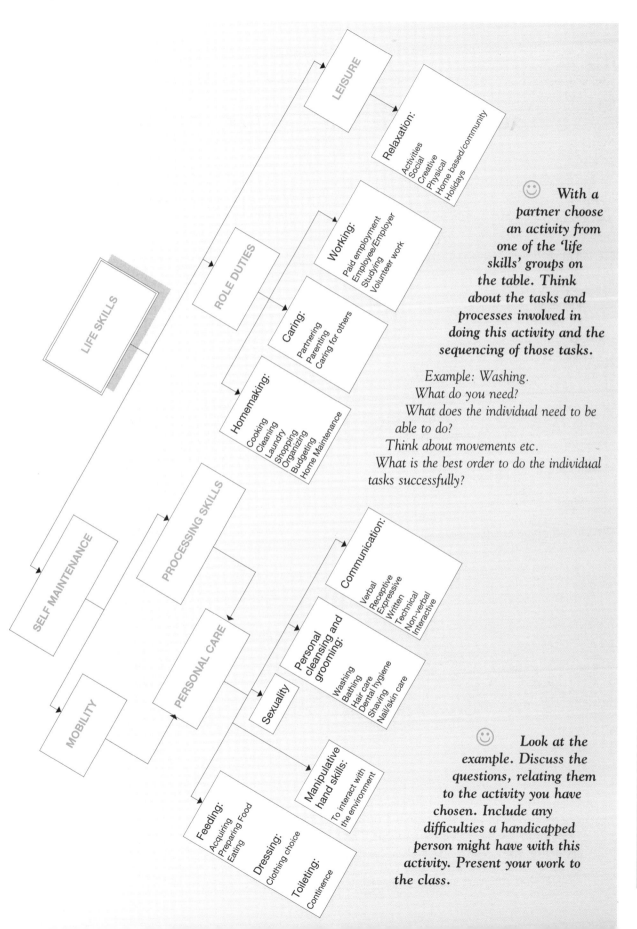

LIFE SKILLS

ROLE DUTIES

LEISURE

Relaxation:
Activities
Social
Creative
Physical
Home based/community
Holidays

Working:
Paid employment
Employee/Employer
Studying
Volunteer work

Caring:
Partnering
Parenting
Caring for others

Homemaking:
Cooking
Cleaning
Laundry
Shopping
Organizing
Budgeting
Home Maintenance

SELF MAINTENANCE

PROCESSING SKILLS

PERSONAL CARE

MOBILITY

Communication:
Verbal
Receptive
Expressive
Written
Technical
Non-verbal
Interactive

Personal cleansing and grooming:
Washing
Bathing
Hair care
Dental hygiene
Shaving
Nail/skin care

Sexuality

Manipulative hand skills:
To interact with the environment

Feeding:
Acquiring
Preparing Food
Eating

Dressing:
Clothing choice

Toileting:
Continence

☺ With a partner choose an activity from one of the 'life skills' groups on the table. Think about the tasks and processes involved in doing this activity and the sequencing of those tasks.

Example: Washing.
What do you need?
What does the individual need to be able to do?
Think about movements etc.
What is the best order to do the individual tasks successfully?

☺ Look at the example. Discuss the questions, relating them to the activity you have chosen. Include any difficulties a handicapped person might have with this activity. Present your work to the class.

REVISION OF VERBS

Look at the groups of 3 pictures and find the matching verbs – write the correct verb under the picture. The verbs on this page start with b, c, d, e or f.

crawl
cry
draw

comb
cook
cough

blow
break
brush

clean
clap
close

dream
drink
drop

dry
eat
fall

☺ *Check your answers with your partner – Which of these activities do you do every day?*

MORE VERBS! *This time from 'c' to 'o'*

cut
hop
jump

have a bath
have a shower
dance

peel
pour
pick up

get dressed
get up
go to bed

iron
kneel
laugh

listen
mend
open

✏️ **Can you write a noun phrase, or an adverb, next to the pictured verbs to make a phrase?**
e.g. get dressed quickly   have a shower in the morning   iron my shirts
How many different phrases can the class think of for each verb?

ARE YOU READY FOR MORE? *Now from 'p' to 'z'*

write	touch	weigh	sew
yawn	turn off	whisper	shake
shave	turn on	whistle	shout
sweep	wake up	sit down	smile
take off	walk	sing	stand up
tie	wash	sleep	stretch
run	wash up	point	
scratch	watch	put on	
scream	wave	read	

✎ Match the groups of 3 pictures with the correct set of verbs from the box.
Conjugate all the verbs illustrated (pages 60–62) that are irregular.
What is the past participle of the regular verbs?

✎ Write sentences using the verbs you need to learn. Are there any others you will find useful?

CONDITIONALS ('IF' SENTENCES)

Introduction to all forms:

1. If I **drop** the ball/glass, what **will happen**?   Time reference: .... Name ....
2. If he **dropped** it, what **would happen**?   Time reference: .... Name ....
3. If he **had dropped** it, what **would have happened**?   Time reference: .... Name ....
4. If you **drop** a glass, it usually **breaks**.   Time reference: .... Name ....

The First Conditional – talking about the present or future – Real Possibilities

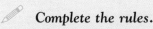 *Complete the rules.*

Use: In the First Conditional both the condition and effect refer to: ....

Form: If + ..., will/........... + ...   (Present, Future or Past time)

The main clause may come before the 'if clause' but remember 'will' is never used in the 'if' clause.

Different forms of the 1st conditional:
– in the 'if' clause *other present tenses* may be used;
– in the main clause, modal verbs or other future forms can be used.

'If' Clause ⟶ Present Simple

Main/Result/Effect Clause ⟶ Future Simple (will/won't)
Present Continuous, be going to or modal verbs: can/could, had better, should, may/might, must/have to

e.g.   **If** you **take** risks, you **will/could have** problems sooner or later.
You'll **have to wait if** the floors **are being washed**.
Children **will/could die if** parents **refuse** vaccinations against childhood diseases.

N.B. If/When/As soon as/Before/After/Until are all used in the same form as a 1ˢᵗ Conditional.

 Match the 'if' clauses in column A with a 'result or effect' clause in B.

A	B
If you have problems learning this,	you'll find him in the bedroom.
If you do that again,	I'm going to take my mother for a drive.
If it's sunny this afternoon,	I'll kill you!
When it looks as though it might rain,	you'd better make an appointment – you should see him soon.
If the fog gets thicker,	I'll help you.
If you break a mirror,	the plane may/might not be able to land in Verona.
If you are looking for Chris,	you'll be grounded (not permitted to go out) for a week!
If you haven't seen the doctor yet,	take an umbrella.
If you don't / Unless you tidy your bedroom,	you'll have 7 years bad luck!

Now, write the reason for using First Conditional, next to each sentence, choosing a reason from the box.

imperative/order	giving advice
a fact/prediction	an intention
a superstition/prediction	speculation
a threat	an offer

The Zero Conditional – is used to talk about *'all time'* – a fact or something that is always true – a universal truth.

Form: **If + present simple, present simple** i.e. the present simple is used in both the 'if' clause and in the 'effect' or 'result clause'. When both clauses in a conditional sentence are in the present tense, this is called the 'Zero Conditional' and the 'if' means the same as 'when' or 'whenever'.

e.g. If you **drop** a glass, it **breaks.**   If you **have** a cold, **don't come** to work.
    If you **heat** ice, it **turns** to water.

🖊 *Practise the First and the Zero Conditionals. Write in the correct form of the verbs.*

1. If/When I .... (go) to the bank, I .... (have) enough money to pay you back.

2. .... (bring) all the books you need, when you .... (come) to lessons tomorrow.

3. If my hours .... (change), I ....(ring) you.

4. You .... (have to wait) until he .... (be) ready.

5. If you .... (not read) more, you .... (never pass) the final exams.

6. An ovum .... (become) a zygote before it .... (implant) in the uterus.

7. We .... (have) a holiday as soon as the exams .... (finish).

8. Mr. James .... (call) if he .... (need) anything.

The Second Conditional – Unreal or Improbable situations in the future – **Imagining.**
Form: **If + simple past tense** is used in the 'if' clause and **would ('d) (n't), could (n't) or might (n't) + infinitive** is used in the main clause.

e.g. If I **were** the doctor, I **would operate** this week.
    He **would go** home if he **had** someone to look after him.
    If she **didn't like** nursing, she **would** probably do a course for kindergarten teachers.

🖊 *Decide which is best – the First or the Second Conditional. Complete the sentences using the correct form of the verbs.*

1. If you .... (make) a cup of tea, I .... (have) one too!

2. He .... (have) more money if he .... (not spend) so much on cigarettes.

3. If everyone .... (eat) a balanced diet, there .... (not be) so many ill people.

4. If I .... (be) you, I .... (study) more before the exams.

5. What .... you .... (do) in the same situation? If I .... (be) you, I ....

6. What time .... you .... (be able) to come and see me on Friday?

7. If the plane .... (be) on time, he .... (get) the connection with the train at 10.30.

8. I .... (give) Mrs. Slade a bath as soon as the doctors .... (go) out of the room.

9. Do you think the doctor .... (change) my medication if he .... (know) how sick they make me feel?

10. .... you........ (feel) more comfortable if I .... (find) you another pillow?

☺ *How many activities can you think of that are risky or dangerous?*

First, think about everyday risks to both adults and children (toddlers are extremely *accident prone*). Think about the home environment, various workplaces, in a hospital and leisure time activities.

e.g. If you don't wash your hands before eating, you will contaminate the food you eat.

If a child took an adult's medication, he would be poisoned – he could die.

If a toddler is left near an open fire, he could fall and be badly burned.

First, write some examples of your own and then with a partner discuss the results of accidents or carelessness.

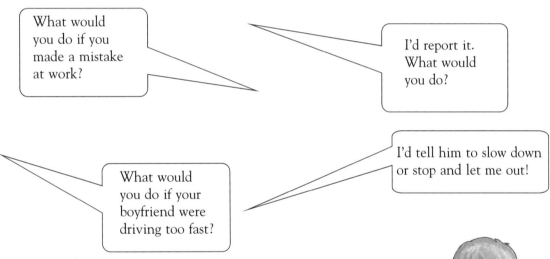

What would you do if you made a mistake at work?

I'd report it. What would you do?

What would you do if your boyfriend were driving too fast?

I'd tell him to slow down or stop and let me out!

What could happen if a young child was left alone at home?

UNIT 1L

65

TAKING RISKS

IT'S BETTER TO BE SAFE THAN SORRY!

☺ *Look at the pictures – Put them in order, according to how dangerous you think the activity is to health and safety. Compare your ideas with a partner. Do you ever take risks? What sort of risks? What risks are these people taking? Find a possible result of these activities below.*

Possible results of these activities.

- burns [bɜːnz] • death [deθ] or serious injury [ˈindʒəri]
- sunstroke [sʌnˈstrəʊk], burns [bɜːnz], skin cancer [kænsə]
- stillborn [stilbɔːn] or underweight [ʌndəˈweit] baby • lung [lʌŋ] cancer [kænsə]
- electrocution [əˈlektrəˈkjuːʃən] • fall [fɔːl] or electrocution [əˈlektrəˈkjuːʃən]
- diabetes [daiəˈbiːtiz], obesity [əˈbiːsəti], high blood pressure [preʃə]
- brain [brein] or head [hed] injury [ˈindʒəri]

✎ *Write the dangers of each activity under each picture at the top of the page.*
How many other dangerous or risky activities can you think of?

- on the road
- at home
- in the workplace
- outdoors

GRAMMAR NOTES
Verb Patterns

The following verbs are used in two distinct 'patterns', i.e. there is a particular 'model' – they are followed by a pronoun, then either the -ing form or the infinitive of the verb.

Learn these verb patterns.

Causative verbs

1. stop
   prevent
   discourage   *somebody from*   *verb + -ing*
   save

2. encourage
   help
   allow   *somebody to* + *infinitive of the verb*
   force
   make it easier *for*

Using the verbs in brackets in the correct form, complete the sentences.

1. Campaigns are used .... the general public .... (discourage/prevent, smoke).

2. You can .... your friends .... to you by being a 'good listener'. (make it easier for, talk).

3. Lorraine can't .... her husband .... long hours, but she is .... him .... more exercise at the weekends. (stop/prevent, work, encourage, do).

4. Nurses can .... patients .... as independent as possible, by ....ing them .... their self–confidence. (help, be, allow, build up).

5. To .... people .... heart attacks, doctors often .... them .... and .... them .... in a more active lifestyle and to change their dietary habits. (save, have, discourage, smoke, encourage, participate).

6. You can't .... people .... so sometimes it is necessary to .... them .... their own decisions. (force, change, allow, make).

 Listening 11a – Public Health   *Listen to the recording and check your answers.*

☺ *Do you know any other verb patterns? Your teacher can give you some more.*

WHY TAKE THE RISK?
YOU KNOW THE DAMAGE AND DISEASE THAT SMOKING CAUSES

📖 🎧 Listening 11b – Smoking

In most countries cigarette packets are now labelled with warnings but these don't seem to discourage people from smoking. Addiction is a hard habit to break. Do young people start smoking to impress their friends? Are they copying someone they admire? Do they know what they are doing to their bodies? Perhaps lung cancer [lʌŋ ˈkænsə], throat cancer [θraʊtˈkænsə], stomach cancer [stʌmək kænsə], emphysema [emˈfaiˈsiːmə], chronic bronchitis [krɒnikˈbrɒŋkaitis], asthma [æsmə] and other respiratory [rəˈspirəˈtri] problems are only words without significance, until the problems start.

YOUR SMOKING CAN HARM OTHERS
Government Health Warning

SMOKING KILLS
Government Health Warning

Nicotine, a drug in tobacco, makes smokers feel they need to smoke. The more you smoke, the more your body will depend on getting nicotine and you may find yourself hooked. It may be difficult to give up smoking once you are hooked on nicotine. For more information, call 13 2130.
Government Health Warning

Winfield
SUPER MILD
25

Winfield
SUPER MILD
25

SMOKING IS ADDICTIVE
Government Health Warning

Tobacco smoke causes cancer and poisons people. People who breathe in your tobacco smoke can be seriously harmed. Your smoking can increase their risk of lung cancer and heart disease. Children who breathe your smoke may suffer asthma attacks and chest illnesses.

In Australia, tobacco smoking causes more illness and early death than using any other drug. Tobacco smoking causes more than four times the number of deaths caused by car accidents.

✏️ *Match the 3 (of many) warnings which appear on the front of Australian cigarette packets with the description which appears on the back of the pack.*

☺ *The following information appears on the side of the packet. Read this and then answer the questions.*

The smoke from each cigarette contains, on average:

- 8 milligrams or less of tar – condensed smoke containing many chemicals, including some that cause cancer;
- 0.8 milligrams or less of nicotine – a poisonous and addictive drug;
- 10 milligrams or less of carbon monoxide – a deadly gas which reduces the ability of blood to carry oxygen [ɒksəˈdʒən].

1. What is tar? What does it cause?
2. How many grams of nicotine [nikəˈtiːn] are there in one cigarette?
3. What does 'on average' mean?
4. Cigarettes contain carbon monoxide [mɒnˈɒksaid]. What else contains carbon monoxide?
5. Do you think all cigarette packets should carry this information?
6. 'Dependency' and 'addiction' mean the same – what do you understand by these words?
7. Find another expression on the back of the cigarette packet that means 'to be addicted'.
8. Name the problems and diseases that smoking can cause. What do you know about these problems? Are they serious?
9. Do you smoke? Why do you smoke? Is that a valid reason?
10. Ask your partner the same questions.
11. How many methods do you know that help people to give up (stop)?
12. Do you know anybody who has successfully given up smoking? How did they do it?

GRAMMAR NOTES

Should [ʃʊd] or Shouldn't [ʃʊdənt]

Should' expresses mild obligation, advice or a suggestion – something that the speaker thinks is right or the best thing to do. 'Shouldn't' is the short form of 'should + not'. It is often introduced by 'I don't think (you should)…' or 'I think (you should)…'

Should is a modal verb and is always followed by the infinitive. It stays in the same form for all persons. Inversion of the subject and the modal verb is used to form questions.

Positive and Negative:	I	
	You	should do more exercise.
	He, she	should see a doctor.
	We	shouldn't smoke.
	They	shouldn't spend so much money on chocolate!

Questions:	Should	I	see a doctor?
		you	
	Do you think	we	should see a doctor?
		they	

Short answer question: Should he see a doctor?   Yes, he should. / No, he shouldn't.

 Match a problem and a suggestion.

Problems	Suggestions
My mother is lonely.	He shouldn't drink so much coffee.
I think I'm getting the 'flu'. (influenza).	You should buy her a pet – a dog or a cat.
John can't sleep.	She should ring him to see what he's doing.
I've got a bad toothache [tuːˈθeik]	She should go on a diet.
She is very overweight.	You should go to the dentist.
Ruth isn't happy – her boyfriend's away on business.	You should go home to bed.

☺ *Practice alternate sentences with your partner.*

🖉 **Turn back to the cartoon pictures of people taking risks on page 66.**
Write two sentences for each picture, one using 'should' and one using 'shouldn't'

1. ....
2. ....
3. ....
4. ....
5. ....
6. ....
7. ....

☺ **Think of a problem and tell your partner about it – ask his/her advice.**

e.g.

A. I have a dentist appointment tomorrow and we have an exam. What should I do?

I think you should cancel or change the appointment. B.

HEALTH AND DISEASE

HEALTH [helθ] was defined by The World Health Organisation as 'a state of complete physical, mental and social well–being and not merely (only) the absence of disease or infirmity (weakness or disability)'.

DISEASE [dizi:z] is an abnormal state in which part or all of the body is not able to perform its required functions.

The WHO definition is idealistic and probably only a few people in the general population could be regarded as absolutely healthy, using these guidelines! However, most people have no detectable [də'tektəbl] abnormality so are thought to be 'healthy'. Some people will be in a 'high risk' category of developing disease for other reasons: genetic influences, living conditions and habits (such as smoking or drug abuse) and obesity (being overweight).

Illness can be categorized [kætəgə'raizd] – that is, put into groups, according to the severity of the illness and the length of time it lasts. Minor illnesses can usually be treated at home, sometimes with help from the local doctor (GP = General Practitioner), chemist, family or friends. An acute disease can be severe, possibly needing medical intervention [intə'venʃən] but does not last for a long period of time. A chronic [krɒnik] disease, on the other hand, may not be very severe but continues over a long period under a doctor's supervision and with ongoing medical and hospital treatment.

☺ **Read the text then answer these questions.**

- How many people are really healthy, using the WHO definition?
- What do people with minor illnesses do instead of going into hospital?
- What puts people 'at risk' of becoming ill?
- What is the difference between an acute illness and a chronic illness?

✎ **Look at the diagrams below. Can you name these important organs? Choose from the following words.**

The lungs [lʌŋz]   *The brain* [brein]   *The kidneys* [kidniːz]   *The heart* [haːt]

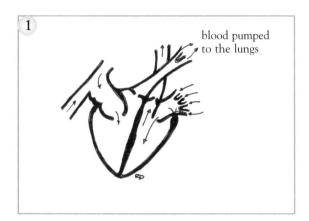

blood pumped to the lungs

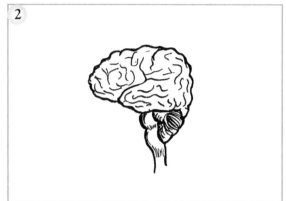

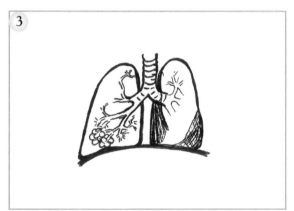

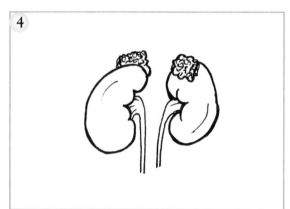

Label the diagrams with the following parts:

the left lung; the bronchi (*plural*); an alveolus (*singular*); the trachea; the diaphragm [daiəˈfræm]

the right kidney [kidni]; the left ureter [juːrətə]; the renal [riːnəl] pelvis; adrenal [ədˈriːnəl] gland

the aorta [eiˈɔːtə]; the right ventricle [ventrikl]; the left atrium [eitˈriːəm]; the pulmonary arteries [pulmənri aːtriz]

the frontal lobe [ləub]; the spinal cord [spainl kɔːd]; the cerebellum [serəˈbelum]; the pons [pɒnz]

Which body systems do these organs belong to?

the nervous [nɜːvəs] *system*
the urinary [juːrinri] *(or excretory* [eksˈkriːtəri]*) system*
the circulatory [sɜːkjuːˈleitri] *system*
the respiratory [resˈpirəˈtri] *system*

SHAPES

☺ Exercise 1. **Match a picture with the name of its shape from the list in exercise 2.**
(Some of them are 2–dimensional and some are 3–dimensional)

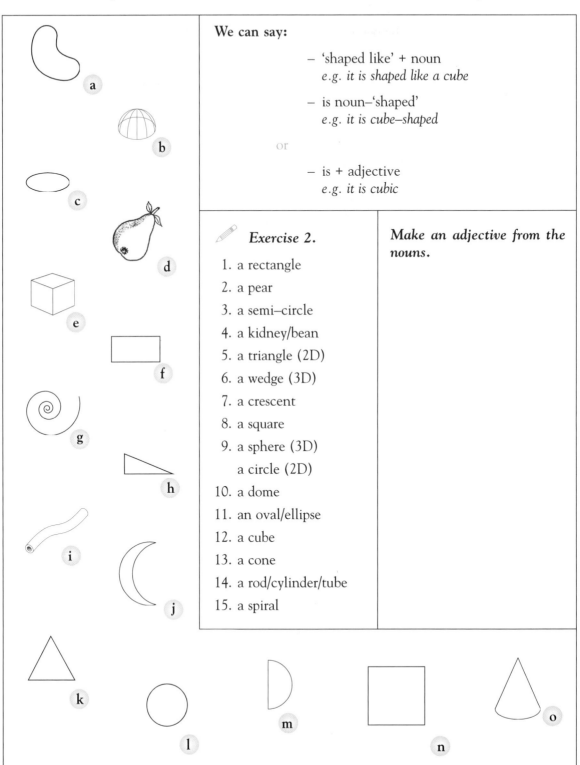

We can say:

– 'shaped like' + noun
e.g. it is shaped like a cube

– is noun–'shaped'
e.g. it is cube–shaped

or

– is + adjective
e.g. it is cubic

✏ Exercise 2.

1. a rectangle
2. a pear
3. a semi–circle
4. a kidney/bean
5. a triangle (2D)
6. a wedge (3D)
7. a crescent
8. a square
9. a sphere (3D)
   a circle (2D)
10. a dome
11. an oval/ellipse
12. a cube
13. a cone
14. a rod/cylinder/tube
15. a spiral

Make an adjective from the nouns.

Exercise 3.
Use an appropriate word to complete these sentences.

Bacteria

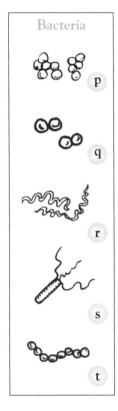

p

q

r

s

t

1. In phases of 'waxing' and 'waning', the moon is often ....

2. Blood red cell content is measured in millions per .... millimetre. (.../cu.mm).

3. The oesophagus is a .... organ leading from the pharynx to the stomach.

4. To play Chess, Monopoly, Chinese Checkers and other board games, you need a .... board.

5. The eye is a small, ... organ.

6. The wafer biscuit used to hold ice–cream and gelati is ....

7. The area of a flat or a house is measured in .... metres.

8. We can say that the excretory organs are ....–shaped, but not ....–shaped!

9. The gallbladder (which stores bile) is vaguely the shape of a pear, that is ....

10. Bacteria are found in three main ....

11. The alveoli look like clusters (or bunches) of berries or grapes, that is they are ....–shaped.

12. What .... are the lungs? I think they are ....

  Exercise 4. **Read this text and label the diagrams of bacteria above.**

BACTERIA *also have different shapes*

Bacilli [bəsili] (bacillus [bəsiləs] – *singular*) are rectangular or rod–shaped cells. Some of these rod–shaped bacteria have fine hair–like projections extending from the cell wall which give them some mobility. These hair–like projections are called **flagella** [flədʒelə].

Cocci [kɒkai] (coccus [kɒkəs] – *singular*) are spherical in shape and are usually smaller then bacilli. They may be grouped in pairs – **diplococci** [diplə kɒkai], in clusters – **staphylococci** [staflə'kɒkai] or in long chains – **streptococci** [streptə'kɒkai].

Spirilla [spirilə] (spirillum [spirilʊm] – *singular*) are the third shape that bacterial cells may take, they are spiral–shapes. They are not as common as rods and cocci and they may also have flagella – like the bacilli.

THE PHYSIOLOGY OF PHYSICAL HEALTH

  Read this.

For an individual to remain physically healthy he requires an adequate intake of oxygen [ɒksiˈdʒən], food and fluid. Oxygen is needed for the metabolic [metəˈbɒlik] breakdown [breik daʊn] of food constituents, called '*cellular respiration*', which provides energy and allows the functioning and replacement of cells throughout the body. Humans need to excrete waste products from the body and to maintain a constant temperature, fluid balance and pH (acid/alkaline–'base' balance). These things are vitally important for all the metabolic processes which take place in the human body, since the *enzymes* [enzaimz] necessary for these processes need an aqueous medium at optimal temperature and pH.

Enzymes are organic compounds, they are an important group of proteins that function as '*catalysts*' [kætələsts] in the hundreds of reactions that occur in metabolism [mətæbəˈlism]. A **catalyst** speeds up the rate of a reaction but is not changed or used up in that reaction. Because they are constantly re–used, only very small amounts of enzymes are needed. Each chemical reaction in the body requires a specific enzyme, so enzymes really control the metabolism [mətæbəˈlism] of the cells. Some of the vitamins and minerals in our daily diet [daiət] are important because they make up parts of the enzymes. The production of each enzyme is controlled by a gene and defects in these genes lead to many hereditary [həˈredəˈtri] disorders.

In its action, the **shape** of the enzyme is important. It must *match the shape* of the substance or substances with which the enzyme combines – in much the same way as a key fits in a lock. (See diagram).

ENZYME   SUBSTRATE   PRODUCT

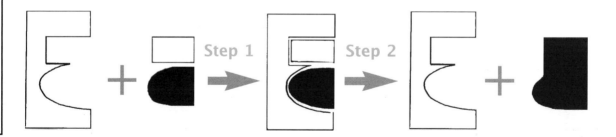

Harsh (severe or difficult) conditions, such as extremes of temperature or pH can alter the shape of an enzyme and stop its action. This is harmful to the cells. You can usually recognise the names of enzymes, because with a few exceptions, they end with the **suffix** *-ase*. Examples are *amylase, lipase and oxidase*. The first part of the name refers to the substance acted on or the type of reaction involved.

Amylase — An enzyme that catalyzes the hydrolysis [haiˈdrɒləsis] of starches.
Amyl comes from *Amido* (a Latin 'root') for **starch** + *-ase* (enzyme).

Lipase — An enzyme that catalyzes the hydrolysis of fats.
Lip(o) – (Latin root for **fats**) + *-ase*.

Oxidase — An enzyme that catalyzes **oxidation** (involving the element **oxygen** [ɒˈksidʒən]).

🖉 *Read these sentences and say whether they are true (T) or false (F).*
Correct the false sentences.

1.	Enzymes are organic compounds necessary for metabolism.	T	F
2.	Enzymes slow down chemical reactions.	T	F
3.	Vitamins and minerals in the diet make up part of the enzymes.	T	F
4.	Enzymes have different shapes depending on the reaction they are involved with.	T	F
5.	Temperature and pH changes in the body are insignificant.	T	F
6.	It is difficult to understand which enzymes are necessary in each chemical reaction.	T	F
7.	Enzyme action is often likened to a key fitting into a lock (or key–hole).	T	F
8.	Some chemical reactions in the body require enzymes.	T	F
9.	Enzymes change during chemical reactions.	T	F
10.	Many hereditary disorders and intolerances [inˈtɒləˈrənsəs] result from defects in the genes that control specific enzymes.	T	F

TO BE OR NOT TO BE? – HEALTHY, THAT IS!

📖 *Promoting good health – and advertising dangers to healthy living – are the modern techniques for the prevention of disease. The World Health Organisation takes responsibility on an international level and all health care workers and various other groups take responsibility on a national and community level. The health of your community is your responsibility.*

Did you see that article on exercise on the MD site on Internet? It's amazing how much blood pressure can be reduced by exercise – I always thought it depended on cholesterol levels and salt intake.
This is the article here: it also appeared in "The Annals of Internal Medicine" on April 2nd, 2002.   **Read it!**

Exercise Helps Everyone's Heart
No Matter Their Race, Fitness Level, or Weight

By Jennifer Warner
WebMD Medical News

If you ever thought your heart and health wouldn't benefit from some exercise, a new study may just change your mind. The overwhelming evidence shows exercise can reduce blood pressure in virtually anyone – regardless of weight, race, or current blood pressure level. Researchers examined 54 studies that measured the effects of exercise on blood pressure in more than 2,400 adults. They found that regular aerobic exercise decreased systolic blood pressure (the top number) by an average of 3.8 mmHg *(millimetres of Mercury)* and the diastolic (the bottom number) by 2.58 mmHg, *(millimetres of Mercury)* in people who were previously inactive.

That may seem like a small reduction, but researchers say it's a bigger effect than has been found in similar studies on other blood–pressure lowering methods such as cutting back on salt, potassium supplementation, and reducing alcohol consumption. About 25% of American adults have high blood pressure, or hypertension, which

can dramatically increase the risk of heart attack and stroke. If left untreated, high blood pressure can also damage the brain, eyes, and kidneys. Generally, a normal blood pressure reading is considered to be lower than 130/85 mmHg. (*one hundred and thirty over/on eighty–five*)

Physical inactivity increases the risk of developing high blood pressure. Although previous studies have shown that regular exercise can lower blood pressure (as well as the risk of diabetes and heart disease), researchers wanted to know if exercise lowers blood pressure equally well in everyone, or if it just works for some groups of people. This study showed that any type of aerobic exercise that improves the body's use of oxygen – such as jogging, swimming, and cycling – has a positive effect on anybody's blood pressure. Exercise lowered blood pressure in all groups of people, including those who had hypertension or normal blood pressure, were obese or normal weight, and were black, white, or Asian.

The authors say that when applied to the population as a whole, even the small average blood pressure reduction found in this study could translate into a dramatic reduction in heart disease and death in the U.S. They say all adults should consider lowering blood pressure as one of the many reasons to exercise for 20–30 minutes several times a week.

 Do you know of any other ways to reduce high blood pressure?
What would you advise someone with high blood pressure to do?

OBSERVATION

Is it enough for the nurse to ask the patient
"How are you today?" or *"How do you feel today?"*

SIGNS AND SYMPTOMS

The answer you get from the patient won't always answer these or other necessary questions.
Good "observation skills" are most important for all health care workers. By observing the patient carefully as you speak, you can watch for reactions and 'body language' which may tell you something quite different from the words the patient uses. By looking for signs and symptoms of pain, discomfort and illness you can understand the patient's condition very much better.

Signs are what you can observe, what you can see (or feel) for yourself.

The nurse can observe – changes in recorded **observations** – blood pressure, temperature, pulse, or respirations

She can see – **a bruise** [bruːz] or **bruising** [bruːzɪŋ] – that is a **'haematoma'** [hiːməˈtəʊmə];

a **rash** [ræʃ], which is an area of red lumps or 'pimples' on the skin, which can be a type of **'erythema'** [erəˈθiːmə] *or* **'urticaria' (allergy rash)** [ɜːˈtɪkˈerɪə] (Some rashes are very **itchy** so the patient wants to **scratch** it);

signs of weight loss or **weight gain** ('losing' weight or 'putting on' weight);

changes in the colour of the skin: 'anaemic–looking' white–pale [peɪl],
'cyanosis' [saɪənˈəʊsɪs] (cyanosed *adj.*) blue–colour,
'jaundice' [dʒɔːndəs] yellow–colour,
'inflammation' [ˈɪnfləˈmeɪʃən] redness;

swelling or **'puffiness'** [pʌfɪˈnəs] (*uncountable noun*) – i.e. extra fluid in the tissues under the skin. *The medical term for swelling is* **'oedema'** [ediːmə] *spelt* **'edema'** *in American English*;

cuts [kʌts], **wounds** [wuːndz] or **lacerations** [læsəˈreɪʃənz]: breaks in the skin (usually caused by an accident).

Symptoms are things that **the patient** feels and **tells the nurse** about.

The patient may say that – he **feels like vomiting** – or feels sick in the stomach – (he is **nauseated**);

he has a **pain** (in his chest, in his calf, etc.);

he cannot sleep (he has or 'suffers from' **insomnia**);

he has **diarrhoea** – frequent, **loose stools/bowel actions**;

he feels **dizzy** or **giddy** (he has **vertigo** [vəˈtaɪˈgəʊ]);

he is very **thirsty** or **dehydrated** [diːˈhaɪˈdreɪtɪd];

he feels **numbness** [nʌmˌnəs] or **tingling** ('pins and needles') – loss of sensation or changed sensation.

77

✎ Exercise 1　Look at the words in bold type on page 77. <u>Underline</u> words you think are <u>not familiar</u> to the patient.

✎ Exercise 2　**Put all the terms into two columns: "1. Understood by the patient" and "2. Used by medical staff".**

✎ Exercise 3　**Now look at the pictures underneath and write** *what is wrong* **with each person.**

a　　　b　　　c　　　d

✎ Exercise 4　**Match a speech bubble below with each picture – then add a phrase stating the sign of the problem.**

e.g.　1.　*He was hit with a base–ball ……he's got a huge (very big) bruise on his arm.*

　　　2.　...

　　　3.　...

　　　4.　...

> 1. He was hit with a base-ball ......

> 3. Look, he's scratching! He must be itchy.

> 2. He's been running a marathon.

> 4. He's got liver disease

☺　**Work with a partner.**
Exercise 5　**Look at the following words and decide if they are signs or symptoms of disease.**

1. an irregular pulse ....

2. stomach–ache [stʌmək'eik] ....

3. thirst [θɜːst] ....

4. hunger [hʌŋgə] ....

5. extreme loss of weight [weit] ....

6. shallow respirations ....

7. dyspnoea [dis'niə] ....

8. pallor (pale *adj.*) ....

9. laceration [læsə'reiʃən] (a cut) ....

10. headache [hedeik] ....

N.B. *Some of the patients complaints may be a*
sign or a symptom.

GRAMMAR NOTES

'have' or 'have got' – 'be' or 'feel'

'Have' or 'have got' can be used to talk about signs and symptoms.

e.g. He's got / He has diarrhoea
or
She's got / She has (a) pain in her left calf.

He hasn't got / He doesn't have a temperature
or
She hasn't got / She doesn't have any chest pain.

Remember 'have got' is only used in the present simple tense and the full verb 'have' is used in all other tenses. *e.g.* He had diarrhoea yesterday. He has had a lot of pain.

'Be' is used with adjectives or states and 'feel' can be used to describe feelings.

e.g. His finger–nails are cyanosed
or
She is / She feels nauseated/tired.

He is very lethargic
or
He feels quite ill.

'Palpitations' (tachycardia [tæki'ka:diə]) **are a symptom** when the patient tells you he can feel his heart 'racing' or 'thumping'. It could **also** show as **a sign** on an ECG (an electrocardiogram).

'Shortness Of Breath' may be visible or only felt by the patient 'On Exertion' (SOB–OE).

✎ *Match the signs and symptoms on the left with a possible diagnosis on the right.*

a. She has lumbar backache and pain radiating down her leg.	hay fever – allergic reaction
b. I have a high temperature and aches and pains all over my body.	hepatitis
c. I have a 'runny nose', itchy eyes and I'm sneezing all the time.	viral infection / influenza
d. He ran home and now he can't breathe – he says his chest feels 'tight'.	lung cancer
e. I've got a headache, I'm tired and I can't concentrate.	appendicitis
f. Her son has really severe pain in the right side of his abdomen, he has to go into hospital for an operation.	sciatica – (vertebral) disc protrusion
g. I've got a burning pain in my chest – too much curry I think!	an insect bite/sting
h. He is a drug addict and his liver function tests are disastrous.	asthma
i. She smoked forty cigarettes a day for over 20 years and now she's coughing up blood.	indigestion – gastritis
j. After working in the garden, her hand became very red and swollen.	middle ear infection
k. The baby is distressed and screaming, she's febrile – she's got a temperature of 39°C.	stress

☺ *Work in pairs, tell your partner some of the signs and symptoms and check that your partner gives you the diagnosis that you chose!*

✎ **What's wrong with the people in the pictures below?**

e.g. The man in picture 1 is sneezing, he must have hay fever, or maybe he's getting a cold.

1 ....

....

2 ....

....

3 ....

....

4 ....

....

5 ....

....

☺ **Your teacher will divide the class into groups and give each group one of the following conditions to discuss. With a partner list as many possible signs and symptoms as you can and then report to the class.**

A heart attack	Liver disease
Influenza (the 'flu)	Malaria
Internal injuries following a car accident	Amoebic dysentery
A deep venous thrombosis	Diabetes
Appendicitis	

You can start your report like this: *When a patient is (feels) very lethargic and complains of (c/o).......*

When you can see .... When he's got ....

.... these are possible signs or symptoms of ....

Think of some more examples of signs and symptoms and ask the class to guess what the problem is.

P

MEDICAL TERMINOLOGY (3)

You may not realise that many medical terms are already part of your vocabulary! Medical terms make up the special language of health care professionals and are based on an understanding of only three basic elements. These are: prefixes, roots and suffixes.

Using these elements in the same way as children build up alphabet blocks i.e. BUILDING BLOCKS, you can build a medical vocabulary.

The root of a word is the part which gives meaning to the whole word and can be 'translated' as the main 'subject' of the word.

A prefix is a letter, or two or three letters, that come before the root and change its meaning in some way.

A suffix is a group of letters that come after the root and also change the meaning of the root–word in some way.

e.g. Prefix: **an-** ('without' or 'no') + Root: **-hydr-** ('water') + Suffix: **-ous** (adjective ending) = **anhydrous,** literally meaning 'without water'

Two 'roots' can be used together like this:
hydr- + 'o' (combining vowel) **+ therapy = hydrotherapy** (treatment in water)
hydr- + 'o' + phobia (fear) **= hydrophobia** (fear of water)

The following words are all combinations of prefixes, roots and suffixes and are probably quite familiar.

abnormal [æb'nɔ:ml]	**ab-** (prefix) means 'away from' so abnormal means *'away from (or not) normal'.*
anaemia/anemia [ə'ni:mjə]	**a-** (prefix) means 'without/no': **-aemia/emia** (suffix) means 'blood condition'. (The literal translation 'without blood' becomes *'not enough red blood cells/Hb!*).
arthritis [a:θ'raitis]	**arthr-** (root) refers to a joint/articulation. The suffix **-itis** stands for 'inflammation'. The word 'arthritis' translates as *'inflammation of a joint'.*
appendectomy [ə'pen'dektəmi]	**append-**(root) refers to the appendix. **-ectomy** (suffix) means 'surgical taking out' or 'excision of...' or 'removal of'. Appendectomy is *'removal of the appendix'.*
electrocardiogram [el'ektrəʊ'ka:diəʊ'græm]	**electr+o** (root) = electric, **cardi+o** (root) the heart, **-gram** (suffix) a recording. An electrocardiogram is *a recording of the electrical impulses of the heart* (an ECG).
hypodermic [haipə'dɜ:mik]	**hypo-** (prefix) can mean 'under' or 'low' and **derm** (root) refers to the dermis or skin, and the **-ic** ending is a suffix making the word into an adjective. A 'hypodermic' injection is given *under the skin* (e.g. a local anaesthetic).
tracheotomy [træki'ɒtəmi]	**trache-** (root) refers to the trachea + **o** + **-tomy**(suffix) means an opening into / a hole, so a 'tracheotomy' is *an opening into the trachea.* (The suffix **-ostomy** is the surgical creation of an opening).

81

Sometimes an extra vowel is used to combine the different parts of the word.

This is called 'a combining vowel' and is usually an 'o.'

e.g. hydrophobia, cardiogram

To make words into adjectives, different suffixes are used. These can be translated as *referring to* or *pertaining to* the root that precedes it.

Adjective endings include:

- **-ic** as in the word hypoderm**ic** (adjective referring to something under the skin)
- **-ous** as in the word ser**ous** (describing something that comes from serum)
- **-al** as in the word or**al** (referring to the mouth)
- **-iac** as in the word card**iac** (referring to the heart)
- **-ary** as in the word pulmon**ary** (adjective pertaining to the lungs)

✏️ *Write a sentence defining these words:*

a. hypoglycaemia [haɪpəʊˈɡlaɪˈsiːmjə] ....

....

....

b. gastrostomy [ɡæsˈtrɒstəmi] ....

....

....

c. appendicitis [əˈpendəˈsaitis] ....

....

....

d. hypoxia [haɪˈpɒksiə] ('ox' = root = 'oxygen' [ɒksidʒən]) ....

....

....

e. cephalic [kefˈælik] or [sefˈælik] ....

....

....

Prefixes	
a-, an-	(absence of, without)
ad-	(to, towards, near, increase)
ambi-	(both)
anti-, contra-	(against)
bi-	(two, both, double)
circum- [sɜːˈkəm] or [sɜːkʌm]	(around)
dia- [daiə]	(across, apart, through)
dys-	(painful, difficult, bad)
em-/en-	(in, within)
endo-	(within)
epi-	(upon, at, in addition to)
ex-, extra-	(out, outside, over)
hyper- [haiˈpə]	(excessive)
hypo- [haipəʊ]	(below, deficient)
inter-	(between)
intra-	(within, inside)
para-	(beside, around, abnormal)
peri-	(around, in the area of)
post-	(after)
pre-	(before, in front of)
pro-	(in front of, before, forward)
re-	(again, back)
retro-	(backward, behind)
semi-	(half)
super-, supra-	(above, extreme)
syn-/sym-	(with, together, beside)
trans-	(across, through, over)
tri- [trai]	(three)
ultra-	(excessive, beyond)

By thinking of these different parts as 'building blocks', you can build an extensive vocabulary.

Study the following word elements and then see how many different words you can make.
The meaning, or meanings, and pronunciation of the part of the word is shown (in brackets).

Roots	
aden [æden] + o	(gland)
angi [æn'dʒi] + o	(blood vessel)
arter + i + o	(artery)
arthr	(joint/articulation)
cardi + o	(heart [ha:t])
cephal + o	(head)
cerebr [serə'br] + o	(brain)
cost + o	(rib)
crani + o	(cranium, skull)
cyst [sist] + o	(sac, urinary bladder)
cyt [sait] + o	(cell)
derm + at/o	(skin)
enter + o	(intestine)
gastr + o	(stomach [stʌmək])
gloss + o	(tongue [tʌŋ])
glyc [glaikəu] + o	(sugar, glucose, sweet)
hem/haem + at/o	(blood [blʌd])
hep + at/o	(liver)
hyster + o, uter + o	(uterus [ju:'tərəs])
mamm + o, mast + o	(breast [brest])
my [mai] + o	(muscle [mʌsl])
nas + o, rhin + o	(nose)
nephr [nef], ren	(kidney)
neur [nju:'r] + o	(nerve)
ocul [okju:l], opthalm [op'θælm] + o	(eye)
or, stoma, stomat	(mouth)
os/te + o	(bone)
ot + o	(ear)
ox + o -oxy-	(oxygen [ɒks'idʒən])
pneum [nju:m], pulmon [pʊlmən], pnea [ni:ə]	
	(lung, air, breathing)
proct + o, rect + o	(rectum)

Suffixes	
-algia [ældʒə]	(pain)
-cele [si:əl]	(hernia, bulging)
-cyte [sait]	(mature cell [sel])
-centesis [senti:sis]	(surgery/procedure –
	aspiration [æ'spir'eifən] or drainage)
-emia/aemia	(blood)
-ectomy	(excision, cutting out)
-iasis	(condition, presence of)
-itis [aitis]	(inflammation)
-malacia [mə'leifə]	(softening)
-megaly	(enlargement)
-oid	(resembling, like)
-oma	(tumour)
-osis	(abnormal condition)
-pathy	(disease [diz'i:z])
-penia	(abnormal reduction)
-phobia [fəubiə]	(exaggerated fear)
-plasty	(mould, form or shape)
-plegia	(paralysis)
-rhage/rhagia	(excess - haemorrhage)
-rhaphy [rəfi]	(suturing, closing)
-rhea	(discharge)
-sclerosis	(hardening)
-scope [skəup]	(examining instrument)
-scopy [skəpi]	(internal examination)
-stomy [stəmi]	(make a permanent opening)
-tomy [təmi]	(make an opening)
-tripsy	(crushing, friction)
-phagia / phagy [feidʒiə] or [feigi]	(eating or
	swallowing)
-uria [ju:riə]	(urine or urination)

83

These are only some of the more common examples – add to the lists as your vocabulary increases.
Examples:

Root + Root

arthr- (joint) + 'o' + scope (surgical instrument) = **an instrument for looking at joints/articulations** *i.e. an arthroscope.*

Root + Suffix

nephr (kidney) + 'o' + -tomy (incision into) = **an incision into the kidney** *i.e. a nephrotomy.*

Prefix + Root + Suffix

en- (in, inside) + cephal (the head) + 'o' + gram (recording) = **A recording of the electrical activity inside the head** *i.e. an EEG or electroencephalogram.*

Write a definition for these words:

a. myocardium [maɪəʊˈkaːdiˈʊm] ....
b. endocardium [endəʊˈkaːdiʊm] ....
c. hepatitis [hepəˈtaɪtis] ....
d. dysuria [disˈjuːriə] ....
e. intracranial [intrəˈkreɪniəl] ....

MEDICAL TERMINOLOGY (4) WHAT'S WRONG WITH ME?

Mrs. Green has chronic cystitis. Please take a CSU and ask path. to ring me with the results. .....

Mrs. Green, Mr. Bailey has the results of your urine test: he told me that you still have an infection in your bladder and he would like another specimen of urine to send to pathology…
We have to pass a catheter this time, it won't be very pleasant but we can take it out again as soon as we have enough urine…

Medical terms used by the staff for conditions and diseases often need to be explained in simpler words to the patient, so he/she understands. The main organs and structures in the human body are discussed in Section 3B.

Translate the following words into phrases that the patient will understand.

1. Nephritis   *e.g. A kidney infection or inflammation of the kidney.*
2. Cystitis   *e.g. An infection or inflammation of the bladder.*
3. Cholelithiasis   *e.g. Stones (calculi) in the gall–bladder i.e. gallstones.*
4. Colostomy   *e.g. Making a surgical opening into the colon/bowel.*
5. Partial gastrectomy   *e.g. Taking out part of the stomach (surgically) i.e. surgical removal of the stomach.*
6. Gastrostomy ....
7. Nephrectomy ....
8. Appendicitis ....
9. Pancreatitis ....
10. Nephrolithiasis ....
11. Gastritis ....
12. Hepatitis ....

ACHES AND PAINS

[eiks]   [peinz]

WHAT IS PAIN?

Pain is a noun and can be described as discomfort or an unpleasant feeling. It is the body's response to an injury or illness.

The word 'pain' is rarely used as a verb – so how can you ask a patient if he has any pain, where it is and what it's like?

 Listening 12 – Pain   *Listen to the recording and complete the following sentences.*

1. "Where .... it ....?"
2. "Have you got any .... in your chest?"
3. "Let me look at your .... (the operation site). I'll just take the dressing off first. That's fine – it's a little inflamed, but that's quite normal. It's O.K. Don't touch it before I put another dressing over it".
4. "When you breathe deeply, does is it .... anywhere?"
5. "Yes, a little in my chest but here, in the back of my leg, it's very ...."

How are these words used?
wound [wu:nd]
sore [sɔ:]
painful [peinful]
hurt [hɜ:t]
pain [pein]

Now, listen again and check your answers.

1. pain [pein]

2. wound [wu:nd]

3. sore [sɔ:]

4. painful [peinful]

5. wounded [wu:ndid]

6. hurt [hɜ:t]

7. ache [eik]

8. aching [eikiŋ]

9. injury [in'dʒəri]

10. injured [indʒəd]

Look at the words in the box on the left.
Are these nouns, adjectives or both nouns and adjectives?
Can they be used as verbs?

  Put each word from the box into a sentence.
   Use a dictionary if necessary.

1. ....
2. ....
3. ....
4. ....
5. ....
6. ....
7. ....
8. ....
9. ....
10. ....

Talking about frequency

How often do you get this pain? When does it hurt?

always
all the time
...when the weather is cold...
never
hardly ever
(not) ever
often
usually
sometimes
rarely
generally
very often
every day (week/month)
2 or 3 times a week
occasionally
frequently

Look at this example:
My shoulder **often** hurts.
or
My shoulder hurts **all the time**.

🖉 *Look at the adverbs and expressions in the box and add one to the sentences below. More than one answer is possible but check the position of the adverb or expression you choose with your teacher!*

1. I can't walk upstairs without a lot of pain.
2. He is tired.
3. I get a bad pain here after I eat something.
4. Do you get indigestion [ɪndəˈdʒestʲjən]?
5. My knee aches [eiks].
6. Is it painful?
7. My nose 'blocks up' in Spring and I can't breathe.
8. My head feels funny and I get a bit dizzy.
9. Do your eyes itch?
10. When I bend like this .... it's very painful .... and during the night.

☺ *Discuss all the different possibilities with a partner.*

Positioning Frequency Adverbs

Remember that adverbs of frequency are put *before all main verbs, but after the verb 'be'.*
e.g. He hardly ever complains – but – He is always tired.

Special note: **The frequency adverbs 'sometimes' and 'usually' can also come at the beginning or end of the sentence as well as in the normal position.**

Time expressions usually come at the end of the sentence.

🖉 *Write some more sentences, using the words from the box which you did not use to complete sentences 1–10.*

....

....

....

....

....

....

🌀 ADJECTIVES THAT ARE USED TO DESCRIBE PAIN

What** is the pain **like**?* – *This question is asking for **a description of the type of pain.
Where** is the pain (exactly)?* – *This question is asking for **the location of the pain.
How long** does it **last**?* – *This question is asking for **the duration of the pain.

🖉 **Work with a partner and divide the words in the bubble into the 3 groups in the table.**

1. to describe the location of the pain
2. to describe how bad the pain is, or the type of pain
3. to describe the duration of the pain

generalised [dʒenˈrəlaizd]
persistent [pəˈsistənt] dull [dʌl] severe [səˈviə]
radiating [reidiˈeitiŋ] stabbing [stæbiŋ] slight [slait]
excruciating [eksˈkruːʃiˈeitiŋ] nagging [nægiŋ]
localised [ləʊkəlˈaizd] sharp [ʃaːp] gnawing [nɔːˈiŋ]
intermittent [intəˈmitənt] occasional [əkˈeiʒənl] burning [bɜːniŋ]
unbearable [ʌnˈberəbl] intolerable [inˈtɒlˈrəbl]
continuous [kənˈtinˈjuːəs]

1. Where is it?	2. How bad is it?	3. Does it last long? How long?

ACHES [eiks]

🖉 **There are only 5 two–part nouns that use the word 'ache' – Can you name them?**

An ache is a pain that is not generally severe but is persistent.

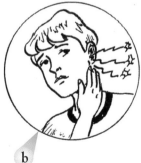
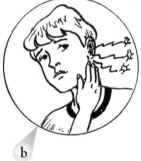

a. ....
b. ....
c. ....
d. ....
e. ....

REVISION EXERCISE

Complete this exercise to test your memory using the correct medical terminology.
The first letter is given to you and also the number of letters in the word.

(a) The technical term for fluid in the tissues is **o_ _ _ _ _**.

(b) A patient whose skin and the 'whites' of his eyes look yellow, is **j_ _ _ _ _ _** d.

(c) When a patient says the pain "won't go away" – the pain is said to be **p_ _ _ _ _ _ _ _ _**.

(d) He's got a very **s_ _ _** throat and a productive cough [prəˈdʌktiv ˈkof].

(e) Following the accident there was a lot of internal bleeding and multiple **h_ _ _ _ _ _ _** s

(f) A patient who has Congestive Cardiac Failure suffers from **s_ _ _ _ _ _ _ _ o_ b_ _ _ _ _** on exertion and often has **o_ _ _ _ _** in his ankles.

(g) After an operation, the **w_ _ _ _** is covered with a sterile dressing to prevent infection.

(h) The soldier was **i_ _ _ _ _ _** by shrapnel when a bomb exploded.

(i) Mr Hill's wound is very **i_ _ _ _ _ _ _**, he should start antibiotics to prevent a systemic infection.

(j) Mr Bradley is complaining of **u_ _ _ _ _ _ _ _ _** pain – his doctor said to give him a dose of IM Pethidine straight away.

(k) Naomi never seems to eat anything, she is **l_ _ _ _ _** a lot of weight and doesn't look well. I think she might be anorexic.

(l) My friend has **u_ _ _ _ _ _ _ _**. She ate something she was allergic to and vomited last night and today she has this awful **r_ _ _** all over her body – it *must* be **u_ _ _ _ _ _ _ _**!

(m) Cyanosis is a **s_ _ _** and diarrhoea is usually a **s_ _ _ _ _ _**.

(n) I had a really bad **t_ _ _ _ _ _ _ _** yesterday so I went to the dentist.

American and British Spelling of Medical Terms

Some words in medical English can be written in two ways – traditional British English and American English – both are correct.
American English is becoming more popular as it is easier!

Compare the spelling of the following words. Which is which? Mark (UK) or (USA).

......foetus/fetus......   ......haematoma/hematoma......   ......mucous/mucus......

......edema/oedema......   ......oesophagus/esophagus......   ......anaemic/anemic......

......disc/disk......   ......anesthesia/anaesthesia......   ......feces/faeces......

accident victims [æksəˈdənt vikˈtimz] (n.) A victim is someone who has been hurt or killed by something. An accident victim has been hurt [hɜːt] or killed [kild] as the result of an accident.

addiction [ədikʃən] (n.) An addiction is the condition of taking harmful [haːmˈfl] drugs and being unable to stop taking them. An addict is a person who is addicted to a harmful substance.

basic information (about the patient) [beisik inˈfɔːmeiʃən əˈbaʊt] (adj. + n. uncountable) Basic information refers to the important or 'necessary to know' facts (about the patient).

bed–making [bed meikiŋ] (n.) The activity of arranging the sheets and covers neatly on a bed.

bomb [bɒm] (n.) A bomb is a device which explodes and damages a large area.

canteen [kænˈtiːn] (n.) A canteen is a dining area in a factory, shop or college where meals are served to the people who work or study there. The staff canteen is the dining area for the hospital staff.

computer [kəmˈpjuːtə] **printout** [printaʊt] (n.) A printout is a piece of paper on which information from a computer has been printed. e.g. Staff are given a printout at handover.

development [diˈveləpˈmənt] (n.) Development is the gradual growth or formation of something. e.g. Midwifery students study the development of the embryo.

explosion [eksˈpləʊʒən] (n.) An explosion is a sudden, violent burst of energy (possibly caused by a bomb).

facets [fæsəts] (n.) A facet of something is a single part or aspect of it. There are many facets of nursing to choose from: public health, children's nursing, medical or surgical nursing and all the specialised areas.

handover [hænd aʊvə] (n.) The handover of something is when control of that thing is given from one group to another, that is, at the time of 'handover' the responsibility for the patients' well–being is passed from the staff on night shift to the staff on morning shift.

hygiene [haiˈdʒiːn] (n.) The practice of keeping yourself and your surroundings clean in order to prevent disease.

illness [ilˈnəs] (n.) A perception of not being in good health, not well. The word 'illness' is also used to mean a disease or disorder. Illness is the opposite of good health.

minor illnesses [mainə ilnəsəz] (adj. + n.) Minor illnesses are disorders that are not serious or complicated.

seasonal [siːzənəl] **illnesses** (adj. + n.) Illnesses that are seasonal appear more in one season than another.

intake [inteik] (n.) Your **intake of** a particular kind of food, drink or air is the amount that you eat, drink, or breathe in. Breathing [briːðiŋ] involves a regular intake of (oxygen) [regˈjuːlə inteik əv ɒksidʒən].

intravenous line (or drip) (adj. + n.) [intrəˈviːnəs lain or drip] An intravenous line or drip refers to the bag, tubing and needle, used to give food or medications continuously into the veins of sick people. Make sure that no air bubbles enter the intravenous line.

personal hygiene [pɜːsənəl haiˈdʒiːn] (adj. + n.) To look after your personal hygiene you keep yourself clean, especially to prevent the spread of disease.

risk [risk] (n.) If something is a risk, it is likely to cause harm. Also (n. phrase): If someone is **at risk**, they are put in a situation where something unpleasant might happen to them.

shift [ʃift] (n.) You work **a shift**, when it is necessary to have groups of people always working and you work for a set number of hours and are then replaced by another group of people.

shrapnel [ʃræpˈnəl] (n. uncountable) Shrapnel consists of small pieces of metal which are scattered after a bomb or shell explodes.

stage [steidʒ] (n.) A stage of an activity, process or period is one part of it. Children express their feelings differently, depending on their age and stage of development, that is on the **developmental** [diveləpˈməntl] (adj.) **stage** of the individual.

supervision [suːpəˈviʒən] (n.) is the supervising of an activity, person or place. That is, a knowledgeable person watches to make sure that the activity is done correctly or that other people are behaving correctly. e.g. Newly trained staff and trainees need supervision by the permanent, experienced staff.

warning [wɔːniŋ] (n.) A warning is something that is communicated, said or written, to tell people of a possible problem or danger.

workplace [wɜːkˈpleis] (n.) or **work place** This is the place where you work.

89

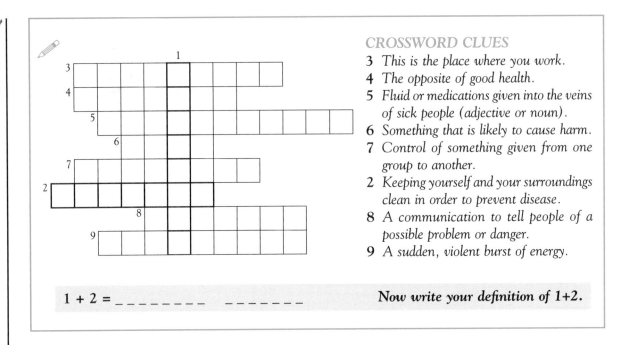

3 *This is the place where you work.*

4 *The opposite of good health.*

5 *Fluid or medications given into the veins of sick people (adjective or noun).*

6 *Something that is likely to cause harm.*

7 *Control of something given from one group to another.*

2 *Keeping yourself and your surroundings clean in order to prevent disease.*

8 *A communication to tell people of a possible problem or danger.*

9 *A sudden, violent burst of energy.*

1 + 2 = _ _ _ _ _ _ _ _   _ _ _ _ _ _ _

Now write your definition of 1+2.

---

overweight [əʊvə'weit] (*adj.*) Weighing more than the normal weight for height. (Body Mass Index).

ongoing [ɒn'gəʊ'iŋ] (*adj.*) An ongoing situation has been happening for quite a long time and seems likely to continue for some time in the future. *e.g. The ongoing treatment seems to be successful.*

indoors [indɔːz] (*adv*) If something happens indoors, it happens inside a building.

outdoors [aʊt'dɔːz] (*adv.*) If something happens outdoors, it happens out in the fresh air, not in a building.

---

to **apply** [əplai] <u>for a position</u> (*v. + prep. + n.*) To *apply* for a job or a position, or membership to an organisation, you ask for it by formally writing a letter of application.

to **attend to** [əten'tuː] **a patient's personal hygiene** (*v. 'to inf.'+ n.*) If you attend to something, you deal with it. If you attend to a patient's personal hygiene, you help the patient to wash, clean his teeth, do his hair and shave.

to be **'due'** [djuː] (*v. + adj.*) If something is due at a particular time, it is expected to happen or to arrive at that time. *e.g. When are the medications due? What time is the 'pre–med' due? When is your sister's baby due?*

to be **given a print–out** [printaʊt] (*v. passive + n.*) If you are given a printout, you are presented with a piece of paper from the computer, giving information about (the patients).

to be **labelled with** something [leibəld wiθ] (*v. passive + prep. + n.*) If something is labelled, there is a piece of paper (or label) attached to it, giving information about it. *e.g. All medications are labelled with directions for use and dosages. Cigarette packets are labelled with warnings.*

to be **'on call'** [ɒn kɔːl] (*v. + phrase*) If a doctor is on call, he/she is ready to go to work at any time if needed, especially for emergencies.

to be **'on duty'** [ɒn djuːti] (*v. + adj*) If someone is on duty, they are working.

to be **rostered on** [rɒstid ɒn] (morning shift) (*v. passive + prep.*) If someone is rostered on then they are working at the time stated on a roster or timetable.

to be **transferred** [træns'fɜːd] (*v. passive*) (to another ward or hospital) If a patient is transferred he is taken from the first place to a second place.

to check [tʃek] (v.) If you check something, you make sure that it is in good working order, or that it is correct and satisfactory.

to check [tʃek] urinary drainage [juːrənˈri dreinidʒ] tubes [tjuːbz] bags (v. + n.) If you check drainage bags and tubes, you make sure they are draining freely, that there are no 'kinks' in tubes (that may block) and also check or measure the amount of urine in the bag.

to complain about [kəmˈplein] (v. + adv.) If you complain about something, you say that you are not satisfied with it. To complain of pain or to complain about a pain in a particular area is to say that the pain is worrying.

to cut down [kʌ(t)daʊn] (the number) (v. + n.) To reduce the number or amount of something. e.g. Cutting down on the total amount of fats in the diet, may help reduce cholesterol levels.

to diagnose [daiəgˈnəʊz] (v.) (Often used in the passive form) If an illness or disease is diagnosed then it is identified. e.g. These people are diagnosed as being weather sensitive.

to do shift [ʃift] work (v. + n.) or to work on (night shift) If a group of people work shifts, they work for a set period before being replaced by another group of workers, so that there is always a group working.

to feed [fiːd] a baby or a patient (v. + n.) When you feed a patient, you give them something to eat and/or drink. e.g. A baby can be breastfed or bottle–fed and an older baby is fed more solid food.

to give sound [saʊnd] advice [ədˈvais] (v. + adj. + n.) If you give a person sound advice, what you tell them to do in a given situation is correct and appropriate.

to give up [givʌp] (smoking) (v. + n.) When you give up doing something you stop doing it.

to go on a diet [daiət] (v. + n.) When you go on a diet, you start eating different food – usually with a reason: to lose weight, to reduce the amount of sugar or fats in your body etc.

to have an infection [inˈfekʃən] (v. + n.) When you have an infection, there is a disease–causing micro–organism present in your body – in the bladder [blædə] = in the urinary bladder.

to lower [ləʊ(w)ə] (blood pressure [blʌd preʃə], cholesterol [kəlˈestəˈrɒl]) To lower something is to reduce it.

to put a dressing on/over the wound [wuːnd] (v. + n.) A dressing is a (sterile) cover used to prevent infective organisms entering an open wound or operation site. e.g. The nurse put a sterile dressing over the suture line when the surgeon had finished operating. (Also: To change a dressing: To remove a soiled dressing and replace it).

to review (a situation) [rivˈjuː] (v. + n.) If you review a situation, you consider it carefully to see what is wrong with it or how it could be changed. e.g. The day after changing the treatment, the doctor reviewed his condition.

to take a dressing off [teikə dressiŋ ˈɒf] (v. + n.) To remove and discard the cover over a wound or IV site.

to take a risk [teik ɑ ˈrisk] (v. + n.) If you take a risk you choose to act in a bold way, possibly with unpleasant or undesirable results.

to treat [triːt] (v.) When a doctor or nurse treats a patient, they try to make them well again. e.g. To treat minor illnesses at home, the patient is not seriously ill and can stay at home and be cared for by his family.

to update [ʌpˈdeit] (nursing care plans) (v. + n.) To add the most recent information.

Matching exercise – Match the words on the left with the correct definition.

indoors	*put a name on something using a piece of paper*
feed somebody	*something is expected to happen at that time*
label	*identify a disease or illness*
due	*to be present in a particular place e.g. a meeting*
diagnose	*a small part of something*
shift	*inside a building*
outdoors	*give a person something to eat and/or drink*
attend	*set working hours (can also mean to move something)*
facet	*make sure something is in order*
addiction	*out in the fresh air, not in a building*
canteen	*being unable to stop taking harmful substances*
check	*a restaurant in a public workplace or university*

**The following words and phrases all use specific prepositions.
Choose the correct preposition from the box.**

	on/off
1. killed ... sb./sth.*	up .... to
	by
2. find out information ... sth./	on
... sb.	down
	off
3. ... the result ... an accident.	to
	of
4. put covers ... the bed.	of
	in
5. serve ... food ... the patients.	on/over
	as ... of
6. look .../... somebody.	for
	of
7. development ... a disease.	up
	by
8. caused ... sth.	on
	of
9. opposite ...	in
	to
10. put ... place.	with
	on
11. replaced ...	by
	on
12. roster .../...	by
	after/for
13. supervised ...	to
	about/for
14. apply ... a job.	to

15. attend ... sth.

16. put a label ... sth.

17. transfer ...

18. complain ... pain.

19. cut ... on the intake of fats.

20. take a dressing ...

21. put a dressing ...

22. unable ...

23. depend ...

24. give ... smoking.

25. ... one season.

26. go ... a diet.

27. formation ...

28. addicted...

29. wrong ... sth.

* sb. = somebody   sth. = something

R

THE PRESENT PERFECT TENSE (1)

In some way relates past time <u>and</u> present time

FORM: **have** ('ve) (haven't)
       has ('s) (hasn't)   + **the past participle**   = **Present perfect simple**
                              (The past participle
                       of regular verbs ends in *-ed*)

e.g *I've been here for a long time, but we haven't known each other for very long.*
     She has worked overseas. He hasn't had an opportunity to travel.

QUESTIONS: Have | I/you/we/they | seen that document?
             Has | he/she/it | worked today?

SHORT ANSWERS: **Use only the subject and the auxiliary 'have' or 'has'.**
N.B. I've, they've, he's etc. cannot be used in short answers.
e.g. *Yes, they have. / No, we haven't.   Yes, he has. / No, he hasn't.*

USES

1. The present perfect expresses what has happened before now, at an indefinite time in the past.
<u>Experience:</u> past ? ? | future Have you ever worked in a nursing home?
                        Now   I've seen 2 operations but I've never assisted in theatre.

(At some time in your life – up to the present – the exact time is not known or is not important)
'ever' and 'never' are commonly used to talk about experience.

2. The present perfect also expresses an action or state which began in the past and continues to the present.
<u>Unfinished time:</u> past | future We've lived in Italy for 16 years.
                     Up to now   She's been in charge of the ward since March.

(The action started in the past, it continues in the present and is still the same. It will probably continue in the future)
'for' and 'since' are commonly used to talk about unfinished time.

3. The present perfect is used to talk about a past action which has results in the present. It is often a recent action.

<u>Presenting News:</u> __x____|____   A plane has crashed into the mountains near here.
                       Now   *(Now it's news – it's important to tell you).*
                                   Has the doctor been yet? (I need to know now because I have some pathology results to show him).

(The action may have happened in the past but is important now, or it's news now, something you didn't know)
The adverbs 'just', 'already' and 'yet' are frequently used with this use of the present perfect.

UNIT 1R

93

WORDS MOST OFTEN USED
WITH THE PRESENT PERFECT TENSE

'FOR' and 'SINCE'

For *is used for a certain* **period** *of time – up to now – up to the present. e.g.* **for** *a long time*

Since *is used for a* **point** *in time* (**colour the dot on the 'i' to help you remember**) *e.g.* **since** *the year 2000*

1. **Put either 'for' or 'since' with the following expressions.**

..... two days ...... five seconds .... yesterday ...... five months .... ever

..... a century ...... 1999 .... the change of the century .... a moment

..... a lifetime ...... last night .... a few minutes .... last Saturday evening

..... ages ...... a long time .... the War in Iraq .... I was at school

..... lunchtime ...... 30 years .... the last time we met .... 6 o'clock

JUST, ALREADY, YET, THIS IS THE FIRST TIME..., EVER, NEVER

I can't go swimming now, I've <u>just</u> had a big lunch. just = a short time ago.

"When are you going on holidays?" "I've <u>already</u> been on holidays." already = sooner than expected.

"Ann's nervous, <u>it's the first time</u> she has driven a car." ... the first time in her experience.

"Have you <u>ever</u> driven on the left side of the road?" at any time in your life up to now.

"No, <u>never</u>. I haven<u>'t</u> been to England <u>yet</u> – but I hope to go there next year." never = not at any time in my life up to now. not ... yet = not at any time up to now but it will happen in the future. yet is only used in negative sentences and questions.

2. **Complete the following sentences with 'just', 'already', 'yet', 'This is the first time...',** **'ever', or 'never'.**

1. I have .... given an injection and I don't think I could.

2. Have you .... eaten Indian food?

3. .... she has ever been in hospital, it is a frightening experience for her.

4. They have .... done the washing–up and cleaned the kitchen, so we can all play cards now.

5. She isn't ready to go to work because she hasn't brushed her teeth ....

6. I have .... had some wonderful news! My son has passed all his exams.

7. Have you finished your homework ....? I would like to know how you did question 24.

8. My next door neighbour has .... left for work, you will see him in the street if you hurry.

9. We have finished everything ...., we thought it would take all night!

10. He said he would love me for .... and ....!

✎ 3. **Choose the correct verb from the box and using the present perfect, complete the text about Nicole** (*see also 1K*).

speak

go (×3)

visit

know

work (×2)

live

sing (×2)

spend

be (×2)

make

do

travel

have (×2)

see

I (1).............. Nicole all her life. Her parents (2)............ very good friends of ours for many years. Although Nicole is only 27, she (3).............. a very interesting life, she loves having new experiences. She (4).... always .... hard and she (5)............ a lot on holidays. She (6).............. to China, she (7)............. Chinese with the Chinese people and she (8).......... the Great Wall of China. She (9).............. to Europe several times and (10)..... even .... on the Orient Express train from London to Bolzano! She (11).............. time in the Dolomites in Italy and she has been sightseeing in many of the main cities in Europe. Her older sister (12).......... in Florence for 7 years, so Nicole (13)............. her there. Nicole has a magnificent singing voice and (14)............... on many important occasions. She (15)......... singing lessons but she (16)..... never ....professionally. Nicole also has a wonderful sense of humour and is very good at telling jokes. She (17)....... often ...... her friends laugh until they cried! Nicole (18).............. a Post Graduate Diploma in Child Health and got top marks in all her exams. She is doing a Master's Degree in Paediatric Oncology at the moment. She (19)........... in Paediatrics for nearly 4 years now and is still working at the Royal Children's Hospital in Melbourne. Her brother has 2 children so Nicole (20)............ an aunt for 8 years – she leads a full, happy and active life.

✎ 4. **Make positive or negative sentences from the following words.**

Nicole is a Registered Nurse.
- work/in 3 different hospitals *e.g. She has worked in 3 different hospitals.*
- not be/on television ....
- travel/a lot ....
- never/be unemployed ....
- sing/since she was 6 ....

✎ 5. **Make questions to ask the following people, using the present perfect.**

(a) A surgeon. e.g. How many operations have you done this week?
(b) The mother of a new baby.
(c) A friend – ask about exams.
(d) An acquaintance about the latest award–winning film at the cinema.
(e) Your sister when she arrives home.
(f) A patient about a particular symptom.

☺ *Discuss your questions with your partner and ask each other about your experiences. How long have you been friends? Test your partner with some irregular verbs! When do you use the present perfect and when do you use the past simple? Ask your teacher for an exercise to practise both tenses together.*

UNIT

2

THE PATIENT AND THE WARD

THE PATIENT AS AN INDIVIDUAL

Patients come in all ages and sizes and from all 'walks of life'. They lead a variety of lifestyles and have different roles to play. Every individual has different skills and abilities applicable to daily life and in normal daily life we do many different activities, each requiring different skills and abilities (refer to the activities of daily living – ADL's in Section 1L).

A patient may be anxious and stressed on admission because he or she is experiencing physical signs or symptoms of a disease or illness and going into a hospital environment, which is cold or unfriendly, will raise his/her anxiety levels. Becoming involved in the patient's concerns and interests, breaks down barriers and reduces stress. Patients must be seen as individuals with individual needs and worries, not as a 'bed number', 'a particular disease' or as 'that patient'! Using the patient's name is a sign of respect. Patients may be in a situation where they have to 'relearn' skills which were part of their daily life but which they can no longer do. Little is known about his family, his home–life, his religion, beliefs or normal responsibilities. He may have one or more of the roles described in Section 1L and will find himself in an unfamiliar and confusing environment where his own skills and capabilities are unimportant and irrelevant.

Due to anxiety and stress, the patient's usual concentration and memory levels may be reduced, so it is often necessary to repeat instructions and information that he needs after the initial "settling in" period.

The nurse should answer any questions that will prevent anxiety and she needs to be able to assess the patient's reactions correctly. The nurse needs to be sympathetic and give encouragement to build trust and companionship. Positive interaction and genuine concern can improve the outcome (and may also reduce the length) of the patient's hospitalisation, build confidence and be both a rewarding and satisfying experience for the nurse and the patient.

Patients often feel they can relate better to junior and trainee nurses. This requires honesty and tact on the part of the nurse when she is unable to help, or to answer questions directly. The junior nurse must not forget her responsibility to the patient when she promises to find a more senior staff member – it is easy to forget or to have something else take your attention.

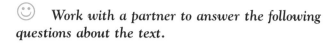

☺ **Work with a partner to answer the following questions about the text.**

1. Compare the phrase '*walks of life*' with '*lifestyle*'. What do you understand by these words?

2. Differentiate between '*skills*' and '*abilities*'.

3. How do people change when they come into hospital? Think about their normal roles, responsibilities and activities.

4. What is the nurse's role when admitting a patient into hospital?

5. How can nurses help the patient to feel more comfortable in the hospital environment and how can they help patients to keep their sense of identity?

6. Put the following age classifications in order, from the youngest to oldest:

old	middle–aged	child	adult	neonate	young adult
elderly	teenager	toddler	pre–schooler	adolescent	baby

7. How old is a teenager? How old is a toddler? How old is a person 'in their 40's'?

8. Look up the meaning of the words *sympathy* (n.) and *sympathetic* (adj.) in your dictionary. How does the meaning differ in your language?

9. Differentiate between '*an active lifestyle*' and '*a sedentary lifestyle*'.

10. Find examples in the text of verbs and nouns or 2 part nouns that are often used together.

   e.g.

   verb and noun

   to be admitted to hospital

   2 part nouns

   home environment

Useful Abbreviations

O/A	stands for:	**On Admission**
C/O	stands for:	**Complaining Of**

B

ADMISSION AND PATIENT ASSESSMENT

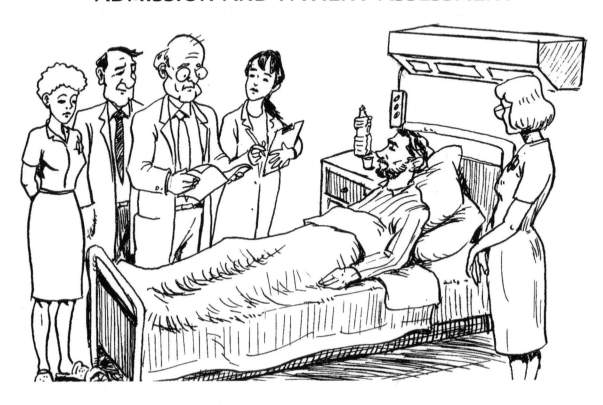

Accepted abbreviations (3)

Do you know what these stand for? Write the full meaning under the letters.

BP	T P R	Y	N
Pt	RIB	PO	O/A
(H)PU	NPU	BO	IV
IM	NAD	O/E	C/O

☺ ***Check with your partner and then your teacher. Practice saying them like this:***
e.g. BP [biːpiː] stands for blood pressure. What does 'TPR' [tiːpiːˈaː(r)] stand for?

📖 Taking 'obs'
(The patient's observations)

B.P. B.P. stands for blood pressure [blʌd preʃə] and is measured in mmHg i.e. millimetres of Mercury [milimi:təz ˈəv mɜ:kˈjəri]. It is usually measured using a sphygmomanometer [sfigmaʊˈmænˈɒmətə]. Normal adult (systolic/diastolic) blood pressure is about 120/80. We say "one hundred and twenty on (or over) eighty". The maximum pressure of blood in the arteries occurs in a systole [sistˈəli] and the minimum in a diastole [daiˈæstəli]. A higher than normal blood pressure is called '*hyper*tension' and a lower than normal blood pressure is called '*hypo*tension'.

T. T. stands for body temperature [temprəˈtʃə]. It is measured in degrees (°) Centigrade [dəgri:z sentiˈgreid] (or Celsius [selˈsi:əs]) using a thermometer [θɜ:ˈmɒmətə] – mercury or electronic, or a heat–sensitive strip. Normal body temperature is considered to be 36.8°C i.e. "thirty–six point eight degrees Centigrade". A patient who is *febrile* [febˈraiəl] has a *high temperature* or '*pyrexia*'. Temperature is normally *lowest* in the morning and *highest* in the evening. Temperature can be measured orally (PO), rectally (PR), in the axilla – under the arm (PA) or in the ear (aurally). '*Hypothermia*' [haiˈpaʊˈθɜ:miə] refers to abnormally low body temperature.

P. P. stands for the pulse rate which is the wave of pressure travelling along the arterial system, created by a contraction of the heart forcing blood into the aorta during ventricular systole. The pulse rate can be counted over major arteries: the carotid artery in the neck, the radial artery at the wrist, the femoral artery in the inguinal canal or the temporal artery on the side of the forehead. The *most convenient* point to *take a* person's *pulse* is on the anterior surface of the wrist; it is *less convenient to take* the apex beat over the heart using a stethoscope. The number of beats per minute (b.p.m.) are counted and recorded. A normal pulse rate *varies between* 68 and 84 b.p.m. Pulse rate is not normally *slower than* 50 b.p.m. The pulse rate is also described as either *regular* or *irregular*.

R. The initial 'R' stands for the patient's respiration rate and is measured in *breaths* [breθs] *per minute*. Normal respiration is approximately 20 breaths per minute. (Respirations are observed *without* the patient *being aware* usually while taking his pulse. If the patient realizes that his breathing is being watched, the rhythm will change and he may '*hold his breath*')

✏️ *What measurements are considered 'within normal limits' for an adult's blood pressure, temperature, pulse and respirations? How do these measurements change with age, in a child or during exercise?*

📖 This is Mark Andrews. He is a 34 year–old married teacher who is waiting to go into hospital for an operation to remove a cancer in his bowel (intestine). The Specialist told him he could go into hospital during the school holidays. He has never been into hospital before.

✏️ *How do you think he feels? Choose suitable adjectives from the following list:*

happy • nervous • surprised • excited • anxious • frightened • depressed • tired • bored • dirty • delighted • lonely • responsible • uncertain • worried • distressed • scared • terrified • fearful • sad

How many nouns can you make from these adjectives? <u>Underline</u> *the negative feelings and put them in order of severity. Can you add any more to the list?*

🎧 **Listening 13 – Julie and Mark at home** *Read the dialogue and listen to the recording.*
Fill in the gaps.

Mark has just arrived home from school and his wife Julie has some news…

Julie: Hello, Love! (1) .... at school?

Mark: Yes, very good really. Most of the students (2) ....in the maths test ... and guess what? We're invited to a holiday break–up dinner in the mountains (3) ....

Julie: I'm glad you had a good day at school. I had a good day too, but I'm afraid (4) .... to the dinner. Mr. Burns' rooms rang today and they told me you can (5) .... on Wednesday afternoon but you (6) .... on Monday morning at 8.30.

Mark: Oh, next week – that's a pity! Bad timing I suppose, but (7) .... I wonder what it will be like! I'll tell the staff tomorrow to take our names off the list for the dinner. I'll have to ask someone to do my lessons next week. There are a couple of relief teachers available, I think. I understood the operation would be in 2 weeks – never mind!

Julie: It will be fine, I'm sure. You should ring your parents and your sisters to let them know that (8) .... for the operation. What do you think you need to take with you?

Mark: Not much really. I'd like to take a couple of books to read and probably two (9) ...., slippers, dressing gown and toiletries. I can't think of anything else. I'll take my CD player and a few disks too. The music has a calming effect.

Julie: Yes, OK. Don't forget to take the MRI (10) ....

Mark: I'll put those in a bag now and I'll pack at the weekend. Will the operation be in the afternoon?

Julie: I don't know really, Mr. Burns' secretary didn't tell me, but I can ring tomorrow and ask her. I'll stay all day but I'm sure you will have lots of beautiful nurses to tell you what to do and (11) ....!

Mark: I hadn't thought of that – but I'll probably be feeling so rotten (12) ....!

Julie: They'll look after you very well I'm sure. You probably won't be able to get out of bed for a couple of days and I'll come in as often as possible so don't worry. Let's go and (13) ....!

Listen again to complete the dialogue. Listen a third time to check your answers, then practise the dialogue with a partner.

☺   *How many family members can you name?*   e.g.   *husband   wife   father   mother*

Draw up a chart with a list of male members and female members.

GRAMMAR NOTES

'will' and 'won't (will not) are modal auxiliary verbs with different uses and are the same in all persons, singular and plural.

PREDICTION – "You <u>won't be able</u> to get out of bed after the operation" "What <u>will</u> it <u>be</u> like?"

WILLINGNESS / INTENTION TO DO SOMETHING – "<u>I'll put</u> them in my bag now..."

A PROMISE – "<u>I'll come</u> in to stay with you as much as possible"

A DECISION MADE AT THE TIME OF SPEAKING – "<u>I'll take</u> my CD player"

<u>**Remember**</u> *'will' is always followed by another verb in the base infinitive (i.e. without 'to')*
*In spoken English the short form '**ll** is used in all persons singular and plural. Will + not = **won't** [wount]*

ADMISSION TO HOSPITAL

On Monday Mark is admitted to hospital and arrives in the Surgical Ward with Julie. They meet the Charge Sister and Sister Joanna, who takes them to a room. Mary, the Ward Help is in the room cleaning the bedside tables. There are 2 beds in the room but both are empty.

Sister Pat:	This is your room Mark – number 612. You will be *on your own* for a couple of days so you can choose the bed near the window or this one near the bathroom. Hello Mary, this is Mr Mark Andrews and his wife Julie.
Mary:	Good morning Mr and Mrs Andrews. Can I get you a bottle of water and a glass?
Sister Pat:	Thank you Mary, but Mark is having more tests today and *can't have anything to eat or drink* until later. Mary is a wonderful help and will help us to look after you Mark.
Mark:	Thank you. I'd like to have the bed near the window if that's all right.
Sister Pat:	Yes, of course. I'll leave you to *change into your pyjamas* and *hop into bed* and then I'll come back in a few minutes to ask you a few questions. You can put your clothes in the cupboard on the left, but it isn't very big so it's probably a good idea to take the suitcase home with you, Mrs Andrews. Mark, you can put *the things you need* in the cupboard near the bed (the locker).
Mark:	Yes, thank you. Jules will take the case with her when she goes – you've got the car, love – so that's no problem. Can my wife stay here this morning, Sister?
Sister Pat:	Yes, that's fine. I'll come back to speak to you both very soon... This is the handset if you need anything just call. This button is the buzzer and this one is to cancel your call – the light over the door turns off – this one is for the overhead light... OK?

🎧 **Listening 14 – Mark at the hospital** *Read the dialogue and listen to the recording to answer the following questions:*

1. Who is Mary?
2. How many patients are in the room with Mark?
3. Does he have a choice of beds? Which one does he choose?
4. What is Julie taking home?
5. Is Mark fasting?

☺ *In groups of 3 practice the dialogue. Discuss the expressions in italics and how you can say them differently.*

STANDARD ADMISSION PROCEDURE

☺ *What is the Standard Admission Procedure where you work? With a partner put the following points into a possible sequence.*

(a) Tell the patient what is going to happen to him/her in the next 12–24 hours.
(b) Co–ordinate between the patient, the doctors and other health care workers.
(c) Put on the patient's name–band and signs necessary on the bed (*e.g. 'nil orally' or fasting*)
(d) Inform the doctor in charge, of the patient's arrival.
(e) Welcome the patient in a calm, friendly manner.
(f) Introduce yourself and the other patient(s) in the room. Introduce other staff and the Ward Charge Nurse where possible.
(g) Complete the Admission form and appropriate charts.
(h) Show the patient where to find the bathroom, the Nurses' Station, the Day Room (Sitting Room) and the location of public telephones (if necessary).
(i) Show the patient which locker is his, demonstrate the handset with the overhead light, and the "call" bell (or buzzer) and show him/her how to use the headphones – if a radio is provided.

C

UNDERSTANDING CHARTS

On the following examination form there are some more abbreviations to guide the doctor's examination and to express the resulting observations – some of the abbreviations are for different body systems. *e.g. R.S. = Respiratory System, CVS = Cardio–Vascular System.*

Can you guess some of the ringed abbreviations?

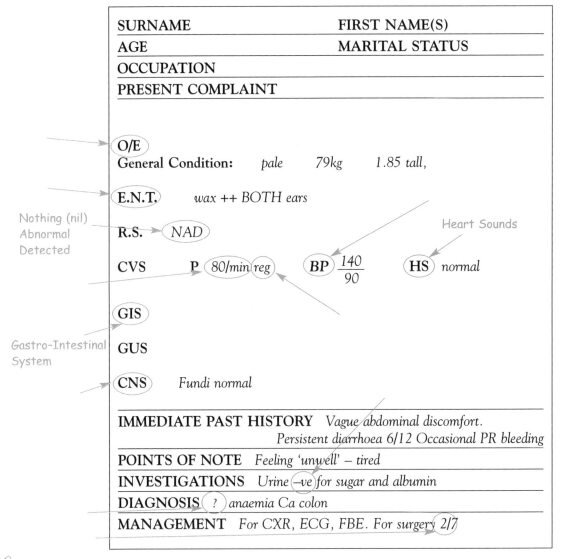

SURNAME	FIRST NAME(S)
AGE	MARITAL STATUS
OCCUPATION	
PRESENT COMPLAINT	

O/E
General Condition: *pale   79kg   1.85 tall,*

E.N.T.   *wax ++ BOTH ears*

Nothing (nil) Abnormal Detected

R.S. NAD

CVS   P 80/min reg   BP $\frac{140}{90}$ Heart Sounds   HS *normal*

GIS

Gastro-Intestinal System

GUS

CNS   *Fundi normal*

IMMEDIATE PAST HISTORY *Vague abdominal discomfort.*
Persistent diarrhoea 6/12 Occasional PR bleeding

POINTS OF NOTE   *Feeling 'unwell' – tired*

INVESTIGATIONS   *Urine –ve for sugar and albumin*

DIAGNOSIS (?) *anaemia Ca colon*

MANAGEMENT   *For CXR, ECG, FBE. For surgery 2/7*

Draw up another chart and fill in as many details as you can for Mark Andrews. Fill in his personal details, the reason for admission to hospital and his diagnosis.

☺ *What are some of the necessary nursing procedures necessary before a patient has abdominal surgery? Discuss your ideas with your partner.*

✎ Look at the following 'Patient Assessment and Care Plan' and think of the questions you would need to ask the patient. Write the questions on the lines under the chart.

Patient Assessment and Care Plan

1 → Name:
2 → Date of Original Admission:
   Date of Admission/transfer:
   Re-admission/s:

Hospital No:

3 → **Observations on Admission:**
   BP
4a → Height
4b → Loss of appetite: ☐ Y
   Temperature
   Weight
   ☐ N

Time of Admission:
Time:
Time:

6 → Communication:
   Vision:
7 → Hearing:
   Speech:
8 → Tissue Viability:
   Pressure Sore Risk Calculator (Norton Scale)

BMI
Recent unintential loss of weight: ☐ Y   ☐ N
Pulse
RSU

5

Table 1   THE NORTON SCALE

Physical condition	Mental condition	Activity	Mobility	
Good 4	Alert 4	Ambulant 4	Full 4	Incontinent
Fair 3	Apathetic 3	Walk/help 3	Slightly limited 3	Not 4
Poor 2	Confused 2	Chairbound 2	Very limited 2	Occasionally 3
Very bad 1	Stuporous 1	Bedfast 1	Immobile 1	Usually/urine 2
				Doubly 1

9 →
Total Score =

I accept full responsibility for my property and decline safe keeping

Patients signature:
(If patient unable to sign give reason)
Staff Signature:
Staff Print Name:
Date: /   /   Grade:

Risk Factor:

5-10 = High
15-19 = Low   11-14 = Medium
20 = No

Assessment completed by:
Signature:
Print Name: Grade:
Date: /   /
Named Nurse: Time:

or

Property in Hospital Safe ☐ Yes   ☐ No
Date: /   /
Receipt Page No: ____

1 of 12

1. ....
2. ....
3. ....
4. ....
5. ....

6. ....
7. ....
8. ....
9. ....

☺ Discuss your questions and possible answers and follow up questions, with a partner. Look at the highlighted section of the chart: What do you understand by the following words?

(skin) tissue viability • physical condition • mental condition
• activity • mobility • continence/incontinence

D

PRESSURE AREAS AND PRESSURE SORES

THE "NORTON SCALE" OF ASSESSMENT

On the "Patient Assessment and Care Plan", on page 105, the Norton scale is highlighted. This is used to calculate the risk of pressure *sores* by recognising a potential risk because sores can be prevented. These pressure sores start as a redness of the skin on the pressure points (or *pressure areas*) on the body – areas where there is not much fat, or 'padding' over a bony prominence. The redness can easily become a sore when the skin 'breaks down'. These used to be called *bed–sores* but can just as easily occur from sitting in a chair for a long period of time without changing position. Some patients are more at risk than others and for this reason the Norton Scale is used for assessment. Very thin people are at risk and those who are in poor nutritional state. Very heavy (obese) people are at risk because they are less likely to be mobile, and unconscious and paralysed patients are at risk because they are unable to move. Incontinent patients are at risk because urine and faeces 'burn' fragile skin tissue and the friction of wet skin surfaces on the bed or chair causes redness and damage to the skin.

Using the Norton Scale

By adding the numbers from each column for the individual patient, the risk factor can be ascertained:

When the total score is   20   there is no risk at all.

When the total score is 15–19 there is low risk.

When the total score is 11–14 there is medium risk.

When the total score is   5–10 there is HIGH risk.

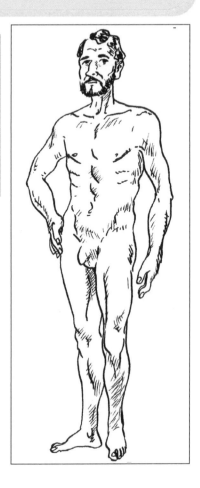

Mark the body parts on the diagram which may be considered 'pressure points' in an unconscious or bedfast patient.

These should include:
1. The rims of the ears.
2. The shoulder blades (not visible on the diagram).
3. The elbows.
4. The sacrum (not visible on the diagram).
5. The hips.
6. The perineum (the area between the genitals and the anus).
7. The back of the knees (not visible on the diagram).
8. The inner sides of the knees.
9. The outer ankles.
10. The heels.

☺ *Imagine a patient you have seen and calculate his/her risk factor for developing pressure sores or use Mark Andrews (post–surgically) as an example.*

☺ **Discuss these statements with your partner.**

🖉 **The statements are either true (T) or false (F). Mark your answers then correct the false statements.**

1. Patients at risk of getting pressure sores have a high score on the Norton Scale.

    T ☐   F ☐

2. All patients in hospital are at risk of getting pressure sores.

    T ☐   F ☐

3. Patients who are incontinent of both urine and faeces are at high risk.

    T ☐   F ☐

4. The first sign of a pressure area is a small red area or an 'abrasion' over a bony surface.

    T ☐   F ☐

5. Fat people are not at risk because they have 'protective padding'.

    T ☐   F ☐

6. Pressure areas can be prevented by keeping the skin clean and dry and by encouraging the patient to move and change his position or by turning unconscious or paralysed patients every 2 hours.

    T ☐   F ☐

7. Ring pads, cushions and pillows can be used to keep the affected part off the surface of the bed.

    T ☐   F ☐

8. Special mattresses, called 'ripple mattresses' are available for immobile or unconscious patients. They are connected to a motor which circulates air inside the mattress and increases the blood circulation.

    T ☐   F ☐

Physical condition	Mental condition	Activity	Mobility	Incontinent
Good 4	Alert 4	Ambulant 4	Full 4	Not 4
Fair 3	Apathetic 3	Walk/help 3	Slightly limited 3	Occasionally 3
Poor 2	Confused 2	Chairbound 2	Very limited 2	Usually/urine 2
Very bad 1	Stuporous 1	Bedfast 1	Immobile 1	Doubly 1

THE BED AND BED LINEN

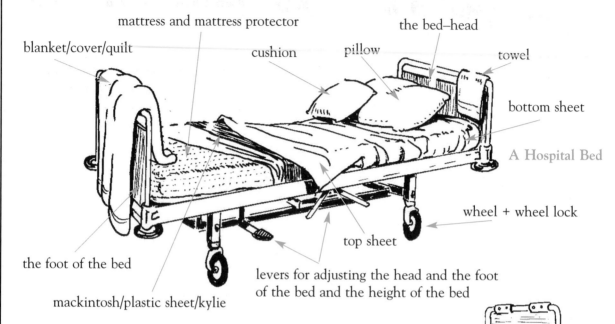

mattress and mattress protector

the bed–head

blanket/cover/quilt

cushion   pillow   towel

bottom sheet

A Hospital Bed

the foot of the bed

wheel + wheel lock

top sheet

levers for adjusting the head and the foot
of the bed and the height of the bed

mackintosh/plastic sheet/kylie

Answer as many questions as you can, then compare your
answers with a partner.

1. What is 'linen'? Can you list all the linen that you would find on
   a bed, in a linen cupboard or on the linen trolley?
2. Label the linen trolley using these words:
   clean linen
   dirty (soiled) linen
   rubbish bag
3. Name 3 different types of sheets.
4. What is a pillow case (or pillow–slip)?
5. What is the difference between a blanket, a quilt and a duvet?

The
Linen
Trolley

6. How can you stop the bed from moving when
   it is in a room?
   How can you 'wheel it along'?
7. What can you do with the levers under the
   bed? (sometimes there is a handle too)
8. What sort of patients need a mackintosh or
   waterproof sheet?
9. List the things you need to
   (a) wash a patient in bed
   (b) change the bed linen
   (c) make a bed for a new admission
10. What can a patient with 'toilet privileges' do?

MAKING THE BED
OF AN UNCONSCIOUS OR BEDFAST PATIENT

📖 *Mark is now convalescing. He doesn't have an IV or a catheter now but he has a colostomy bag which he is learning to look after himself. Tomorrow he can wash in the bathroom but today he washed himself in bed. Pat is changing all the bed linen and explaining to Annie what to do. Read the directions Pat gives to Annie.*

✏️ *Use your own words to explain to Mark what you are going to do.*

1. First Annie, ask Mark if he has finished, if he shaved and if he was able to wash his private parts, legs and feet! Then, explain that you would like to wash his back and that he needs to turn onto his side.

✏️ ....
....

2. While he is lying on his side and when you have finished washing his back, roll the soiled sheet up lengthways along Mark's back, take the clean bottom sheet and tuck the top and bottom corners neatly under the mattress, rolling the other half lengthways next to the soiled sheets. Pull back the mackintosh and take a 'draw sheet' or 'half–sheet' and place it over the plastic sheet, tucking the end of both sheets under the mattress. (Some hospitals use a *kylie* which is a disposable '2 in 1' waterproof sheet)

✏️ ....
....

3. Next, help Mark to turn back to the other side, rolling over the pile of bed linen in the middle of the bed. Make sure he is comfortable lying on the other side and holding the side of the mattress if he needs to. Now, pull out the soiled sheets from behind Mark's back and pull the clean sheets through. First pull the bottom sheet and tuck it into the mattress – 'mitre' the corners under the mattress, they look so neat! Now pull the waterproof sheet through and the half–sheet and 'tuck them in' under the mattress.

✏️ ....
....
....
....

4. Now, put the soiled top sheet in the bag and get a fresh sheet off the trolley. Mark's clean pyjamas are in the bedside locker, we'll dress him together. That's it. We'll sit Mark up for breakfast, put on the top sheet and tuck it in at the bottom (mitred corners again) then the blanket and the quilt. ... You can take the trolley, Tony, we've finished in this room…

🎧 **Listening 15 – Changing bed sheets** *Now listen to the recording. How does your dialogue compare?*

😊 *Can you and your partner 'do a demonstration' for the teacher?*

THE PRESENT PERFECT (2) AND OTHER PERFECT TENSES

(The Present Perfect tense is discussed in Section 1R)

Continuous tenses and passive tenses both need the auxiliary 'be' – so in Perfect Continuous and Perfect Passive the past participle 'been' is used:

Present Perfect Passive

(Passive is needed when the subject of the sentence is not the agent of the verb)

Form: have ('ve) (haven't)
has ('s) (hasn't) **+ been + the past participle =** **Present perfect simple passive**

e.g. *His dressing <u>hasn't been done</u> yet. She has <u>been seen</u> by the doctor.*

Present Perfect Continuous

(All continuous tenses are used to talk about activities, with the present perfect we are talking about activities 'up to now' or activities in the recent past that have a significance now)

Form: have ('ve) (haven't)
has ('s) (hasn't) **+ been + the <u>present</u> participle =** **Present Perfect Continuous**

1. The action continues to the present. *e.g. He's been waiting for ages.*
2. Referring to an action that has results in the present. *e.g. She's (is) sunburnt – she's (has) been working outdoors.*

Past Perfect

(relates an earlier past time with the past)

Form: **had** ('d) (hadn't) **+ the past participle = Past perfect**

Relates the past <u>to an earlier past</u>. *e.g. He had spoken to the doctor before he came into hospital.*

Past Perfect Passive

(used to talk about an action in 'an earlier past' when the subject of the sentence is not the agent of the verb)

Form: **had** ('d) (hadn't) **+ been + the past participle = Past Perfect Passive**

e.g. *She had a bowel resection yesterday. She <u>had been operated</u> on 6 months ago but that operation wasn't successful.*

> ## Past Perfect Continuous
> (used for an activity in an earlier past up to a specific past time)
>
> *Form:* **had** ('d) (hadn't) + **been** + the **present** participle = **Past Perfect Continuous**
>
> The past perfect continuous describes an activity that started at a time earlier to the past time referred to.
> e.g. *Mrs Dooley was admitted for elective surgery yesterday. She had been waiting for a bed for three months.*

🖊 *Test yourself by completing the following sentences using the present perfect, the present perfect continuous, the present perfect passive, the past perfect or the past perfect continuous tense. Use the verbs in brackets.*

1. His blood pressure ....(take). It was 116/76.

2. Mrs Roberts vomited all night, she ....(feel) nauseated all day yesterday.

3. Mr Andrews ....(admit) for surgery later this week.

4. .... Mr Burns (the surgeon) ....(see) him yet?

5. .... Mr Andrews....................................(take) any medication at home?

6. He...(take) vitamins regularly but not any prescription medicines.

7. .... he .... (lose) any weight recently?

8. .... his valuables ....(put) in the locked cupboard?

9. What happened? Mr Thornton .... (take) back to the operating theatre.

10. He was getting much better and he ....(eat) normally.

11. What ....you ....(do)? You look exhausted.

12. Where .... you ....(go)? I .... (wait) for ages.

13. I wanted to visit my sister and her new baby, but she .... (feed) the baby and .... (fall) asleep, so I left a message and said I would call back this evening.

14. Miss O'Donovan is incontinent of both urine and faeces. She .... (have) problems for quite a long time.

THE WARD AND THE ROOMS

The wards and the patients' rooms are designed [dəˈzaind] so that patients can be as comfortable [kʌmfˈtəbl] as possible and have their own privacy [praiˈvəsi]. Medical staff need to have easy access [ækˈses] to the patient and there needs to be enough space around the patient to carry out necessary procedures [prəˈsiːdjəz].

All the rooms are cleaned thoroughly [θʌrəli] (very well) and staff have to wash their hands thoroughly before attending to each patient, because there is always a risk of 'cross–infection' (the transferring of infection from one patient to another).

Most rooms have a separate bathroom with a shower, washbasin, toilet and bidet but there is usually a large communal [kəmjuːnəl] bathroom for patients who 'have bathroom privileges' [privˈlədʒəz] and so the staff can bathe [beið] or shower patients if necessary.

All these things can be found in the ward. Number the items in the box under the pictures.

dangerous drugs [deinˈdʒərəs drʌgz]		cupboard [kʌbəd]		chair [tʃeə]		switch [switʃ]	
magazine [mægəˈziːn]		toilet [tɔiˈlət]		drug trolley [drʌg trɒli]		bidet [bidei]	
sofa/couch [səʊfə/kautʃ]		shower [ʃauwə]		locker [lɒkə]		wheelchair [wiəlˈtʃeə]	
bedpan & urinal [bedˈpæn & juːrənəl]		TV [tiː viː]		desk [desk]		washbasin [wɒʃ beisən]	
telephone(phone) [teləˈfəun]		linen trolley [linən trɒli]		(history) chart trolley [histri] [tʃaːt trɒli]		bed [bed]	
table [teibl]		heater [hiːtə]		bath [baːθ]		sterilizer [sterəˈlaizə]	

112

✎ *Where could you find the things pictured?*

- In the patient's room.
- In the Pan Room or Work Room.
- In a store room.
- In the corridor.
- In the Office or Nurses' Station.
- In a bathroom.
- In the 'day room' or sitting room (lounge room).

GRAMMAR NOTES

Conjunctions (Linking words): and, but, because, so/so that

Notice how and, but, because, so *and* so that *are used to join sentences.*

- 'and' *joins two similar ideas:* Patients can be comfortable and have privacy.
- 'but' *joins two different ideas:* Most rooms have a bathroom but there is also a communal bathroom.
- 'because', 'so' *and* 'so that' *give a reason:* Rooms are designed so that staff have easy access to patients.

✎ *Use a 'linking word' to make five sentences using your choice of objects in the pictures.*

1. ....
2. ....
3. ....
4. ....
5. ....

✎ *Use a 'linking word' to complete the following sentences, matching part A with part B (not in order).*

A		B
1. A Day Room is provided		dirty linen is put immediately into a bag.
2. Most rooms have bathrooms		patients need to be able to contact their family.
3. The door–ways are wider than normal	**and**	patients like to have somewhere to relax.
4. The beds are arranged		patients in wheelchairs can pass through.
5. Furniture and fittings are designed	**but**	bedpans are sometimes called 'pots' or 'potties'.
6. Telephones are available on each floor	**because**	staff can see the patients from the doorway.
7. Visiting hours are usually restricted	**so**	there is also one for dangerous or addictive drugs.
8. There is a locked cupboard in the Nurses' Station which is used for keeping valuables	**so that**	close family members are sometimes allowed to come in at other times.
9. Urinals are sometimes called 'bottles'		a lot of patients wash independently.
10. Clean linen is stored in a cupboard or on a trolley		they can be cleaned easily.

☺ *Compare possible answers with a partner, then check with your teacher.*

113

WHAT IS IT AND WHAT'S IT FOR?

 Here are 12 (twelve) different objects found in a ward of a hospital.

First, identify the pictures using the words in the box, then using the words or expressions under the pictures, describe what each thing is used for.

e.g. A towel is used for drying (hands or bodies!)

Remember

The 'ing' form of a verb is used after a preposition.

A urinometer [ju:rən'ɒmətə]	A wheelchair [wiəl tʃeə]	A razor [reizə]
A towel [taʊəl]	A dressing gown	A crutch [krʌtʃ]
A bra [bra:]	[dresiŋ gaʊn]	*or* walking stick [wɔ:kiŋ stik]
A toothbrush [tu:θ brʌʃ]	Scissors [sizəz]	A urinal [ju:rənəl]
A bedpan [bed pæn]	Forceps [fɔ:səps]	

1. A towel is (used) **for** dry**ing** hands or bodies.
2. ....
3. ....
4. ....
5. ....
6. ....
7. ....
8. ....
9. ....
10. ....
11. ....
12. ....

support breasts (a 'nursing' mother
   needs a 'maternity' one)
shave (clear an area of hair)
wear over pyjamas
help lame [leim] *or* unstable patients
   to walk

collect faeces
transport patients who are
   unable to walk
cut various materials
~~dry hands or bodies~~
clean your teeth

test the 'specific gravity' (SG) of
   urine
pick things up using a
   'no–touch' technique
pass urine (micturate/urinate) in
   bed – males only!

THE PASSIVE TENSE

General - ALL FORMS

Form

Different Passive tenses are formed by using
the different tenses of 'BE' (is, was, is being, have been etc.) + the PAST PARTICIPLE

The rules for choosing *tenses* in the passive are the same as in the active.
That is, to talk about something in progress now, we use the 'present continuous'.
e.g. *The road is being repaired at the moment.*

Passive Tense	Structure	Example
Present simple	am/are/is + past participle	*Medications are given as directed.*
Present continuous	am/are/is + being + past participle	*His urine is being tested for glucose.*
Past simple	was/were + past participle	*He was operated on yesterday.*
Past continuous	was/were + being + past participle	*Diet cards were being given out …*
Present perfect simple	have/has + been + past participle	*They have been filled out correctly.*
Past perfect	had + been + past participle	*Everyone had been told how to do them.*

Active or Passive

***Compare these active and
passive sentences***

Active
Someone cleans the
waiting room every evening.

Passive
The waiting room is cleaned
every evening (by someone)

Active
Someone has invited Tony to
the party

Passive
Tony has been invited to the
party (by someone)

* Note that the object of an
active verb (e.g. the waiting
room, Tony) becomes the
subject of a passive verb.

Use of the Passive

I) We often use the passive when we do not know
who or what does something.
My mobile phone was stolen last night. (I do not
know who stole the phone.)

II) We also use the passive when we are not
interested in who or what does something.
This hospital was built in 1981.
Tony has been invited to the party.
In these sentences we are interested in the
hospital and Tony, not who built the hospital,
or who invited Tony. Include note (iv) here –
We are interested in the procedure, not the
person who does it.

III) We also use the passive when we do not want
to say who or what does something!
Compare:
Active: *The surgeon made a mistake.*
Passive: *A mistake was made!*

IV) Also to describe: a process, a procedure, an
experiment or an operation – it is important
to know **how** the procedure is done, not **who**
does it.

✎ *On the floor plan of a ward, pictured on the right, label the corridor, the patients' rooms, the office, the stairs and the lifts.*

☺ **Work with your partner.**

Student A: Look at diagram A below. Decide which rooms you have, then ask your partner which rooms he/she has in diagram B. Tell your partner what 'things' could be found in those rooms.

Student B: Look at diagram B. Tell your partner which rooms in the ward you have in your picture, then write or draw all the 'things' your partner describes. When you have a complete list, ask your partner which rooms he/she has and then tell him/her all the 'things' you would find in those rooms. Now it is your partner's turn to write or draw.

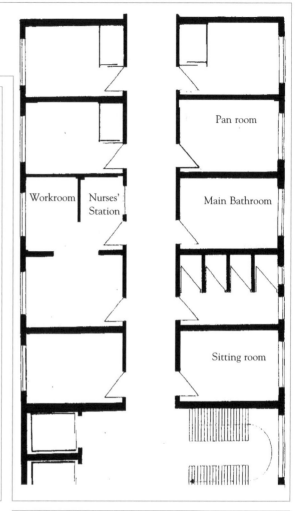

STUDENT A   STUDENT B

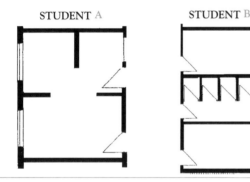

☺ ROLE PLAY

Imagine that there are 6 patients' rooms in a newly renovated ward of a small private hospital where you are working. Each room is tastefully decorated in a different colour:
one is red, one is white, one is bright green, one is bright yellow, one is light blue and one is pink.

Four patients are being admitted today:

• *a female psychiatric patient, suffering from severe depression*
• *a young lady who is having her first baby*
• *a male teenager, convalescing after surgery for a ruptured appendix and peritonitis*
• *an elderly male suffering from terminal cancer of the prostate*

Work with a partner. Read your role–card and decide what you are going to say.

STUDENT A

You are one of the four patients arriving at the hospital.
Decide which room you would like and the reasons for your choice.
Explain to the admitting officer what your problems are and why you would like that particular room.

STUDENT B

You are the admitting officer at the hospital. Consider the problems of the patients who are arriving today and decide which rooms are best for each.
Discuss this patient's choice and tell him/her which room you have chosen and why it is best.

DIRECT AND REPORTED SPEECH

📖 *Look at the sentences.*

> 1. "I spend most of my free time reading," he said.
> 2. He said that he spent most of his free time reading.

Which sentence is in direct speech and which is in reported speech? What happens to the tense of the verb spend in reported speech? What other differences are there between the two sentences?

Reported Statements

Direct statement	Reported Statement
"I'm a police officer."	He said/told me (that) he was a police officer.
"I live in Sydney."	He said/told me (that) he lived in Sydney.

Reported Questions

Direct questions	Reported questions
"When can we meet?"	I asked when we could meet.
"Are you frightened?"	She asked the girl if she was frightened.

Focus

➡ Reported speech is often introduced by *say* and *tell.*

➡ *Tell* is always followed by a name or an object pronoun:
He *told me* he was a police officer.

➡ When the reporting verb is in the present tense, there is no change in the tense:
"I *don't want* to come." He says *he doesn't want* to come.

➡ 'That' is always optional after verbs of speaking.

➡ In reported questions the word order of the original question is changed:
"*What's your name?*" She asked the patient what *her name was.*

1. *Move the tenses used in direct speech 'back one step into the past' to complete the sentences using reported speech.*

DIRECT SPEECH			REPORTED SPEECH
I know quite a lot of people here	**Present Simple**	Simple Past	He said that he .... quite a lot of people *there*.
John is feeling much better	**Present Continuous**	Past Continuous	He said that John .... much better.
I enjoyed my holiday in Australia	**Simple Past**	Past Perfect	He said that he .... his holiday in Australia
Rosanna wasn't feeling well	**Past Continuous**	Past Perfect Continuous	He said that Rosanna .... feeling well.
They've been in the new cable car	**Present Perfect**	Past Perfect	He said that they .... in the new cable car.
I've been waiting for ages	**Present Perfect Continuous**	Past Perfect Continuous	She said that she .... for ages.
I had been wanting to come to see you	**Past Perfect Continuous**	Past Perfect Continuous	She said that she .... to come to see me.
will, can, may, shall, must	**Other Changes**		
this, today, tomorrow, here	**Other Changes**		

REPORTED SPEECH

2. *Re–write the following text using reported speech. The beginning has been done for you.*

"My name's Vera, and I'm from Russia. I came to Italy about 5 years ago and I've been living in Verona since then. When I lived in Moscow, I was a journalist, but now I'm working at a hospital here and I quite enjoy it. I'm not sure if I will go back to Russia now but I may go back for a holiday. I haven't seen my family for a long time and I know they want me to visit them."

I met a very interesting woman the other day. She said that her name was Vera and that ....

DIRECT SPEECH

3. *Re–write the following example of reported speech using the words that the speaker actually said.*

Mr John Hepburn, the cleaner who won a record $4 million with one lottery ticket, said that he had been amazed to win so much money but that he wouldn't let it change his life. He wanted to continue working in the same job, which he enjoyed, but he said he would buy a new van, as the old one had broken down. He said that he was going to Scotland to visit relatives, which was something he had been planning to do for a long time. He said that when he got back he would go straight to work again.

" *I was amazed to win so much money...................*

✏ 4. *Now write the following statements in reported speech – watch for changes other than tense changes.*

1. "John will ring tomorrow, "he said to the group.
   e.g. He told the group (that) John would ring the next day.
2. "I can help you," she said to me.
3. "We may go to Munich, " they said to her.
4. "What shall we do?" they asked me.
5. "She must leave early today, "said the mother to the teacher.
6. "This is a good video, " he said to his friend.
7. "I want to study today," she said to her boyfriend.
8. "It's Jackie's birthday tomorrow, " my mother reminded me.
9. "I'll meet you here," she said.
10. "He's bought a new car," she said.
11. "He's going to watch TV," his parents said.
12. "My appointment is at 8.30 tomorrow morning," she told her husband.
13. "We moved to the country a couple of years ago," they said.
14. "I may sell my computer," she said.
15. "I can't think of anything to write about," the boy said to the teacher.

☺ *Think of the different ways can you offer someone a cup of coffee in English? Using the 'verbs of reporting' listed below, make as many sentences as you can.*

Verbs of Reporting

Apart from say, tell and ask, there are many other verbs which report speech. Here are some of them with the structures which follow them.

- ◆ **verb + object + full infinitive:** advise • remind • ask • tell • persuade • warn
  They advised me to leave at once.
  He warned me not to stay.

- ◆ **verb + that + clause:** say • explain
  I explained that I wasn't feeling well.

- ◆ **verb + two objects:** introduce • offer
  She introduced her husband to me.
  He offered me a cup of coffee.

- ◆ **verb + full infinitive:** agree • refuse • promise
  They agreed to come

- ◆ **verb + -ing form:** suggest
  They suggested meeting at the pizzeria.

- ◆ **verb + preposition+ing form:** apologise
  He apologised for being rude.

- ◆ **verb + object:** accept • refuse
  They accepted the invitation

119

PLANNING FOR DISCHARGE [dis'tʃa:dʒ]

 An example of the Core Standard Procedure for patient discharge.

PATIENT DISCHARGE: STANDARD STATEMENT:	All patients will receive a fully planned discharge from hospital commencing from the time of admission.	
RESPONSIBILITY:	Ward Charge Nurse	

CONSIDERATIONS – STRUCTURE	PLANNING PROCESS	DESIRED OUTCOME
Patient and involved person (family member or other)	Patients are fully involved with all discharge plans	Patient is well informed and involved in discharge (1)
Qualified Nurse	Coordinates patient discharge with all members of the multidisciplinary team, the patient and carers	Appropriate members of the multi–disciplinary team will be involved with planning the discharge
Discharge Assessment	Planning is commenced and all appropriate documentation is used	Patient's and relatives' wishes have been considered (2)
Discharge Check List	All members of the multidisciplinary team, the patient, relatives/involved people are notified	Check List or Discharge Assessment form has been completed, dated and timed
Multidisciplinary team – Patient education booklets/pamphlets	The patient is advised and educated appropriately to meet his/her needs	Patient will have received all appropriate information and/or booklets or pamphlets specific to his/her condition (3)
Property & General Office Check	The patient's *bed space* is checked and all property and valuables are returned to the patient	The patient returns home or to his/her community with all personal property

Write 'yes/no questions' to ask the patient about the details numbered above.

1. ....

2. ....

3. ....

☺ 🐛 *With your partner, look at the example page (below) of a 'Planning for Discharge and Discharge Checklist' form and make questions to ask the nurse organising this patient's discharge.*

(N/A stands for 'not applicable' – and in different circumstances it can mean 'not available')

---

1. Name of nurse planning discharge................[N/A]   Name of Care Manager ....[N/A]

2. Patient involved in discharge planning   Yes/No   Relative/Carer involved in discharge planning   Yes/No

3. **Transport:**   Transport arranged   Yes/No   Date booked..........................
   Transport by ....   Type........................... Ref. No...............
   Transport booked for ....(day and date)   ....(time a.m./p.m.)

4. **Preparation:**   General Office notified – Valuables returned to patient .... (time and date) [N/A]
   Date of home visit .... Date aids to be delivered .... [N/A]
   Letter written/sent to Community Nurse/Local Doctor........... Date homecare commences.... [N/A]
   Have patient/relative or carer been taught the necessary skills? Lifting and handling   Yes/No [N/A]
   Other (please specify e.g use of equipment)..

   Discharge address: **Preparation of home**
   ....   Food parcel arranged   Yes/No   [N/A]
   ....   Heating turned on   Yes/No   [N/A]
   ....   Key available – arranged   Yes/No   [N/A]
   ....   Equipment/Aids arranged   Yes/No   [N/A]

5. **Medications:**   How does the patient manage medications at home? ....
   Use of a pre–prepared pill–box   Yes/No   [N/A]
   Specific problems (tick if applicable):
   Opening bottle tops ☐   Pouring liquids ☐
   Reading labels ☐   Instilling eye drops ☐
   Managing blister packs ☐   Using inhalers/spacers ☐
   Understanding what they are for ☐   Getting more supplies ☐
   Understanding special instructions or equipment ☐
   Understanding times and/or dosages ☐   **None of the above** ☐
   'Take home' medications written up and ordered   Yes/No   [N/A]
   Medications explained to patient/carer   Yes/No   [N/A]
   Specialist medications (e.g. syringe driver) available   Yes/No   [N/A]

6. **Transfer letter written**   Yes/No   [N/A]

7. **OPD appointment made/referral letter sent**   Yes/No   [N/A]

General Information: (specify information sheets, booklets or other)

Additional Information:

☺ *Plan Mark Andrews discharge from hospital using the information you have about him.*

> Has this patient got transport to go home?

> Can he manage his own medications and his colostomy when he goes home?

> Do his relatives know what time he can go?

EXPRESSION and WORD LIST

1. to **build trust**, companionship, confidence etc.
2. a **wave of pressure** travels along the arterial system
3. there are a couple of **relief teachers** available
4. to change into **your own** pyjamas
5. to **cause** redness and damage to the skin
6. a **bedfast patient** (or a bedridden patient)
7. a thin patient **is at risk of** developing pressure sores
8. to **have an abrasion** over a bony surface
9. to **prevent** bed sores
10. to **wheel along** a hospital bed
11. to **roll** the soiled sheet **up** lengthways along the patient's back
12. there is **a risk** of cross infection
13. to help **lame** or **unstable** patients
14. (measurements) are considered **within normal limits**
15. to **provide** a day room
16. **dirty linen** has to be put into a bag

First translate the underlined words into your own language, then write a sentence in English using the words written in italics.

Pronunciation

Minimal Pairs

Look at the three words in each line and decide which one is pronounced differently.
The vowel sounds used are written in phonetics.
Put a circle around the one word with different pronunciation.

(a)	day	die	wide	[ai]	or	[ei]
(b)	walk	short	work	[ɔ:]		[ɜ:]
(c)	sit	seat	sheet	[i]		[i:]
(d)	halve	have	part	[a:]		[æ]
(e)	look	lock	drop	[ʊ]		[ɒ]
(f)	cleans	please	pins	[i]		[i:]
(g)	good	book	food	[ʊ]		[u:]

 When you listen to the recording circle the word(s) you hear.

1. She can walk / work when she goes home.
2. Sit / seat his relatives in the day room.
3. He can have / halve his medications.
4. Look at / lock the drug cupboard.
5. The title of the essay is "Today – In Peace" / "To Die – In Peace"

  Listening 16 – Exercise *Listen to the recording to check all your answers.*

UNIT
3

THE HUMAN BODY
Inside and Out

LEVELS OF ORGANISATION

Everyone is interested in the human [hju:mən] body, what happens when it is affected by disease [dəzi:z], and how to stay healthy [helθi]. Articles on health and medicine appear daily in newspapers and magazines. Ordinary people who are not specifically trained in science are frequently asked to make decisions on scientific matters which affect society.

The scientific [saiən'tifik] term for the study of **body structure** is *anatomy* [ən'ætəmi]. Part of this word means to 'cut' because early anatomists *dissected* (cut) the human body to learn about its structure. The practice of any health care professional requires a basic understanding of anatomy and most anatomic data is now obtained through the use of **computed tomography, magnetic resonance imaging and positron emission tomography,** rather than through experimental studies.

Physiology [fizi'ɒlədʒi] is the **study of how body parts function** including their chemical and physical processes. Anatomy and physiology are closely related. Anything that disturbs the normal working of the body is considered a **disease** [dəzi:z] and is studied as the science of *pathology* [pəθ'ɒlədʒi].

All living things are organised from very simple levels to more complex levels. Living matter begins with simple chemicals [kemikəlz] which are formed into the complex substances that make living **cells,** which are **the basic units of life** [laif]. **Groups of specialised cells** form **tissues** and **different tissues function together to form organs.** Various organs function together to make up the **systems** of the human body.

All the 'human sciences' study different aspects of the human body, its structure and function, its behaviour and its association with its

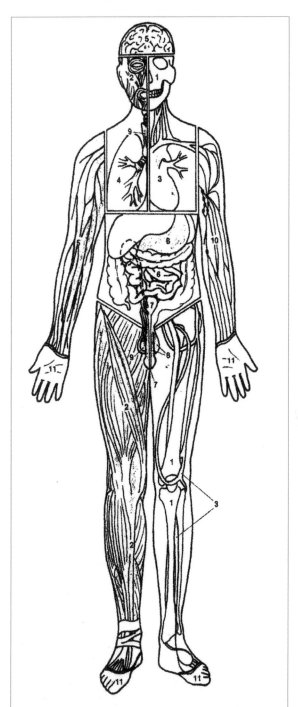

Dover Pictorial Archive Series (1982) – Margaret Matt Human Anatomy Coloring Book

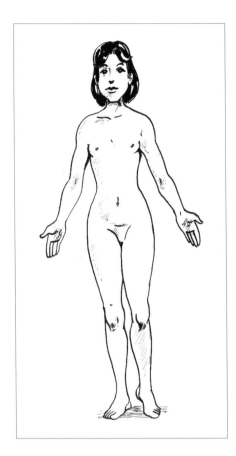

environment. To study the awesome complexities of the human body it is necessary to 'break it down' into sections that can be examined in detail, remembering that all the parts must interact with one another successfully to ensure our survival.

To study different parts of the body, we can divide the body in various ways to give us position or location. General divisions are **the head, the thorax, the abdomen, the pubes** and **the limbs or extremities.**

Diagrams are shown with the figure standing in the **anatomical position** unless stated otherwise. The pictures show figures in the anatomical position with hands facing the front and feet slightly apart.

N.B. Standing in this way the **anatomical right** is on the left of the diagram and the **anatomical left** is on your right!

The human body is marvellously complex and it is amazing how well it works most of the time. How does it start and how does it develop?

The human 'gametes' or 'germ cells' are the ova (*pl.*) **ovum** (*s.*) in the female and the **sperm cells (spermatozoa/spermatozoon)** in the male. **Meiosis** occurs during their formation **(oogenesis)**, when these germ cells develop with a *haploid number* (half the number) of chromosomes. All other cells in the body, contain the full number of chromosomes and are called *diploid cells.*

During **fertilisation** the two haploid cells fuse together and become a **zygote** with the complete number of chromosomes, so a **female germ cell + male germ cell = zygote =** the beginnings of a human life.

Other cells reproduce by **Mitosis,** which is the equal division of nuclear material (*karyokinesis*), followed by division of the cell body (*cytokinesis*). The result of this division is two 'daughter cells' each containing 23 pairs of chromosomes (i.e. 46 chromosomes altogether).

Because all tissues increase in size during childhood, a lot more cells divide in a growing child than in an adult.

Specialised groups of cells form tissues [tiʃuːz]	cell + cell = tissue
Tissues functioning together are organs [ɔːgənz]	tissue + tissue = organ
Organs functioning together for the same general purpose = body system [sistəm]	organ + organ = body system

B

THE STRUCTURE AND FUNCTION OF BODY SYSTEMS

STRUCTURE

Structure

refers to the arrangement of parts, organs, tissues, cells or particles.

Function

is the normal, unique [juːniːk] activity.

A cell

is the basic structural and functional unit of any living organism. Cells may be different shapes and sizes and perform a variety of functions.

Tissue

is made up of a specialised group of cells. There are 4 basic types of tissue:

- **Epithelial** [epiˈθiːliəl] tissue forms the skin that covers the body, lines cavities and forms glands.

- **Connective** [kənektiv] tissue is extensive and forms the support and framework of the whole body. Bone, cartilage, tendons, fat, blood and lymph are all made up of different types of connective tissue.

- **Muscle** [mʌsəl] tissue is designed to produce movement by forcible contraction and includes three different groups: skeletal muscle, smooth (or 'visceral' [visərəl]) muscle and cardiac muscle.

- **Nervous** [nɜːvəs] tissue makes up the communication network of the body. The central agency is the brain and each structure in the body is in direct communication with the brain by nerves which come together to form the spinal cord.

An Organ

is made up of groups of specialised tissues, working together with a specific function.

A System

is a group of organs working together with the same specialised function.

☺ *Can you name any of the major organs in the human body?*

✏ **Matching Exercise.**

Put the words in the box below in the space provided to complete the definition.

cartilage [ka:təlidʒ]

tissue [tiʃu:]

myocardium
[mai'əuka:diəm]

epithelium [epi'θi:l'iəm]

cell [sel]

function [fʌŋkʃən]

brain [brein]

organ [ɔ:gan]

smooth–muscle
[smuð mʌsl]

mitosis [mai'təusis]

1. The process of cell division involving the DNA which doubles itself to produce identical 'daughter cells' is called ....

2. A group of specialised cells with the same function is called ....

3. The thick, muscular [mʌsk'ju:lə] layer of the heart wall is known as the ....

4. The largest mass of nerve tissue in the body – the 'central agency' for communication with the rest of the body, is an organ called the ....

5. A type of hard connective [kənektiv] tissue that acts as a 'shock absorber' and reduces friction between bones in moveable joints (or articulations) of the body is called ....

6. The tissue that forms a protective covering for the body and also lines the intestinal [intest'ainəl] tract, the respiratory [rə'spirə'tri] tract and the urinary [ju:rənri] passages is called ....

7. The basic unit of life is the ....

8. Different tissues working together, with the same function form an ....

9. The action of peristalsis [peri'stɒlsis] – the movement of food down the oesophagus [ə'sɒfəgəs] and through the intestine – is formed by 'involuntary' or ....

10. The normal, unique [ju:ni:k] activity of various body parts is its ....

Although each body system cannot work independently, we can look at the structure of each and its various complicated functions to see how the body works as a single unit.

✎ *Study the picture with the body systems marked with numbers one to eleven on page 124 and name them using the following names: (Write them again under 'name of system' below).*

Nervous System [nɜːvəs]

RESPIRATORY [rəˈspirəˈtri] SYSTEM

Circulatory [sɜːkˈjuˈleitri] System

[diˈdʒestiv] Digestive System

Lymphatic [limfætik] System

Endocrine [endəʊˈkrin] System

Skeletal [skəˈliːtl] System

Muscular [mʌskˈjuːlə] System

Reproductive [riprəˈdʌktiv] System

Skin (Integumentary [integˈjuːˈmentri] System)

Urinary [juːrənri] System

NAME OF SYSTEM	STRUCTURE (is made up of..)
1. .... Function(s):	bones [bəʊnz], (+ cartilage, ligaments)
2. .... Function(s):	skeletal, cardiac and smooth muscles [mʌsəlz] (+ tendons)
3. .... Function(s):	heart [haːt] & blood vessels (arteries, veins and capillaries)
4. .... Function(s):	lungs [lʌŋz] and air passages. Nasal passages, uvula [juːvˈjʊlə], pharynx [fæˈrinks], larynx [lærinks], trachea [trəˈkiə], bronchi [brɒŋki], bronchioles [brɒŋkiˈɒlz], alveoli [ælˈviˈɒli]–(air sacs)
5. .... Function(s):	brain, spinal cord and nerves
6. .... Function(s):	mouth (teeth, tongue and salivary glands), epiglottis, oesophagus [əˈsɒfəgəs], stomach [stʌmək], intestines [inˈtestənz] + **accessory organs**: liver [livə], gallbladder [gɔːlˈblædə], pancreas [pæŋˈkriəs]. *Parts of this system are sometimes referred to as 'the gut'.*
7. .... Function(s):	kidneys [kidniz], ureters [juːrətəz], bladder [blædə], urethra [juːˈriːθrə]
8. .... Function(s):	Male: testes, ducts/seminal vesicles, Prostate gland, Penis Female: ovaries, Fallopian tubes (oviducts), uterus [juːtəˈrəs], vagina [vəˈdʒainə], breasts [brests]
9. .... Function(s):	Glands: Pituitary [pitjuːˈitri], Pineal [pinˈiəl], Thyroid [θaiˈrɔid] and Parathyroid [pærəˈθaiˈrɔid], Thymus [θaiməs], Adrenal [ədriːnəl], Pancreas [pæŋkˈriəs], Ovaries [əʊvəˈriz] & Testes [testiz].
10. .... Function(s):	lymph nodes, (tonsils and adenoids [ædə ˈnɔidz]), lymph vessels, valves [vælvz], the spleen [spliːn]
11. .... Function(s):	epidermis, dermis, sebaceous [səˈbeiʃəs] (oil–producing) glands, sudoriferous [suːdəˈrifərəs] (sweat–producing) glands

🎧 Listening 17 – Body systems *Listen to the recording and check your answers.*

GRAMMAR NOTES

Talking about structure

'to be made up of' 'consists of' *or* 'to be composed of'

There are subtle differences in the use of the above phrases:

'to be made up of' is used for a detailed breakdown of a part or a structure
e.g. The joints (or articulations) are made up of bones, cartilage and ligaments.

'consists of' is used in a general way when all the main parts of a structure are named
e.g. The respiratory tract consists of the pharynx, trachea, lungs, bronchi, bronchioles and alveoli.

'to be composed of' is used when the materials or substances from which the structure is formed,
are named.
e.g. Both the brain and the spinal cord are composed of nerve cells and fibres.

 Now complete the following sentences.

1. The pharynx .... the naso–pharynx, the oro–pharynx and the laryngo–pharynx.
2. The brain stem .... the mid–brain, the pons and the medulla.
3. The intestines .... two parts, the large and the small intestine.
4. The duodenum, the jejunum and the ileum .... the small intestine.
5. What does the skeletal system ....? Bones, joints and ligaments.
6. The female reproductive system .... the ovaries, the oviducts, the uterus and the vagina.
7. The skin .... epithelial tissue, collagen fibres, nerves, blood vessels and glands.

☺ **With a partner, look at question 5. Make question for the other sentences.**
Using the information you have, ask your partner some questions about the structure of other systems.

VERBS AND NOUNS

Complete the table with the missing word.

Verb	Noun	Verb	Noun
transport	*transportation*	circulate [sɜːkˈjuleit]	
regulate [regˈjuleit]			digestion
	formation	remove	
secrete (directly into the bloodstream)			elimination
	destruction	filter	
excrete (into a duct)			production
	reproduction	conceive	
defend			lining
	cover(ing)	develop	
provide			protection
	storage	situate	
dilate			function(ing)

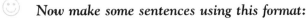

☺ **Now make some sentences using this format:**
e.g. The circulation of blood to the tissues is the function of the heart.

The excretion of waste products		
Blood circulation		the liver
Waste excretion	is a/the* function of	the kidneys
Water regulation		the heart
Production of bile		
Storage of protein and glycogen		

(**The function** *is used when it is the only* **function,** *a* **function** *indicates one of several functions*)

✎ Function(s):

Read the description of the functions of each body system. Identify the system and label each. Now turn back to page 128 and write a brief summary of the function(s) of each body system.

(a) [   ]

The purpose of this system is to take in air, filter it and take it to the tissues responsible for gas exchange. Oxygen [ɒksiˈdʒən] is then transported by the blood to all the tissues in the body. Carbon Dioxide, a waste [weist] product is re–absorbed into the blood and then excreted from the body.

(b) [   ]

This system forms the basic framework of the body – it supports and protects all the internal organs. Bones serve as levers (with the attached muscles) for movement, produce blood cells and store calcium [kælˈsiːəm] salts which can be absorbed into the blood when there is not enough calcium in the diet.

(c) [   ]

The secretion of hormones [hɔːˈməʊnz] which regulate the body's functions chemically, is the function of this system.

(d) [   ]

This system is also called the *excretory system* and filters body liquids, eliminating chemicals and excess fluids from the body.

(e) [   ]

This system contains an important organ which pumps blood round the entire body. This is necessary to supply cells with nutrients and oxygen and to transport waste products for excretion.

(f) [   ]

This system is essential for reproduction and the production of hormones, sex cells (gametes) [gæmiːts] and it also enables conception [kənˈsepʃən] and permits the carrying and birth of babies (offspring).

(g) [   ]

The system which converts (changes) food into simpler substances for the cells to use for energy also takes away (or eliminates) waste products from the body.

(h) [_____]

This complex system which is also thought of as an organ, protects the body from disease, helps to regulate body temperature and acts as a sensory receptor.

(i) [_____]

A system which runs parallel with the veins throughout the body, drains fluid from the tissues and helps to defend the body against infection and disease.

(j) [_____]

We need this system to produce movement, both voluntary and involuntary, and to keep our hearts beating to keep us alive [əlaiv].

(k) [_____]

This is the most complex system in the body and its functions are to regulate all the other systems in the body, receive and send messages and to provide us with information about our environment [enˈvaiˈrənˈmənt].

Complete the sentences using the correct word(s) from the box.

ovaries
reproduce
lines
are situated
urinary system
blood
pancreas
cartilage
conception
regulate
covers
bone
kidneys (×3)
liver (×2)
secrete
oxygen
excrete
heart
are produced
form
are composed of
division
excretory system
is made up of
secretes

1. The .... carries .... through the arteries to the body cells.
2. One function of the .... is to .... the amount of water in the body.
3. The .... also .... 'urea' [juːriːə] (a nitrogen waste product) from the body.
4. The .... functions as both an organ of digestion and excretion.
5. The .... is an accessory organ of digestion.
6. The .... beats 80 times per minute on average.
7. The .... are only found in females. They are endocrine glands which .... hormones and ova .... here.
8. An accessory [ækˈsesəˈri] organ of digestion, which is also an endocrine gland, ... insulin and is called the ....
9. All the bones in the skeletal system .... from a fibrous connective tissue called .... This tissue eventually hardens with calcium deposits to become ....
10. The ....s, the ureters, the urinary bladder and urethra make up the .... which can also be called the ....
11. Both the spinal cord and the brain .... of nerve cells.
12. Cells .... by .... – a process called mitosis.
13. The skin which .... the outside of the human body .... cells, sweat glands, oil–producing glands, blood vessels and nerve endings. Epithelial tissue also .... all the systems that have 'tracts' opening onto the surface of the body.
14. The heart and lungs .... in the thoracic cavity.
15. A zygote is formed at the time of .... – it is the union of the male and female sex cells, or gametes.

DIRECTIONAL TERMS

It is necessary to have special words to talk about the position or location of organs and parts and to talk about direction in the human body. The words 'left' and 'right', 'back' or 'front' are not specific enough and the use of 'north' and 'south' would be inappropriate! The directional terms used refer to the body in the **anatomic position.** Three **imaginary planes** are used to describe the structural plan of the body and the anatomic relationship of one part to another. These **planes** cut through the body at right angles to each other.

PLANES OF DIVISION

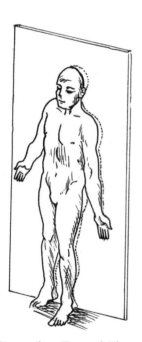

Coronal or Frontal Plane

Divides the body into front and back halves.

Directional terms used:
Frontal / Ventral or Dorsal
Anterior or Posterior

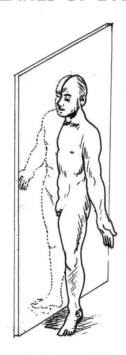

Midsagittal Plane

Divides the body into right and left halves.

Directional terms used:
Medial or Lateral
A Sagittal plane lies away from the midline and divides the body into right and left parts

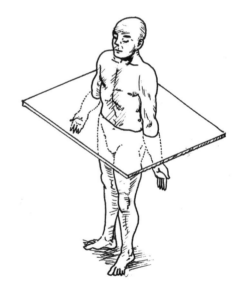

Transverse Plane

Divides the body into parts above or below.

Directional terms used:
Superior or Inferior
Cranial or Caudal

 Draw a cross–section of each of the planes of division.

DIRECTIONAL TERMS

🖋 *Now label the 'directional term' diagram below with all the following 'directional terms', matching the words that have opposite meanings.*

Draw the **midline (1)** – an imaginary line close to the middle of the body – there is no opposite to this!

anterior/ventral (towards the front)
distal (farther away from the body)
inferior/caudal (below or lower than...)
medial (nearer to an imaginary midline plane)

lateral (further from the midline/towards the side)
superior/cranial (above or in a higher position)
proximal (nearer to the main part of the body)
posterior/dorsal (towards the back)

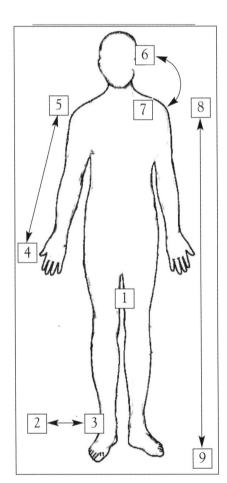

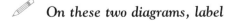

🖋 *Study the directional terms and complete the following sentences.*

*e.g. The hand is **distal to** the shoulder*

1. The thorax is .... to the abdomen.

2. The nose and the mouth are in a .... position on the face.

3. The elbow is .... to the wrist.

4. The knee is .... to the back of the thigh.

5. The ears are in .... positions on the head.

6. The buttocks are .... to the pubic region.

7. The navel (or umbilicus) is at the ....

8. The femur (the long bone in the thigh) is .... to the tibia and fibula.

9. The knees are .... to the hips.

10. The brain is .... to the spinal cord.

11. The oesophagus is .... to the stomach.

📖 A lot of muscles and blood vessels are named using *directional terms* so that their location and relationship to other parts is easily understood.

🖋 **On these two diagrams, label**

1. the right eye: (a) Inferior rectus muscle
(b) Superior rectus muscle
(c) Medial rectus muscle
(d) Lateral rectus muscle

2. the heart: (a) Inferior vena cava
(b) Superior vena cava

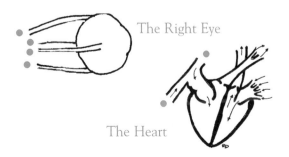

The Right Eye

The Heart

A cavity is any hollow space. *Body cavities* are areas which confine organs and systems that have related functions. The two major body cavities are the **dorsal cavity** and the **ventral cavity.**

The Dorsal Cavity is subdivided into the *cranial cavity* (containing the brain) and the *spinal cavity* (containing the spinal cord).

The Ventral Cavity is divided into 3 parts: the *thoracic cavity*, the *abdominal cavity* and the *pelvic cavity*. The abdominal and pelvic cavities together are called the *abdominopelvic cavity.*

Label the body cavities and the organs situated in the abdominopelvic cavity.

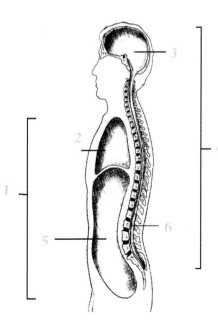

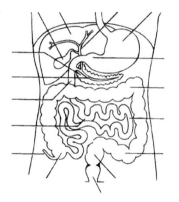

Complete these sentences.

1. The heart and the lungs are situated in the ....

2. The dome–shaped muscular organ that separates this cavity from the abdominal cavity is the ....

3. The spinal cord is located in the ....

4. The brain and the spinal cord are situated in a space known as the ....

5. The abdominal and pelvic cavities together are known as the ....

6. Where are the different parts of the digestive system located? Look at the diagram of organs located in the abdominal cavity and write an approximate position for each on the list, using directional terms (*e.g. The oesophagus passes through the diaphragm and its inferior end lies medially in the abdominal cavity*):

- *The stomach* [stʌmək] ....
- *The liver* [livə] ....
- *The appendix* [əpˈendiks] ....
- *The pancreas* [pænˈkriəs] ....
- *The transverse colon* [trænzˈvɜːs kəʊlɒn] ....
- *The duodenum* [djuːəˈdiːnəm] ....
- *The ascending colon* [eiˈsendiŋ kəʊlɒn] ....
- *The descending colon* [diːˈsendiŋ kəʊlɒn] ....
- *The gallbladder* [gɔːlˈblædə] ....
- *The bile duct* [baiəlˈdʌkt] ....
- *The caecum* [siːkəm] ....

CLINICAL DIVISIONS OF THE ABDOMEN

For the purpose of clinical examination and reporting, the abdomen is divided into four corresponding regions called *quadrants*. The umbilicus [ʌmbəˈlaikəs] (or 'navel') is the intersecting point.

 On diagram (1) mark:

the Right Upper Quadrant (RUQ)
the Right Lower Quadrant (RLQ)
the Left Upper Quadrant (LUQ)
the Left Lower Quadrant (LLQ)

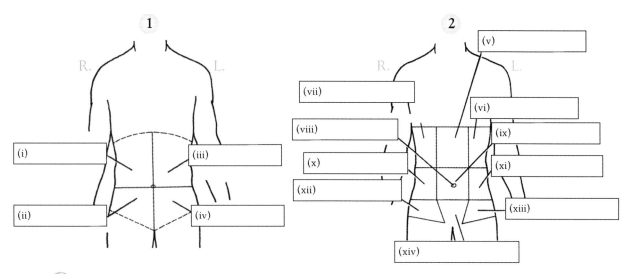

Listening 18 – Exercise *Practise saying the words in the box before listening to the dictation. Now, listen to the recording. Use it as a dictation to help you label diagram 2.*

Now test yourself and mark the anatomic regions in the box on diagram.

☺ *Do you know how the word 'hypochondriac'* [haipauˈkɒndriæk] *is usually used? What is the reason do you think?*

☺ *Think of some questions to ask your partner. Look at the examples and formulate some questions before you start.*

Where would a patient with acute appendicitis feel the most pain?

In the Right Lower Quadrant or the Right Iliac Region of the abdomen... Where is the Liver located?

In the Right Hypochondriac Region! ...What organs are situated in the Hypogastric (or pubic region)?

The umbilicus
[ʌmˈbilikəs] or [ʌmbəˈlaikəs]

The Umbilical
[ʌmˈbilikl] or [ʌmbəˈlaikl]
Region

The Pelvic/Pubic [pjuːbik] **or Hypogastric** [haipauˈgæstrik]
Region

The Right and Left Lateral [lætrəl] **Regions**

The Right and Left Hypochondriac
[haipauˈkɒndriæk]
Regions

The Left and Right Inguinal [iŋˈgwinəl] **or Iliac** [iliːˈæk] **Regions**

The Epigastric [epiˈgæstrik]
Region

135

THE SKELETAL SYSTEM

📖 *Read the text before attempting the written exercises.*

The skeletal system includes all of the bones of the body shown on the right and includes cartilage (*fibrous connective tissue*), joints (*articulations*) and ligaments (*fibrous tissue bands* that connect bones or cartilage). The study of bones is called **osteology**.

There are 206 bones in the adult human skeleton and their function is to give the body its shape, to support the body and protect all the delicate internal organs. The skeleton also provides places for the attachment of muscles and the bones act as *levers* to provide movement of skeletal muscles.

The cavities inside long bones store fat in the yellow marrow and bones also store the minerals, calcium, magnesium, phosphorous, potassium, sulphur and sodium. Red blood cells are formed (*haematopoiesis* [hemˈætəʊˈpɔiˈːsis]) in the *bone marrow* of certain bones.

Bones are individually classified as organs and bone tissue is capable of a process which forms new bone. *Osteoclasts* are responsible for the re-sorption (or breakdown of bone) and *osteoblasts* build it and assist in the growth a bones.

Bones are classified according to their shape. There are 5 main classifications:
- **long bones** e.g. humerus, ulna, femur;
- **short bones** e.g. wrist & ankle bones;
- **flat bones** e.g. ribs, sternum, scapulae;
- **irregular** e.g. vertebrae, face bones;
- **sesamoid** bones are small bones which **form in tendons** e.g. patella.

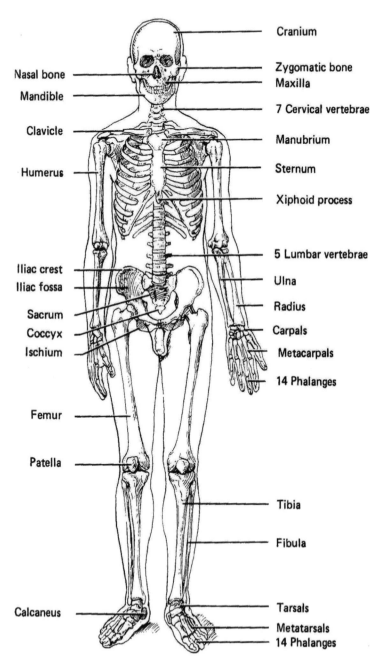

Cranium
Zygomatic bone
Maxilla
7 Cervical vertebrae
Manubrium
Sternum
Xiphoid process
5 Lumbar vertebrae
Ulna
Radius
Carpals
Metacarpals
14 Phalanges
Tibia
Fibula
Tarsals
Metatarsals
14 Phalanges

Nasal bone
Mandible
Clavicle
Humerus
Iliac crest
Iliac fossa
Sacrum
Coccyx
Ischium
Femur
Patella
Calcaneus

✏️ *Label the scapulae* (pl.) *on the diagram.* (*scapula – singular*)

The Structure of a Long Bone

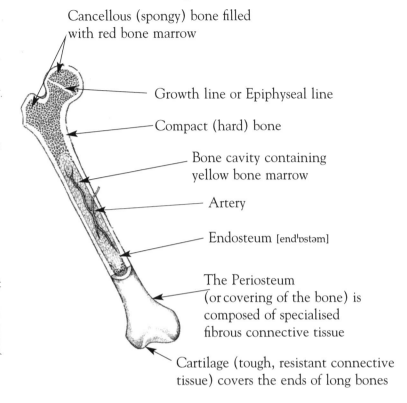

Cancellous (spongy) bone filled with red bone marrow

The Proximal Epiphysis [əˈpifəˈsis]

The Diaphysis [daiˈæfəsis]
or
Bone Shaft

The Distal Epiphysis [əˈpifəˈsis]

Growth line or Epiphyseal line

Compact (hard) bone

Bone cavity containing yellow bone marrow

Artery

Endosteum [endˈɒstəm]

The Periosteum (or covering of the bone) is composed of specialised fibrous connective tissue

Cartilage (tough, resistant connective tissue) covers the ends of long bones

Each bone can be labelled using its <u>markings</u> – that is the depressions, grooves, openings (foramina), processes and projections that can be seen on the surface of bones and are used as reference points.

Divisions of the Skeleton

1. The Axial [ˈæksiəl] Skeleton:
is composed of the skull, the vertebral column and the bones of the thorax – the rib cage and sternum.

2. The Appendicular [eipenˈdikjuːlə] Skeleton:
includes all the bones of the extremities (the arms and the legs) and the bones these are connected to: i.e. the *shoulder girdle* and the *pelvic girdle*.

The *skull* includes all the bones of the head: the cranial bones and all the facial bones.

The *vertebral column* consists of 26 irregular bones, the vertebrae (*pl.*), divided into sections by their position from the base of the skull to the caudal end: 7 cervical vertebrae (C1 to C7), 12 thoracic vertebrae (T1 to T12), 5 lumbar vertebrae (L1 to L5), 5 fused vertebrae which make a triangular bone called the sacrum (which also makes up part of the pelvic girdle or 'pelvis') and a smaller triangular bone consisting of 4 fused vertebrae called the coccyx [kɒksiks].

The *rib cage* (or bony thorax) consists of the 12 thoracic vertebrae dorsally, the 12 pairs of ribs laterally and the sternum and costal cartilages anteriorly. The first seven or eight pairs of ribs are connected to the sternum by cartilage and are referred to as *true ribs*. The remaining 5 pairs of ribs are called *false ribs*.

Complete the following sentences.

1. The adult skeleton has .... bones.

2. Bones are a 'storehouse' for .... and ....

3. What are the functions of the skeletal system?

4. List the 5 classifications of bone: ....

....

....

5. A long bone is divided into the shaft or .... and the ....

6. Name two types of bone tissue: ....

7. Name the two main divisions of the skeleton: ....

8. The bones of the thorax include the 12 pairs of ...., the 12 .... and the ....

9. Identify the site where growth occurs in long bone: ....

10. Name the two bones of the vertebral column that are made up of fused vertebrae: ....

....

🎧 Listening 19 – The skeletal system   **Listen to the recording and check your answers.**

Now match the following words with the correct definition.

1. The fatty substance inside the central cavity of long bones: ....

2. The bones of the head and face together are called the ....

3. The material that forms the skeleton in an embryo: ....

4. The 5 biggest vertebrae are located in the .... region of the vertebral column.

5. The tough (strong) connective tissue that covers bones is called the ....

6. Blood cells are produced in the ....

7. The shaft of a long bone is also called the ....

8. The lining (the inside surface) of a bone cavity is called the ....

9. The tail part of the lower vertebral column, consisting of four or five small, fused bones is called the ....

10. The bone located on the side of the thumb in the forearm is the ....

11. The end of a long bone is its ....

12. The scientific name for the knee–cap is the ....

13. An adjective which means 'between the ribs': ....

14. The type of connective tissue that connects one bone to another: ....

ligament

epiphysis

yellow marrow

diaphysis

coccyx

patella

cartilage

radius

red marrow

skull

lumbar

periosteum

endosteum

intercostal

JOINTS

📖 *Read the text.*

> *Where two or more bones come together and usually need to move or 'articulate'* [aˈtikˈjuːleit]*, there is a joint* [dʒɔint] *(or 'an articulation'* [əˈtikˈjuːleiʃən]*) which is held together with strong, flexible bands of fibrous connective tissue called* ligaments [ligəmənts]*. Joints are classified according to the amount of movement permitted, that is* immovable *– a synarthrosis (singular),* slightly moveable *– an amphiarthrosis (singular) or* freely moveable *– a diarthrosis (singular).*

1. **IMMOVABLE or FIBROUS joints (synarthroses** [sinˈaːθrəʊsiːz] *plural*) are those joints that are fixed, such as the joining of the skull bones – the lines at these joints are called *sutures* [suːtʃəz].

2. **SLIGHTLY MOVEABLE or CARTILAGINOUS joints (amphiarthroses** [amfiˈaːθrəʊsiːz] *plural*) have only a minimal amount of movement – the vertebrae [vɜːtəbri] are examples of these. Between the vertebrae there are disks of another strong connective tissue called **cartilage** [kaːtilidʒ]. This acts as a cushion, reducing *friction* and 'wear and tear' of the bones. (Cartilage is also found on the ends of long bones). Another example of these **cartilaginous** joints is the symphysis pubis [simfəsəs pjuːbəs] – the anterior pelvic joint, which softens during pregnancy to allow more movement.

3. **FREELY MOVEABLE or SYNOVIAL joints (diarthroses** [daiˈaːθrəʊˈsiːz] *plural*) have a variety of different movements, so they can also be named according to the type of movement. A freely moveable joint is referred to as a **synovial** [sinˈəʊviəl] joint because there is a cavity between the joints containing a sticky synovial fluid (secreted by the synovial membranes *lining* the joint) which prevents *friction* between the bones.

🎧 Listening 20 – Joints **Look at the pictures of joints below and listen carefully to the recording to describe each one.**

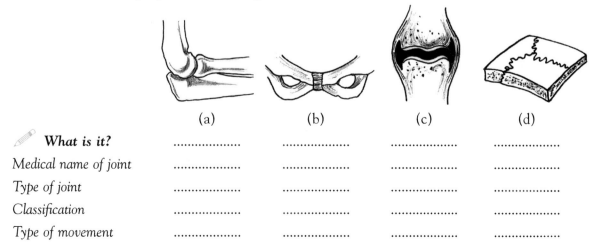

	(a)	(b)	(c)	(d)
✏️ **What is it?**	....	....	....	....
Medical name of joint	....	....	....	....
Type of joint	....	....	....	....
Classification	....	....	....	....
Type of movement	....	....	....	....

Further classifications of
Freely Moveable (Synovial) Joints or Diarthroses

 Write an example of each on the line.

BALL AND SOCKET JOINTS: These give a lot of freedom and allow movement on two planes.

....

HINGE JOINTS: This type of joint restricts movement to one plane.

....

PIVOT JOINTS: This type of joint allow the bones to rotate on one another.

....

 Listen again and check your answers.

FRACTURES

A fracture [fræk'tʃə] is any break or rupture in a bone. Severe force can cause a fracture in almost any bone. The word 'fracture' is often written as the symbol '#' e.g. # NOF = 'fractured Neck of Femur'.

The bones of a baby or a young child are not as hard as an adult's bones (because there are less calcium salts and they consist of a lot of cartilage). They are softer and more elastic so do not break easily. Very often the injury seen in a child is a 'greenstick' fracture i.e. the bone does not break right through but is only injured on one side. Imagine bending a branch of a tree that is not dry or dead – it may bend and partially split but does not separate into two pieces.

There are 4 general classifications of fractures and a number of more specific classifications:

1. **Simple** – the bone is broken but there is no break in the skin.

2. **Compound** – the skin over the fracture has been punctured or torn or another organ is also damaged.

3. **Comminuted** [kɒminju:tid] – the bone is fractured in one or more places, is splintered or crushed.

4. **Greenstick** – the bone does not break right through but is only injured on one side.

CAUSE AND EFFECT

What happens in the human body when a bone is fractured?

CAUSE		SIGN OR SYMPTOM
An increase in circulation to the injured part	→	redness, a sensation of heat
Fluid and leucocytes (white blood cells) leave the blood stream and enter the tissues – there may also be bleeding into the tissues	→	swelling
The pressure on nerve–endings increases	→	pain
The body attempts to keep the part still	→	loss of mobility (function)

Look at the following example and make sentences to answer the questions.

When a bone is fractured, why do you notice redness around the area?

Because redness **is caused by** an increase in circulation.

or **Because** an increase in circulation **results in/causes/leads to** redness.

1. Why does the injured part start swelling?
2. Why do you feel pain when a bone is fractured?
3. Why is there a sensation of heat when a bone is fractured?
4. Why is there loss of function when a bone is fractured?
5. What does a deficiency in Calcium cause?
6. Why are the bones of old people more likely to break?
7. Why is exercise important for the body, the skeletal system in particular?

 Ask your partner these questions.

1. What are the three main classifications of joints?
2. What is the name of the connective tissue that joins one bone to another?
3. What is the name of the strong, connective tissue that surrounds all bones?
4. What are the four main classifications of fractures?
5. What has happened to a bone if it is classified as a 'comminuted [kɒminjuːtid] fracture'?

F

MOVEMENT, POSTURE AND LIFTING

Skeletal muscles are attached to bones and move the skeleton. There are more than 650 individual muscles in the skeletal muscle system. Each muscle is a distinct structure but muscles usually act in groups to execute body movements. Because it is under *conscious control*, skeletal muscle is also called *voluntary muscle*.

All muscles in the body needs **energy** to *contract* or shorten. This energy is supplied in the form of **ATP** (adenosine–tri–phosphate) which is the result of the cells 'burning' or using nutrients, causing oxidisation.

For the cells to produce ATP they must have an adequate supply of Oxygen, Glycogen and other nutrients.

If the body uses more Oxygen than is available for strenuous exercise, *lactic acid* (a waste product of metabolism) builds up (or accumulates) in the muscles, causing cramps and muscle fatigue. After strenuous exercise we need to breathe faster and our hearts beat faster so that more oxygen is pumped to the tissues. This helps the lactic acid to be reabsorbed and to be used for other metabolic activities.

POSTURE [pɒsˈtʃə]

The way we stand, sit and move is important to our general good health. For the skeletal muscles to strengthen and support the body and its internal organs, they have to function correctly. When the axis of the body and the axial skeleton are almost the same, good posture is achieved.

Label the figures.

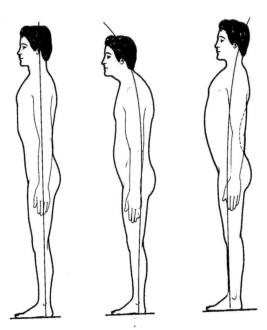

☹ 1 *'standing straight' with the shoulders pushed back and the abdomen pushed forward*
This causes the abdominal muscles to become weak and may result in digestive, respiratory and/or back problems including an abnormal curvature of the spine with *an excessive lumbar curve*, called **lordosis.**

☹ 2 *with his head pushed forward to balance his body*
(He has to tilt his pelvis or 'hip girdle' forward. This results in rounded shoulders and strained back muscles which prevent correct breathing.) This posture can lead to **kyphosis** (sometimes called *hunchback*) which *is an exaggerated curvature of the thoracic curve of the spinal column.*

☺ 3 *standing with good posture*
He is standing comfortably with his ear, hand and foot on the same axis.

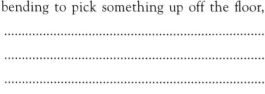 *Look at the pictures below and complete this sentence.*

When exercising or lifting heavy items or even bending to pick something up off the floor,

....

....

....

don't move too quickly

don't use jerky movements

keep your back (the vertebral column) straight

bend your knees

watch what you are doing

balance yourself, with a hand on your thigh if necessary

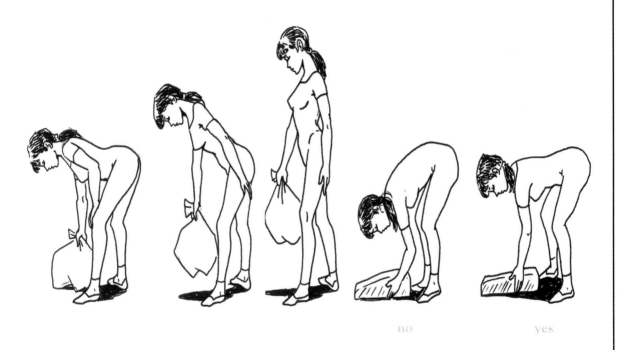

no   yes

☺ *With a partner discuss 'good posture' when moving, sitting and lifting.*

If unnatural movements are avoided – sudden twisting and turning – we avoid damaging the delicate alignment of our bodies that keeps it functioning well.

Exercising regularly, at least 3 times a week, can improve our general health by strengthening muscles and bones, keeping blood pressure at a normal level and by lowering blood cholesterol levels. During exercise, the heart beats faster and the volume of blood pumped per beat (the stroke volume) increases. The rate and depth of respiration also increase, filling the lungs completely and increasing the amount of oxygen available to the tissues. Exercise and training programmes also increase the power and endurance of muscles by repeating and practicing complex movements. Overall, the body reacts positively to regular, short periods of exercise and it brings a feeling of 'well–being' mentally and physically.

G

DISEASE

Disease is an abnormal state in which part or all of the body is not able to perform its required functions.

  Common medical terminology used in the study of disease.

Read the following text – the words in italics are terms frequently used in English when discussing disease.

To treat *disease*, the type of illness has to be assessed – that is, a *diagnosis* is made according to the various *signs* and *symptoms*. Signs are visible to the nurse or physician and can be observed (such as rashes, oedema etc.) whereas symptoms are noted by the individual himself (changes in *temperature*, weight, pain etc.). Often a definite group of signs and symptoms accompanies a disease and this is called a *syndrome*. The nurse's *role* in observing signs and finding out the *patient*'s symptoms, recording this information and reporting it to the *physician*, is invaluable. The information available is assessed and the appropriate *therapy* or *treatment* is ordered.

The study of the cause, or the theory of the cause(s) of disease is called *etiology*. When the origin of a disease is not known it is termed an *idiopathic* disease. The study which relates both the physiologic aspects and the pathologic aspects of disease is called *pathophysiology*.

Diseases are often classified on the basis of severity and on how long they last: *Acute* illnesses are quite severe but usually only last a short time. *Chronic* illnesses may be less severe but continue for a long time, or recur over a long period of time. *Subacute* illnesses are not as severe as 'acute' illnesses nor as long–lasting as 'chronic' illnesses. A *'communicable'* (or *'infectious'* disease), is one that can be transmitted from one person to another. The infected person is said to be *contagious* – usually before signs and symptoms appear.

If a disease is continuously found in a certain region it is said to be *endemic* and most childhood diseases, such as Mumps

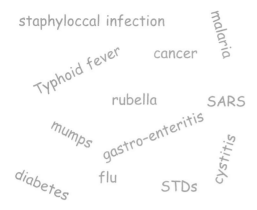

staphyloccal infection

malaria

Typhoid fever cancer

rubella SARS

mumps gastro-enteritis

cystitis

diabetes flu STDs

(parotitis), Chicken Pox (varicella), Measles (rubeola *virus*) and German Measles (rubella), fit into this category.

When a large number of people in a certain region get a disease at the same time, it is said to be *epidemic* (e.g. *outbreaks* of the Ebola virus – in Zaire in Africa – have been acute and deadly but relatively short–lived epidemics. Ebola causes haemorrhagic fever and immediate death). Influenza, often endemic, can also often reach epidemic proportions.

A disease found over a much wider area, throughout an entire country, continent or the world, is *pandemic* – AIDS is now pandemic – and the recent SARS outbreaks appear to be pandemic for several months.

Promoting good health and advertising dangers to healthy living are the modern techniques for preventing disease. The World Health Organisation takes responsibility on an international level and all health care workers and various other groups take responsibility on a national and community level.

There are marked variations in the *extent* of a disease and its effect on the individual. These depend on where the organism entered the body – the *'portal of entry'* – the *virulence* or aggressiveness of the organism, the ability of the organism to produce *toxins* or poisons, the *dose* (or quantity) of the organism and the condition or *predisposition of* the person.

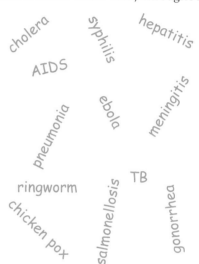

cholera syphilis hepatitis

AIDS

ebola meningitis

pneumonia

ringworm TB

chicken pox salmonellosis gonorrhea

 How quickly can you complete the table with a word from the text in italics? Define each word.

S	I	E	S
S	D	C	C
S	P	T	V
P	E	A	P
R	I	C	V
O	P	D	P

☺ **With a partner discuss what you know about some of the diseases named on this page.**

PRE-DISPOSING FACTORS
IN THE OCCURRENCE OF DISEASE

The following pre–disposing factors may not <u>cause</u> disease but can increase the probability of illness occurring.

Living Conditions and Habits   Physical Exposure   Psychogenic Influences   Sex
Heredity   Occupation   Pre–existing Illness   Age

Write the correct pre–disposing factor from above, next to its definition.

1. .... Degenerative processes in older people can be a direct cause of disease, but certain age groups are often more likely to get a particular disease – for example measles [miːzəlz], caused by the rubeola virus, is more common in children.

2. .... Males are more likely to develop heart disease and Females are more likely to develop diabetes.

3. .... Some diseases seem 'to run in families' – allergies for example, and also diabetes.

4. .... People who are 'workaholics', don't get enough sleep, use drugs or smoke or don't have a balanced diet, are at risk. Also areas which are overcrowded and have poor sanitation are predisposing factors.

5. .... Certain jobs may predispose people to disease. Working with chemicals, radiation, dust in coal–mines or asbestos–dust in building materials, is hazardous to health.

6. .... Being exposed to both excessive heat or excessive cold for long periods can be a starting factor of disease.

7. .... When the body's immune system is weakened by an illness, or even a slight 'cold', the chances of contacting another disease are much higher.

8. .... Emotional stress and anxieties can affect the 'psych' [saik] (the mind) which can result in physical signs such as headaches, indigestion and lethargy.

THE BODY'S "LINES OF DEFENCE" [diˈfens]

The Human Body is very well organised to protect itself from disease and disease–producing organisms.

The barriers (the things that prevent disease from entering or attacking the body) are considered as 'lines of defence' in an order that helps to protect us.

Chemical and Mechanical Defences Against Disease

The first lines of defence are:

SKIN: The skin and the mucous membranes are *mechanical barriers* that prevent disease from entering the body, but only when <u>they</u> are intact. All the mucous membranes (also epithelial tissue) that line the various tracts opening onto the body's surface, secrete mucous <u>which</u> traps (catches) any foreign material and the cilia (hairs) help to expel <u>these</u> impurities from the body.

SECRETIONS: Tears, perspiration, saliva and gastric secretions help to wash away disease–causing organisms and most secretions contain chemicals that can destroy <u>them</u>.

REFLEX ACTIONS: Sneezing and coughing expel any micro–organisms from the respiratory tract and vomiting and diarrhoea expel <u>them</u> from the digestive tract.

The next lines of defence are the white blood cells:

PHAGOCYTOSIS: Some of the white blood cells are able to absorb and destroy foreign and waste matter by a process called phagocytosis [feɪˈɡəʊˈsaɪˈtəʊsɪs]. <u>This process</u> is mainly carried out by cells called *neutrophils* [njuːˈtrəʊˈfɪlz] and *macrophages* [mækrəʊˈfeɪdʒɪz].

NATURAL KILLER CELLS (NK CELLS): <u>These</u> cells are a type of *lymphocyte* [lɪmfəʊˈsaɪt] that can recognize cells with abnormal membranes, such as tumour cells or cells infected with a virus, and can kill <u>them</u> on contact.

INFLAMMATION: *Inflammation* is a reaction that assists the body to expel an irritant, not only infective micro–organisms. Other irritants may be burns, friction, cuts, X–rays or chemicals. An *inflammatory reaction* occurs when the irritant is an infective organism and <u>this</u> is then called an *infection*. An inflammatory reaction shows four classic symptoms and <u>these</u> are: heat, redness, swelling and pain.

FEVER is an increase in body temperature above the normal and is a sign that the defence mechanisms are in order because the phagocytes release substances that raise body temperature.

INTERFERON: <u>This</u> is a substance released by infected cells which stops other cells becoming infected. <u>It</u> prevents viruses from multiplying and also stimulates the body's immune system.

IMMUNITY: The body's final 'line of defence'.

Immunity is the body's final line of defence and may be Inborn or Acquired (Naturally Acquired or Artificially Acquired).

Immunity is the individual's personal ability to resist or 'fight off' the effects of a particular micro–organism or other harmful agent. <u>It</u> is a selective ability which may be successful against one agent but not another.

🖉 *Read the above text and look at the <u>underlined</u> words. Put a circle around the words that these refer to. Now re–write the sentence using the name instead of the pronoun or determiner.*

STERILISATION, DISINFECTION AND ANTISEPSIS

STERILISATION [sterəˈlaizˈeiʃən] **kills all living micro–organisms on an object.** In operating theatres, delivery rooms and when other 'sterile' [steraiəl] procedures are performed, as much of the equipment as possible is sterilised – this includes all the instruments and tools and also the clothes (gowns, gloves etc.) and drapes that are used.

Methods

Live steam under pressure using an *autoclave* is the most commonly used method of sterilisation.

Dry heat and *Irradiation* are also used.

Gas – Ethylene oxide is used to sterilise things which cannot withstand high temperatures.

Boiling for at least 4 minutes. This is mostly effective but may not kill spore–forming organisms which need a much higher temperature and take a longer time to be destroyed.

DISINFECTION [disˈinfekʃən] **kills all pathogens except spores but not all harmless micro–organisms.** Most disinfecting agents are chemicals and are used to disinfect *non–living surfaces* only. Other terms used for these chemicals are *disinfectant*, *bactericide* and *germicide*.

Disinfectants

Chlorine compounds (including household bleach), phenol (carbolic acid) and others.

ANTISEPSIS [æntiˈsepsis] **prevents pathogens from multiplying but does not necessarily kill them.** Because *antiseptics* are not as powerful as disinfectants, they are safe to use on living tissue. Antiseptics may be a diluted disinfectant and they create a state called *bacteriostasis* [bækˈtiːriəʊˈsteisis] – where the micro–organisms are kept in a 'steady' state and cannot multiply.

ALTERNATIVE MEDICINE

📖 *(From Chambers Dictionary of Science and Technology)*

Systems of medicine such as *acupuncture* [ækjuˈpʌŋktʃə], *chiropractice* [kaiˈrəʊˈpraktis], *herbal medicine*, *homeopathy* and *osteopathy*, are able to alleviate symptoms for reasons which are poorly understood. The methods used for treatment of disease have not usually been subjected to testing by a randomized clinical trial and are often not fully accepted by orthodox medical science.

'Old wives' tales' are treatments that are accepted in communities and passed down through generations. Massage, Medicinal teas, various oils, flowers, herbs and spices, in different forms, are used for a variety of illnesses and are often quite effective. Faith healing has helped a lot of people and many are now looking into the results of traditional Chinese medicine.

Keeping healthy and fit by careful attention to diet and exercise is more important than deciding on which treatment to have. When problems arise don't wait too long before asking for medical advice.

alignment [əˈlainˈmənt] (*n. uncountable*) The alignment of something is its position in relation to something else or its correct position.

alternative medicine [ɔːlˈtɜːnəˈtiv medsən] (*adj. + n.*) describes a different form of medicine, in contrast with traditional forms.

bacteria [bækˈtiəriə] (*n. pl.*) Micro–organisms, some of which cause disease.

behaviour [bəˈheivjə] (*n. uncountable*) The way that people or animals do things. **behave** (*v.*) [bəˈheiv].

bone [bəʊn] (*n*) The hard parts inside the human body that form the skeleton.

cartilage [kaˈtəˈlidʒ] (*n. uncountable*) Cartilage is a strong flexible substance in the human body, found especially at the ends of long bones and in joints.

cell [sel] (*n*) A cell is the smallest part of a plant or animal that is able to function independently.

classification [klæsəˈfikˈeiʃən] (*n.*) A division or category so that things with similar characteristics are in the same group.

complementary medicine [kɒmpləˈmentri medsən] (*adj. + n.*) Referring to different forms of medicine which can be used together and 'complement' [kɒmpləˈment] each other.

cramp [kræmp] (*n.*) A sudden, strong pain caused by a muscle suddenly contracting.

defence [dəˈfens] (*n.*) ('*defense*' *in American English*) Defence is action that is taken to protect against attack.

deposits [dəˈpɒzəts] (*n. pl.*) These are substances that have been left somewhere as the result of a chemical process.

depression [dəˈpreʃən] **1** (*n. uncountable*) A mental state of sadness and not being able to enjoy anything. **2** (*n.*) A depression in a surface is an area which is lower than the parts surrounding it.

disease [dəˈziːz] (*n. + uncountable*) A disease is an illness which affects people, animals or plants.

drain [drein] (*n.*) A drain is a type of pipe or tube that takes away liquids, causing it to flow somewhere else. **drain** (*v.*) If you drain something, you dry it by causing water (or liquid) to drain out of it.

environment [enˈvairənˈmənt] (*n.*) **1** Someone's environment is all the circumstances, people, things and events around them that influence their life. **2** Your environment consists of the particular surroundings in which you live or exist. **3** The environment (*n. uncountable*) is the natural world of land, sea, plants and animals.

exchange [eksˈtʃeindʒ] (*n.*) A passing from one area to another in different directions at the same time. *e.g. gaseous exchange.*

fatigue [fəˈtiːg] (*n. uncountable*) A feeling of extreme physical or mental tiredness.

foramen [fəˈreimən] (*n.*) A natural opening in a bone or other body structure. **foramina** (*n. pl.*) [fəˈræminə].

framework [freimˈwɜːk] (*n.*) A framework is a structure that forms support or frame for something.

function [fʌŋkˈʃən] (*n.*) The function of something is the useful thing it does or is intended to do.

gamete [gæmˈiːt] (*n.*) A sex cell, which is either the sperm of the male or the ovum (egg) of the female.

groove [gruːv] (*n.*) A deep line cut into the surface of something.

haematopoiesis [hemˈætˈəʊˈpɔˈiːsis] (*n. uncountable*) (or **haemapoiesis, haematogenesis, haematosis**) The differentiation process by which new blood cells are made.

hormone [hɔːˈməʊn] (*n.*) A chemical substance which occurs naturally in the human body and stimulates other organs.

joint [dʒɔint] (*n.*) A place where two main parts come together. In the body, it is where two bones meet and move together.

ligament [ligəˈmənt] (*n.*) A band of tough [tʌf], fibrous, partly elastic tissue – important components of joints.

meiosis [meiˈəʊsis] (*n. uncountable*) The type of cell division that occurs in the ovaries and testes during the reproduction of gametes.

mitosis [maiˈtəʊsis] (*n. uncountable*) The type of cell division in which the chromosomes within the nucleus of the cell are exactly duplicated into each of two daughter cells.

muscle [mʌsəl] (*n.*) A structure composed of bundles of specialized cells capable of contraction and relaxation to create movement.

offspring [ɒfˈspriŋ] (*n. uncountable*) Human and animals' young (babies/children) can be referred to as their offspring.

organ [ɔːˈgən] (*n.*) A collection of various tissues integrated into a distinct structural unit to perform specific functions.

pathology [pəθˈɒləˈdʒi] (*n. uncountable*) The study of disease – its causes, mechanisms and effects on the body.

physiology [fiziˈɒlədʒi] (*n. uncountable*) The study of body functions, including physical and chemical processes of cells, tissues, organs and systems, and their various interactions.

posture [pɒsˈtʃə] (*n.*) The relative position of parts of the body at rest or during movement. Good posture consists of balancing the body weight around the body's centre of gravity in the lower spine and pelvis. Maintaining good posture helps prevent neck and back pain.

protection [prəˈtekˈʃən] (*n. uncountable*) If something gives or offers protection, it prevents people or things from being harmed or damaged.

structure [strʌkˈtʃə] (*n.*) The way in which something is made, built or organized.

support [səˈpɔːt] (*n.*) The provision of something to help a person or thing stand alone. **to support** [səˈpɔːt] (*v.*) To provide what a person or thing needs to stand alone.

survival [səˈvaivəl] (*n. uncountable*) Managing to live and not die following difficult circumstances.

system [sistəm] (*n.*) The body's organs and other parts that are grouped together to perform a particular function.

tendon [tenˈdən] (*n.*) A strong, flexible, fibrous cord that joins muscle to bone or muscle to muscle but is inelastic.

tissue [tiˈʃuː] (*n.*) A collection of cells specialized to perform a particular function.

virus [vaiˈrəs] (*n.*) The smallest known type of infectious agent. It is debatable whether viruses are truly living organisms or just collections of molecules capable of self–replicating under specific conditions. Outside living cells, viruses are inert.

fibrous [faiˈbrəs] (*adj.*) Referring to a substance that contains a lot of fibres, or looks as if it does.

imaginary [imˈædʒˈinri] (*adj.*) Referring to something that exists in your mind but not in real life.

strenuous [strenˈjuːəs] (*adj.*) Refers to an activity or action which involves a lot of energy or effort.

unique [juːˈniːk] (*adj.*) The only one of its kind.

to break down [breikˈdaʊn] (*v. + prep.*) To form smaller parts or particles.

to protect [prəˈtekt] (*v.*) To prevent someone or something from being harmed or damaged.

🖉 **Match an idiom in column A with its meaning in column B.**

e.g. (1) Use your head → (i) Think about what you are doing.

A

1. *Use* your *head!*
2. Don't *stick your neck out!*
3. It was a real *eye–opener!*
4. I knew I had *hit the nail on the head!*
5. *Give* me *a hand.*
6. He *lost his head!*
7. She *paid lip service to* the idea!
8. They *pulled the wool over* my *eyes!*
9. *Keep your fingers crossed!*
10. *Take heart!*
11. She always *puts* her *foot in* her *mouth!*
12. I'll *play it by ear!*
13. He *got cold feet!*
14. *Give* him the *cold shoulder!*
15. She *can't stomach* [stʌmək] it!

B

(a) It was a most surprising fact.
(b) Please help me.
(c) Don't do anything risky.
(d) They deceived me, their intentions weren't clear.
(e) Be hopeful (positive) – I'm sure you will get what you want.
(f) I did the right thing – I guessed correctly.
(g) He got *extremely* angry!
(h) She seemed to like the idea but then did nothing about it.
(i) Think about what you are doing.
(j) Ignore him.
(k) She can't endure or tolerate it.
(l) Be encouraged, more confident.
(m) I don't know what to do but I'll work it out as I go along.
(n) He decided not to do it at the last minute – he was afraid.
(o) She always says the wrong thing.

🖉 *Use the idiomatic expressions in the following sentences, changing the verb tenses when necessary.*

1. I thought she was very lazy until yesterday – she had finished everything when I arrived – it was a ....!

2. My friend decided to study art, she said she couldn't .... nursing or medicine!

3. Can you .... me .... to turn Mr. Biggs and attend to his pressure areas?

4. He .... about going to the doctor, saying that it really wasn't necessary.

5. I may be .... my ...., I know it's taking a risk but I really have to do it.

6. Take each day as it comes, you are making good progress. You can .... in these results!

7. That was an unnecessary thing to say, he was most offended. You are always .... your .... your .... !

8. Martin lied about his qualifications and will lose his job – he doesn't .... his ....!

9. When the boss discovered the lies he accused Martin of .... his ....

10. When I have a problem, I think about it, work out a solution then .... my ....!

11. When Lisa heard that her friend was nauseated nearly every morning and guessed that she was pregnant, she had ....!

12. Michael's son had an accident when driving the family car home from a party. Michael .... his .... when he found out that his son had been drinking.

13. Annette .... to the group's holiday plans but later decided to have a different holiday with her boyfriend.

14. After making this decision, everyone in the group .... her ....

15. I don't know if my friends can *put me up* when I go to London, so I'll just .... it ....

✎ *Now use a dictionary and add derivatives from the words listed.*
Choose one of these words, write a sentence and then translate it into your own language.

e.g.   deceived [dɪˈsiːvd] (v. pp.) – **deceit** (n.), deceitful (adj.), to deceive (v.)
    Deceit *is behaviour that is intended to make people believe something which is not true.*

approved [əˈpruːvd]   ....

decide [dɪsaɪd]   ....

discover [dɪsˈkʌvə]   ....

encouraged [enˈkʌrədʒd]   ....

endure [enˈdjuːə]   ....

hopeful [həʊpˈfʊl]   ....

ignore [igˈnɔː]   ....

know [nəʊ]   ....

risky [riski]   ....

surprising [səˈpraɪsɪŋ]   ....

CROSSWORD

✎ *Look at the clues across (→) and down (↓) to find internal and external parts of the human body.*
(The number in brackets tells you how many letters there are in each word.)

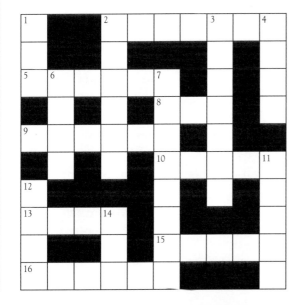

Down:
1. A common word used for the digestive or alimentary tract. (3)
2. This is a long, narrow marking on a bone – in the ribs they contain inter–costal nerves and blood vessels. (6)
3. The largest endocrine gland, situated in the neck. Its function depends on the amount of iodine in the blood. (7)
4. One of the two main organs of the respiratory system. (4)
6. The back or posterior part of the foot (or of a shoe!) (4)
7. One of the male gonads, contained in the scrotum. (8)
11. The main organ of the circulatory system – described as 'a pump'. (5)
12. This body part lies at the distal end of the leg. (4)
14. One of the lower extremities. (3)

Across:
2. The pubic area is also called the .... area. (7)
5. The inside of the neck is called the .... (6)
8. The external auditory (hearing) apparatus. (3)
9. This is the name given to the bony area that consists of the hips, sacrum and the symphysis–pubis. (6)
10. The upper anterior part of the leg. (5)
13. ...... hygiene means keeping the mouth and teeth clean. (4)
15. An incredible organ that stores glycogen, vitamins and iron, produces bile and blood plasma proteins, destroys old red blood cells and removes poisonous (toxic) substances from the blood. (5)
16. Our sense of taste is located by receptors in the .... (6)

UNIT

4

DIET AND NUTRITION

A

FOOD AND FOOD GROUPS

1. *Can you name one piece of fruit and one vegetable* starting with "b" ....
starting with "m" ....
starting with "p" ....
starting with "c" ....?

2. *Can you name two or three berry fruits?* ....

3. *Name three citrus fruits:* ....

4. *How many tropical or "exotic" fruits can you name?*

5. *Translate the following names into your language:*

    a. a pineapple   d. a cauliflower
    b. a lettuce   e. a passion fruit
    c. grapes   f. a cabbage

6. *With a partner discuss the answers you have written and then answer the following question:*

What is the difference between a plum and a prune?

7. *Now, with your partner, label all the foood products you can identify on this page.*

8. *Circle the 'odd one out' in each of the following groups? Give a reason for this choice.*

1. grapes	raspberry	strawberry	blackberry
2. banana	mango	apple	pineapple
3. pumpkin	tomato	zucchini	carrot
4. mushroom	onion	courgette	passion fruit
5. pear	lemon	orange	grapefruit
6. calf	beef	pork	lamb
7. salmon	crayfish	trout	cod
8. prawns	lobster	octopus	crabmeat
9. salami	ham	chicken	bacon
10. flour	sugar	butter	rice

Make lists of food under the following headings. Can you pronounce all these correctly? Use phonetic symbols to help you remember.

fruit [fruːt]	vegetables [vedʒˈtəbəlz]	meat and fish [miːt ᵗn fiʃ]	carbohydrate foods [ka:bəʊˈhaidreit]	oils and fats [ɔiəlz n fæts]

MEALS
[miːəlz]

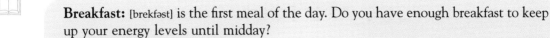

Breakfast: [brekfəst] is the first meal of the day. Do you have enough breakfast to keep up your energy levels until midday?

Lunch: [lʌntʃ] is a light meal eaten in the middle of the day. When you don't have a long break, or if you are not using a lot of energy, a sandwich or yoghurt and fruit is enough.

Dinner: [dinə] is the main meal of the day and can be eaten at midday or in the evening.

Supper: [sʌpə] is a light meal eaten in the evening when the main meal was at midday.

A Snack: [snæk] is not a 'meal' but is eaten between meals, mid-morning or mid-afternoon or late in the evening! A snack should be light and nourishing and not reduce your appetite for a meal.

A Salad: [sæləd] in English is not only lettuce, or varieties of lettuce, but includes cold meat, cheese, hard-boiled eggs or seafood, cold or raw [rɔ:] (uncooked) vegetables, pickled [pikəld] (bottled in vinegar) vegetables and sometimes fruit.

Dressing: [dresiŋ] usually refers to 'salad dressing' – a combination of oil and vinegar, mustard and/or mayonnaise.

Food intake

Food intake is essential if cells are to receive nutrients for energy production. Foods can be solid or liquid and the choice is individual and voluntary but **appetite is controlled by the hypothalamus** in the brain. **Proteins, carbohydrates, fats, minerals and vitamins** are all essential if health is to be maintained. If any vital food is missing from the diet, the body will suffer from *malnutrition or deficiency.*

A well-balanced diet is simple. Nothing is forbidden, but some foods need a higher profile than others. Because proteins are not stored in the body in the same way as carbohydrates and fats, protein foods should be eaten on a regular basis.

☺ *Your teacher will show you how to make 'a food and drink network' to help you learn and remember vocabulary. Using the 'network' throughout this section, start by listing as many beverages as you can. Divide them into hot and cold, alcoholic and non-alcoholic drinks.*

Fluid intake

Fluid intake is as important as food intake. The normal proportion of body water varies from 50% to 70% of a person's weight. Water is important to living cells as a solvent, as a transport medium and as a participant in metabolic reactions.

Most people drink when they are thirsty, about 6 to 8 **beverages** [bev'ridʒəz] a day. Total fluid intake is normally about two and a half litres and comes from drinks and food, especially soups, fruit and vegetables. The control centre for 'the sense of thirst' is located in the **hypothalamus** [haipˈəuˈθæləməs] in the brain. Drinks containing **alcohol** [ælkəˈhɒl] or **caffeine** [kæfiːn] should not be included in this total because they act as **diuretics** [daiˈjuːˈretiks] and increase water loss. When exercising vigorously and/or in very hot weather, the body can **dehydrate** [diːˈhaiˈdreit] very quickly. In a person whose health is normal, the intake of fluids is approximately equal to the **output** but this amount varies considerably from day to day and from person to person.

☺ *What is the difference between a prescription* [presˈkripʃən], *a receipt* [riˈsiːt] *and a recipe* [resəˈpi]?

THE HEALTHY DIET PYRAMID

[pirə'mid]

A healthy diet contains amounts of all the substances shown in the pyramid and an adequate intake of fluid.

The pyramid illustrates that grains, cereals, fruit and vegetables need to be eaten in larger quantities than other kinds of food and that a limited intake of fats, oils and sugars is recommended. It has been advised that calories [kælə'riz] *(or kilojoules) from the 3 main classes of nutrients are distributed as follows:*

Fats: less than 30%, Carbohydrates: 58% and Protein: 12%.

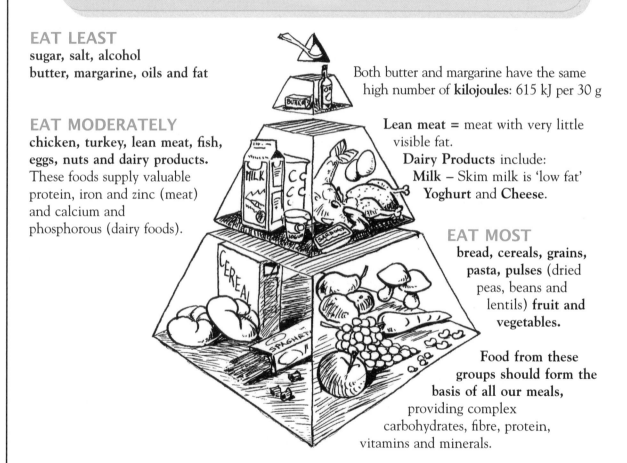

EAT LEAST
sugar, salt, alcohol
butter, margarine, oils and fat

Both butter and margarine have the same high number of **kilojoules**: 615 kJ per 30 g

EAT MODERATELY
chicken, turkey, lean meat, fish, eggs, nuts and dairy products.
These foods supply valuable protein, iron and zinc (meat) and calcium and phosphorous (dairy foods).

Lean meat = meat with very little visible fat.
Dairy Products include:
Milk – Skim milk is 'low fat'
Yoghurt and **Cheese.**

EAT MOST
bread, cereals, grains, pasta, pulses (dried peas, beans and lentils) **fruit and vegetables.**

Food from these groups should form the basis of all our meals, providing complex carbohydrates, fibre, protein, vitamins and minerals.

Can you name the five main categories of food necessary in a well-balance diet?

(1) _ _ _ _ _ _ _ _ _ _ _ _ _ (13 letters), (2) _ _ _ _ _ _ _ (7 letters), (3) _ _ _ _ _ (5 letters – This used to be called 'roughage'), (4) _ _ _ _ _ _ _ _ (8 letters) and (5) _ _ _ _ _ _ _ _ (8 letters: these two substances are counted together) and (6) _ _ _ _ (4 letters)

Listening 22 – The healthy diet pyramid *Listen carefully to the recording and follow the instructions to update it.*

WHAT TO EAT AND HOW MUCH

☺ *Choose from the following groups, and working with your partner, plan a healthy daily diet.*

A BALANCED DIET PLANNER	
EAT MOST	
6 serves daily	**Bread** (wholemeal/wholegrain for extra fibre), rolls, toast, crackers. **Cereal:** preferably wholegrain. Cooked or ready-to-eat. **Rice, pasta:** preferably wholegrain.
6 serves daily	**Vegetables and/or fruit and fruit juices.**
1 serve daily	**Legumes and pulses** (beans, peas, lentils, chick peas etc.) if vegetarian.
EAT MODERATELY	
about 125 g.	**Lean meat** (with the skin or fat cut off). Veal, pork, beef, lamb or organ meats: liver, brain, kidneys etc. Chicken, turkey, duck (or other **poultry**). **Fish**, Prawns, lobster and oysters or other **seafood**. or **Eggs** (1 egg replaces 25 g. meat).
1 serve daily	**Nuts** (if vegetarian).
300 ml. daily	**Milk products** (low fat or skim milk is preferable for adults). Yoghurt. Cheese – (about 50 g. Ricotta or Cottage cheese replaces 200 mls. milk) 40 g. of hard cheese replaces about 300 mls. milk.
EAT LEAST	
30 ml. (1 Tablespoon)	**Oils and fats:** cooking oil or salad oil, mayonnaise, butter, margarine, cream, sour cream
Not required! (a glass of soft drink or a small serve of other sweets supplies about 300 kJ = 70 calories)	**Sweets:** sugar, honey, jam, marmalade. (*What's the difference between jam and marmalade?*) **Confectionary:** (sweets or bon-bons) caramels, toffees, chocolate etc. **Soft drinks:** Coca Cola, lemonade etc. **Cakes and desserts, sweet biscuits.** **Snacks:** potato crisps, corn chips, cheese savouries, mixed nuts etc. **Alcohol:** Wine, Beer, Spirits.

✎ *Make a list of what you ate yesterday. Was it well-balanced?*
Can you plan a well-balance diet that you could eat nearly every day using the 'updated food pyramid'? An occasional indulgence is allowed, including wine if it is not contraindicated!

☺ *Interview your partner and find out what meals he/she has and what he eats most days.*
Ask "What do you have for breakfast? Do you have snacks during the day?"
Discuss your likes and dislikes and decide if you and your partner have a <u>healthy</u> diet.

GUIDELINES FOR A HEALTHIER DAILY DIET

♦ Enjoy a *wide variety* of nutritious food.
♦ Eat plenty of bread and cereals (preferably wholegrain), vegetables (including legumes) and fruit.
♦ Eat a *diet low in fat*, especially low in saturated fat.
♦ *Maintain a healthy body weight* by balancing physical activity and food intake.
♦ If you drink *alcohol, limit* your intake.
♦ Use only a small amount of *sugar* and eat only a small amount of food containing added sugar.
♦ *Choose low salt* food and try not to add extra salt to food. (Herbs can flavour food and decrease the need for salt. They also supply vitamins and minerals).
♦ Encourage and support new mothers to *breast-feed* their babies.
♦ Eat food containing *calcium*. This is particularly important for girls and women.
♦ Eat food containing *iron*. This is particularly important for girls, women, vegetarians and athletes.

HOW NUTRITION AFFECTS YOUR HEALTH

DIET PROBLEM	ASSOCIATED DISEASE
Too many kilojoules (calories)	Overweight, obesity Insulin dependent diabetes Cancer of the breast and uterus Heart Disease
High intake of saturated fat	Heart Disease
High intake of fats	Bowel (intestinal) cancer Breast cancer Endometrial (uterine) cancer
High sugar intake	Overweight Dental cavities (caries)
High salt intake	High blood pressure Stroke (CVA) – Intracranial haemorrhage or occlusion of intracranial blood vessels
Low fibre intake	Constipation Haemorrhoids Cancer of the bowel and breast Diverticular Disease
Excess alcohol	High blood pressure Cirrhosis of the liver Dietary deficiency diseases
Low iron intake	Anaemia
Low calcium intake	Osteoporosis

Make some sentences using the tables on these pages to talk about the quantities of food needed or that should be avoided to prevent certain illnesses and diseases. Use the following quantifiers:

more or less   the most or the least   a lesser amount or more (a larger amount)

QUANTIFIERS

COUNTABLE NOUNS

apples	girls	children
numbers	chairs	dishes
enzymes	toilets	cups

How MANY ....?

...too many

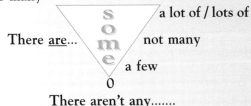

There <u>are</u>...   ~~some~~   a lot of / lots of

not many

a few

0

There <u>aren't any</u>.......

<u>Are</u> there <u>any</u>..........?

UNCOUNTABLE NOUNS

rain	money	air	meat
gold	electricity	blood	oxygen
information	water	flour	pressure

How MUCH ....?

...too much

There <u>is</u>...   ~~some~~   a lot of / lots of

not much

a little

0

There <u>isn't any</u>........

<u>Is</u> there <u>any</u>...........?

Exercise 1. *Write 'a' / 'an' or 'some'*

(a) .... book
(b) .... air
(c) .... rain
(d) .... atom
(e) .... sugar
(f) .... molecule
(g) .... information
(h) .... five dollar note
(i) .... snow
(j) .... apple
(k) .... exercise

Exercise 3. *With partner, think of all the expressions of quantity that can be used in the following sentences.*

1. There has been .... rain this month.
2. The river is flooding – .... water is coming down from the mountains.
3. There is still .... snow above 2000 metres.
4. You can't pick .... apples until they are bigger.
5. How .... meat can you eat?
6. I would like .... Coca Cola please.
7. There are .... violent programmes on TV.
8. I've got .... free time this weekend.
9. Vegetarians don't eat .... meat.
10. He doesn't know .... of the answers.

Exercise 2. *Complete the questions using 'much' or 'many'*

(a) How .... people are there in here?
(b) How .... money have you got?
(c) How .... calories are there in an egg?
(d) How .... beer is there in the fridge?
(e) How .... gold is in that ring?
(f) How .... children have you got?
(g) How .... petrol is in the car?
(h) How .... food groups are there?
(i) How .... information did you get from that new text book?

Now match a suitable answer with one of the questions:

1. It's full.
2. More than enough to do the homework.
3. Not much – about 5 Euros!
4. There are 5 main groups.
5. It's 18 carat – about 30 grams I suppose.
6. We've got 3 sons.
7. 6 cans and 1 bottle.
8. Ninety.
9. Nine, 3 men and 6 ladies.

SPOT THE DIFFERENCE – IS/ARE THERE ANY LEFT?

A

☺ With your partner, look at pictures A and B and see how many differences you can find.

	Picture A	Picture B
Orange juice		
Grapefruit juice		
French bread		
Beef Curry		
Rice		
Hamburgers		
Pizza		
Steak		
Chips		
Sausage rolls		
Doughnuts		
Cheesecake		
Fruit Salad		
Apple Cake		
Chocolate Cake		
Crisps (Chips)		
Cheese sandwiches		
Chicken sandwiches		
Cheese rolls		
Salad		
Tomatoes		
Hard-boiled eggs		

B

EXPRESSIONS OF QUANTITY

> *Two young people were interviewed by a market research company and asked about the types of food they buy each week. Both Michael and Karin made mistakes using the expressions of quantity.*

Underline the incorrect grammar and re-write the dialogues.

e.g.   Michael says: *I buy <u>many meats</u>, because I need <u>a few energy</u>...*
            CHANGE TO: *I buy* **a lot of meat,** *because I need* **a little energy...**

Michael: What do I buy most? Well, I buy <u>many meats</u>, because I need <u>a few energy</u> to go to the gym and for leading a pretty busy life. It's easy to cook and I buy any vegetables from the freezer at the supermarket, I don't buy some fresh vegetables because I only have a little fridge. I buy much packets of ready-to-eat meals so I have time to do other things in the evenings. I have very few time for cooking and I love pasta dishes and fresh fruit. I buy several fruit at the market on my way home from work. I eat too many bread too, but I usually buy wholemeal bread or the bread rolls with seeds and grains in it, so I think that's quite good for me really.

Karin: I am quite a fussy shopper! I like to buy much things at the health food shops and I buy 'free range' eggs and things like that. I don't buy many chocolate or much sweets but I love ice-cream! I'm allergic to any chemicals and colourings in food, so I look at the labels and look at all the ingredients before I buy something. I like cooking for my friends and because much of them are vegetarian I always serve many fresh fruit and vegetables too. They like fish so I buy fresh salmon or trout and cook it with too many butter and lots of almonds – it's delicious but probably has far too much calories! I always have breakfast – I enjoy having yoghurt and fruit and a big cup of milk coffee while I watch the news before I go to work. I'm cooking any chicken for supper tonight, with much potatoes, some spinach and baby carrots – sounds good, doesn't it?

161

D

WEIGHT STATUS – THE BODY MASS INDEX

There is no exact correct weight for good health but there is a healthy weight range. Women in some modern Western societies think that 'thin is beautiful' but the problems of anorexia and bulimia nervosa and other eating disorders have shown that this is not the case. It is not healthy to be fat either but if you have a small frame (small skeletal structure) and don't have much muscle, then it is better to aim for a steady weight in the lower half of the healthy weight range. On the other hand, if you have a large frame or do a lot of exercise and have an increased muscle mass, then you can aim to have a higher level in the normal healthy range. Problems with appetite can be made normal with regular exercise and by using the 'diet pyramid' as an every day food guide.

WEIGHT–FOR–HEIGHT CHART

For men and women from 18 years onwards
Based on Body Mass Index (BMI) in Range of 18, 20, 25, 30

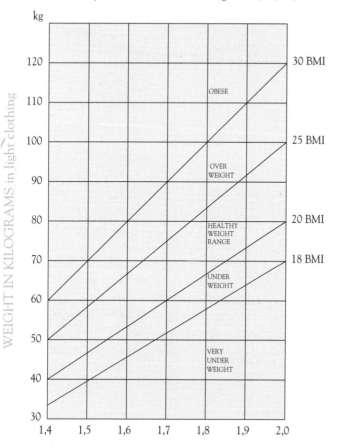

HEIGHT IN METRES without shoes

THE BODY MASS INDEX (BMI)

The Body Mass Index (BMI) is the most valid indication of weight status. It is calculated as follows:

$$\text{divided by } \frac{Weight\ in\ kilograms}{(Height\ in\ metres)^2}$$

The following classifications are used:

Below 18 = very underweight
  18–20 = underweight
  20–25 = healthy weight range
        (least risk of disease and death)
  25–30 = overweight
Over 30 = obese

☺ *Using the chart, discuss the healthy weight ranges with your partner. Do you think you should change anything in your lifestyle?*
Chart the height and weight of all the class members.
What conclusions can you come to about the average dietary habits of the class?

THE DIGESTIVE SYSTEM

First number the pictures: Left 1, 2, 3 Centre 4, Right 5 and 6.

Label the diagram with as many of the following organs and parts as you can.
(The numbers in brackets tell you which picture(s) to label.)

The Diaphragm (4) • The Small Bowel/Small Intestine (Ileum, Jejunum) (4) • The Spleen (3.4)
The Gallbladder (4.5) • The Liver (4) • The Oesophagus (2.4) • The Transverse Colon (4.6)
The Stomach (2.3.4) • The Appendix (4.6) • The Pyloric Sphincter (2) • The Duodenum (2.5)
The Oesophageal Sphincter (2) • The Descending Colon (4.6) • The Ascending Colon (4.6) • The Anus (1.4)
The Common Bile Duct (5) • The Pancreas (3) • The Sigmoid Colon (1.6) • The Pancreatic Duct (5)
The Cystic Duct (5) • The Caecum (4) • Rectal valves (1.4) • The Lower Oesophageal Sphincter (4)

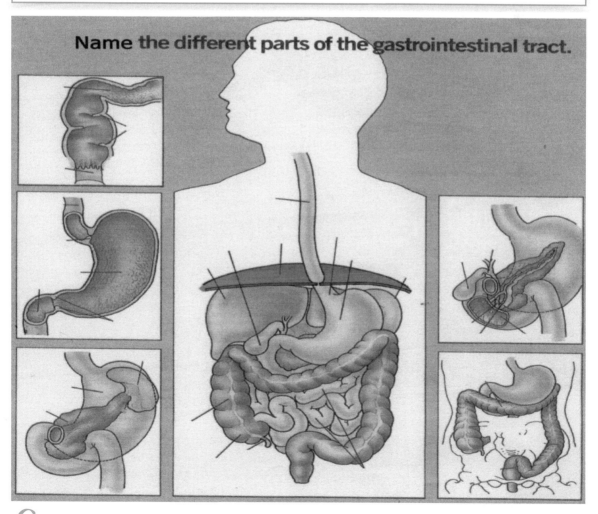

Listening 23 – The digestive system *Listen to the text, add the names that are still missing and check that the pictures are labelled correctly.*

THE DIGESTIVE [dɪˈdʒestɪv] SYSTEM

The **digestive system** consists of all the organs that ***ingest*** [ɪnˈdʒest] (take in) and ***digest*** [daɪˈdʒest] (break down into smaller particles) the food we eat. It also ***excretes*** [eksˈkriːts] (gets rid of) any ***waste products*** [weɪstˈprɒdʌkts], that is, substances that the body does not need.

Eating

1. Salivary glands
2. Tongue
3. Epiglottis
4. Esophagus
5. Trachea
6. Teeth

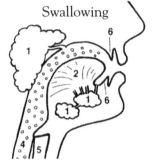

Swallowing

The primary organs of digestion are the mouth, the ***tongue and palates*** – hard and soft – (the roof of the mouth), the ***pharynx*** [færɪnks], the ***oesophagus*** [əˈsɒfəgəs], the ***stomach*** [stʌmək] and the ***large and the small intestines*** [ɪnˈtestˈaɪnz]. Food is ingested, chewed and softened in the mouth and then swallowed. The muscular soft palate and the attached ***uvula*** [juːvjələ] move upwards closing the entrance to the nasal cavities and trachea and food passes into the oesophagus. This is a muscular tube, lined with mucous membrane. Food is moved down the oesophagus by waves of muscular contractions called *peristalsis* [periˈstɒlsis]. Peristalsis starts in the oesophagus and continues in the stomach and in the intestines. The mucous membrane lining *secretes* [səˈkriːts] mucous which provides lubrication for the movement of food during this process. The stomach is a bag–like organ with muscular rings at the openings called *sphincters* [sfinkˈtəz]. Food enters the stomach from the oesophagus through the ***cardiac sphincter*** and leaves the stomach to pass into the small intestine through the ***pyloric sphincter***. While food is in the stomach, Hydrochloric [haɪdrəˈklɒrik] acid (HCl) and the enzyme [enˈzaɪm] Pepsin are mixed with the food by the 'churning movements' of the stomach. Pepsin is a protein-digesting enzyme. Food leaves the stomach in a semi-liquid form and is then called *chyme* [kaɪm]. The first part of the small intestine is the ***duodenum***, and both the pancreatic duct and the bile duct have openings into the duodenum. The duodenum measures about 25 cm and the following ***jejunum*** [dʒeˈdʒuːnəm] is about 2 and a half metres long. Together with the lower section, the ***ileum***, the small intestine measures over 6 metres! The large intestine is larger in diameter than the small intestine, but smaller in length, about one and a half metres long. The large intestine consists of the ***caecum*** [siːkem], the ***colon*** [kəʊˈlɒn] and the ***rectum*** [rektəm]. The function of the large intestine is to eliminate waste from the body and to prevent *dehydration*. To do this, the large bowel re-absorbs most of the water secreted into the digestive tract to help with digestion.

The accessory organs of digestion include **the teeth** (for chewing and grinding food into smaller particles), the salivary glands (which secrete saliva and the enzyme *ptyalin* [taiə'lin] that starts the digestion of starches – carbohydrates), the **liver**, the **gallbladder** and the **pancreas.** The liver is the largest gland in the body. It is a vital organ with many important functions. It secretes *bile* [baiəl] that is important in the digestion of fats, stores glucose [glu:'kəuz], forms blood plasma proteins (albumin, globulin and clotting factors), it synthesises *urea* [ju:'riə] – a waste product of protein metabolism, destroys old red blood cells, stores some vitamins and iron and removes or 'de-toxifies' [di:'tɒksifaiz] poisonous substances such as drugs or alcohol. The pancreas is both an endocrine and an exocrine gland. The pancreas produces *insulin* which controls carbohydrate metabolism.

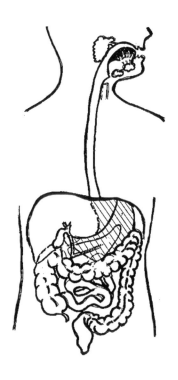

☺ *Work with a partner to answer the following questions about the function of the organs of the digestive system.*

1. Which accessory organs are the first to break food up into smaller pieces? Name two of the actions used to do this.

2. How does the soft palate help in the process of swallowing food? What sort of 'tissue' is it?

3. Name the 'wave-like' contractions that help food to travel down the oesophagus and through the intestines.

4. What happens to food when it arrives in the stomach?

5. The whole digestive 'tract' is lined with mucous membranes. In fact, all the body systems that open to the outside of the body are lined with mucous membranes. What is their function?

6. How many functions of the liver can you list?

7. What two parts are the intestines (also called 'the bowel) made up of?

8. What does the pyloric sphincter do?

9. An enzyme is an organic catalyst. A catalyst speeds up chemical reactions. Enzymes enable metabolic reactions to occur at a fast rate to maintain life. Many different enzymes are needed, because each one works only on one specific substance. There are two enzymes mentioned in the text. What are they and what do they do?

10. Where is bile secreted? Where is it stored? How does it reach the intestine? What does it do?

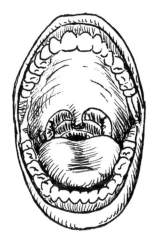

THE FUNCTIONS OF THE LIVER

📖 *The liver is the largest glandular organ in the body and is composed of four lobes, a large right lobe with two smaller inferior (lower) lobes and a smaller left lobe. It is an incredible organ and has so many important functions that only some are mentioned here.*

Glycogen, iron and vitamins are stored

Harmful substances are detoxified

Food substances are removed from the blood and are converted to glucose
Old red blood cells are destroyed and eliminated in the bile

Vitamin A forms

Urea is synthesised

Bile is manufactured

Fats are modified to be used efficiently by cells all over the body

Blood plasma proteins are manufactured by the liver
Food substances are carried to the liver in the blood via the Portal Vein System

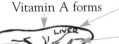

✎ **Look at the diagram and complete the following description using the words in the box.**

When food has been .... into the blood from the intestine, it is .... to the liver, where it is .... from the blood and .... Certain carbohydrates are .... into glycogen in the liver and Vitamin A is .... from substances in vegetables and blood proteins. Glycogen, iron and the vitamins A, D and B are .... in the liver, to be available when needed by the body. Bacteria and 'worn-out' red blood cells are .... and other toxic or harmful substances in food are .... by complex processes in the liver. Urea, a waste product of protein metabolism is .... in the liver. Another important function of the liver is the secretion of a digestive juice known as .... which .... fats into smaller particles called fatty acids.

breaks down
stored
formed/manufactured
bile
carried
detoxified
removed
stored
converted
absorbed
destroyed
synthesised

Check the answers with your teacher.

Medical terms

used by medical staff for conditions and diseases, often need to be explained to the patient in simpler words for the patient to understand. The names of main organs of the body are usually understood. Refer to the 'building blocks' in Section 1.

Gastroenterology

Remember that the 'root' is the main part which can be understood:

Prefixes (at the beginning of the word) and suffixes (at the end of the word) change the root in some way.

gastr- = stomach   *chole-* = gallbladder

oesoph- = oesophagus   *splen-* = spleen

hep- = liver

🖉 *Match the prefix and suffixes to the correct meaning.*

-scope	surgical removal of	-rhea	inflammation or infection
-ectomy	an opening into	-itis	visual examination
-iasis	through, complete	-oma	discharge, flow
dia-	instrument to view	-scopy	tumour or growth
-otomy	a condition or 'the presence of'		

Look at the names of the following conditions (affecting the organs of the abdomino-pelvic cavity) and the example explanations, then write the others in words that a patient will understand.

Appendectomy ....

Cholangitis [kɒlˈænˈdʒaitis] *Inflammation of the common bile duct – the tube draining from the liver and gallbladder.*

Cholecystitis *Acute or chronic inflammation of the Gallbladder.*

Colostomy *Making a (temporary or permanent) surgical opening into the Colon.*

Gastroscopy ....

Gastrotomy ....

Hepatoma ....

Ileostomy ....

Laparotomy ....

Lobectomy ....

Oesophagitis ....

Paralytic Ileus ....

Peptic (Gastric ulcer/ation) ....

Sigmoidoscope ....

Splenectomy ....

Ulcerative Colitis ....

📖 *Some medical terminology has slightly different spelling in American English, both forms are correct. Look at these examples.*

British English	American English
oesophagus	esophagus
haematology	hematology
caecum	cecum
disc	disk
leukocyte	leuco

The meaning of some medical terms can be entirely misunderstood through incorrect spelling. The following examples are very different in meaning but there is only one letter different!

The Ileum   is the lower part of the small intestine (small bowel [baʊəl]).
The Ilium   is the hip bone, part of the pelvic girdle.

Abduction   is a movement away from ...   Arteritis   is inflammation of an artery.
Adduction   is a movement towards ...   Arthritis   is inflammation of a joint (an articulation).

DIFFERENT HOSPITAL DIETS

There are four main classifications for hospital diets:

1. A FULL (or 'normal') diet, where the patient can choose his food for each meal from the menu.
2. A LIGHT (or 'soft') diet containing very little fibre and food which is easily digested, i.e. foods made from refined flour and not including whole grains or seeds.
3. A 'FREE' LIQUID (or 'FLUIDS ONLY') diet includes all liquid foods such as soups (strained, creamed or puréed), drinks and cooked refined cereals such as 'porridge/gruel', plain ice-cream, sorbet and semi–liquid desserts made with milk or gelatine.
4. A CLEAR LIQUID diet includes only water, flavoured or plain water ice, strained fruit juices, vegetable water, clear consommé (soup) and different varieties of tea or coffee without milk.

Look at the different food and drinks in the box under the table, then list the food that a patient is allowed to have (is permitted to have / can have) on these diets.

FULL	SOFT/LIGHT	FLUIDS ONLY	CLEAR FLUIDS ONLY

porridge (rolled oats) • ice-cream • minestrone-vegetable and grain soups • mayonnaise
milk/cream/yoghurt • clear soup • eggs-raw/cooked • banana and walnut cake
meat/fish/poultry • sugar • custard • rice • vegetables • fruit • mashed potato (purée)
wholegrain or wholemeal bread • spaghetti with meat sauce • biscuits
lettuce and tomatoes • fruit juices • butter/cheese • nuts
refined white bread • tea/coffee • dry biscuit/crackers • semolina • muesli
cordial/clear fruit syrup drinks • dried fruit • chocolate

📖 TALKING ABOUT OBLIGATION (OR LACK OF OBLIGATION)

If you 'are allowed' to do something, someone in authority has given you permission to do it.
If something is 'not allowed' then someone in authority has said 'permission is <u>not</u> given'.
'To be allowed', or 'not allowed' are always followed by the full infinitive (i.e. + 'to')
e.g. *A patient on a liquid diet <u>is not allowed to</u> eat solid food.*
    A diabetic <u>isn't allowed to</u> have sugar in his tea or coffee.
    A patient on a full diet <u>is allowed to</u> eat anything he chooses.
The modal verb 'must' or 'mustn't' is also a verb for strong obligation from someone in authority, or for indicating strong obligation to yourself.
The modal verbs 'must', 'mustn't', 'can' and 'can't' are followed by the infinitive without 'to':
e.g. *A patient with a gastric ulcer <u>must not drink</u> alcohol.*
    Personal allergies <u>must be</u> written on the patient's case notes and the dietician <u>must be</u> notified.
    I <u>must remember</u> to ring the dietician's office.

✏️ *Now, using* (to be) allowed to **or** (to be) not allowed to, must, mustn't, can **or** can't *complete the following sentences.*

1. Both the patients in this room .... choose from the 'Full' Menu.
2. Mr. Campbell is on a Soft Diet so he .... eat the nuts his wife brought in.
3. There are 2 patients on Fluids Only – they .... both .... have the strained vegetable soup, and the puréed apples and custard for lunch.
4. Doctor has just written orders for Miss Klein to fast – she .... have anything to eat or drink until after the operation.
5. Mrs White has just come back from the Recovery Room and she .... start having sips of clear fluids – she would probably like some ice to suck.
6. Patients on a Light Diet .... eat fruit and vegetables that are high in fibre.
7. Milk and milk products .... on a Clear Fluid Diet.
8. Patients on Full Liquid Diets .... have milk and egg drinks, vegetable and fruit purée and cooked cereals (but they must be 'creamed').
9. Mr. Campbell .... have wholemeal bread or bread with grains in it.
10. Mrs White .... have a meal yet, she is still on fluids only.

☺ *Look at the signs and words in column A and match them with a phrase or a sentence from column B. Add another sentence to each of the pictures.*

A		B	
1	🚭	(i)	This patient must not have anything to eat or drink.
2	DIABETIC	(ii)	This patient is not allowed to drink milk.
3	NIL BY MOUTH / NIL ORALLY	(iii)	Smoking is not allowed.
4	Fluid Balance Chart	(iv)	This patient is on a 'special' diet.
5	CLEAR FLUIDS ONLY	(v)	Keep an accurate record of fluid intake and output.

169

G

SPECIAL DIETS

Special Diets may be ordered as treatment for a disease, to eliminate certain substances from the diet or to supply a specific nutrient in the case of a 'deficiency disease' (for example: Iron deficiency anaemia is treated with a diet rich in iron).

An individual's choice of food may be based on ideals, customs or religious dietary restrictions.

Exemples of Special Diets are:

◆ Diabetic Diet
◆ Low–Cholesterol (Low Fat or Fat–Free) Diet
◆ Low Fibre Diet or a High Fibre Diet
◆ Gluten–Free Diet
◆ High Protein Diet or a Low Protein Diet
◆ Iron rich Diet – and many others.

A Vegetarian Diet may be a personal choice or it may be based on cultural principles found in many Eastern religions. Some regimens are nutritionally adequate and others are not.

A lacto–ova–vegetarian diet consists of grains, fruit and vegetables, supplemented with milk, cheese and eggs. A lot of nuts and legumes are included and used in a variety of ways.

Vegans, who don't eat any animal products at all and have **only fruit and vegetables, nuts and grains** in their diets, need to plan their meals very well to have a nutritionally adequate diet. A vegan diet, when planned properly, can supply a good balance of essential amino-acids, and adequate amounts of calcium, riboflavin, iron, vitamin A and vitamin D. Vitamin B12 can be taken as a supplement or obtained from soy milk fortified with this vitamin.

☺ *Discuss these diets with your partner. Can you answer the following questions?*

What is the difference between a vegetarian and a vegan?
Do you know what types of food contain a high level of cholesterol and what can be eaten instead?
Do you know how a patient can increase his intake of fibre?

THE FLUID BALANCE CHART (FBC)

The nurse is responsible for keeping clear, accurate fluid balance charts. Patients with actual or potential problems of fluid balance have this chart attached to their nursing notes. All fluids given orally and/or administered by intravenous infusion and all fluid lost by vomiting or in liquid faeces or wound drainage or excreted as urine, must be measured accurately and recorded at that time.

Alert patients are very often given responsibility for their own intake – they can be instructed on the quantity of liquid a cup or a glass holds and be shown how much to record. They can keep an accurate record, knowing when they drink a full glass or if the glass or bottle was taken away before it was finished. Allowing the patient to participate in his own care does not lessen the responsibility of the nurse to ensure that accurate records and charts are kept. The total intake and total output are calculated every 24 hours.

		Unit No.					
		Surname					
		First names					
	Intake			Output			
	All measurements in ml.						
Hour	Mouth	Intravenous		Urine	Vomit	Aspirate	Other
		Fluid	Volume				
0900							
1000							
1100							
1200							
1300							
1400							
1500							
1600							
1700							
1800							
1900							
2000							
2100							
2200							
2300							
2400							
0100							
0200							
0300							
0400							
0500							
0600							
0700							
0800							
Total							
	Grand Total for intake				Total output		
				Allowance for insensible loss			
Record intravenous fluid volume when each bottle has been infused				Grand Total for output			
Date				Balance			

JEWISH PEOPLE – Jewish dietary laws are taken from rules laid down in the Bible and *mainly concern the selection and killing of animals and the preparation of meat*. Animals allowed to be eaten are those with 'cloven' hooves that 'chew cud': cattle, sheep, goats and deer are all considered 'clean'. Most poultry, that is, chicken, duck, turkey etc. is included if it has been declared free of disease and is killed according to specific rules. *All meat and poultry must be 'koshered'* which removes all blood from the meat before cooking. This involves soaking the meat in water, salting it thoroughly, then washing it three times. *Only Fish with fins and scales can be eaten* – this excludes shellfish, octopus and eels. *Meat and milk cannot be combined in the same meal.* Milk and milk products can be eaten immediately before a meat meal, but not with it or for six hours after it. Eggs can be eaten, but not if they contain blood spots.

Bread and other bakery products must be produced under acceptable Kosher standards.

The most important day is Saturday, *the Sabbath, when no food can be cooked or heated.* The meal on Friday night is usually quite substantial and extra food is either kept warm or refrigerated for the following day. Other holy days are festivals with special delicacies used to celebrate. Ten days after Rosh Hashanah – celebrating the new year– is a day of *absolute fasting* called Yom Kippur (the Day of Atonement). *Abstinence from all food and drink*, including water, must be observed from sundown on the eve of the holiday to sundown on the holiday. Pregnant women and people who are ill do not fast. *During Passover*, a commemorative festival in spring which lasts for eight days, *no bread or cake is allowed that uses a raising agent (baking powder/yeast)*. 'Matzo' is unleavened bread which is not allowed to be salted during Passover. Cakes are made using ground matzo or potato flour and egg whites. Matzo can be fried, cooked in oil, or made into pancakes.

ZEN BUDDHISTS –

divide food into 'yin' and 'yang' and balance their diet in this way. This is known as the *Zen Macrobiotic diet*. There are different levels of severity of this diet and the most extreme levels have been known to cause deaths and vitamin deficiencies.

MUSLIMS –

are *forbidden to eat pork* (pig meat) and pork products such as gelatine, sausages and ham. They are *not allowed to drink alcohol* or alcohol products, such as vanilla extract. Any *animals killed to eat, must be prepared using a special religious ritual:* as the blood is drained from the animal, the name of God must be spoken. (Many Muslims use 'Kosher' meat prepared for Jewish people, as this is prepared in a similar way.) *Some food has to be included:* especially olive oil, milk, seafood, dates and honey.

Muslims fast during the month of Ramadan every year – this varies with the lunar calendar. During Ramadan, Muslims fast all day and will eat only twice a day: before the sun rises and after it goes down at night. They are also encouraged to *fast for three days every month* but menstruating, pregnant or lactating women don't have to. Muslims are advised not to eat to capacity and to always share food.

ROMAN CATHOLICS –

are expected to observe the *laws of abstinence on Ash Wednesday and on the Fridays during Lent.* On these days no meat, gravy or soup made from meat can be eaten.

Laws on fasting have changed in recent years and days of fast vary. On days of fast, only one full meal is allowed. Two other light meals without meat can be eaten to maintain strength as necessary. When health or the ability to work would be seriously affected, the laws of fasting do not apply.

SEVENTH DAY ADVENTISTS –

are advised by the church to follow a *vegetarian diet including milk products and eggs,* but may elect not to.

☺ *Discuss these diets with your partner. What facts did you find interesting? Summarise the rules (using the words in italics) for each religion. In groups make a daily menu for either a Muslim or a Jewish patient.*

PATIENTS AND THEIR PROBLEMS

> Doctor Singh and the Ward Charge Nurse are doing their morning round of the patients.
>
> Five patients are describing their problems. Read and listen to the dialogues and then complete the table following the conversations, with the patients' problems and what action will be taken.

🎧 **Listening 24 – Exercise**

Dr Singh:	Good morning, Mr White. How are you today?
Mr White:	I feel much better thank you doctor.
Dr. Singh:	I have the results of you blood tests and I'm afraid your cholesterol levels are much too high. You will have to go on a diet.
Mr. White:	A diet? What sort of a diet? My weight never changes.
Dr. Singh:	It's a special low fat diet – reducing the amount of saturated fats and cholesterol you eat. I will ask the dietician to talk to you and she will tell you what you should eat and what you should avoid. She can help you to plan your meals each day.
Ward Nurse:	Would you like me to telephone the dietician, doctor?
Dr. Singh:	Yes, please – try to get an appointment for this morning.

Doctor Singh:	Good morning, Mr Mane. How are you today?
Mr. Mane:	Good morning, doctor. I'm feeling a little better but I can't 'open my bowels' – I can't go to the toilet. It's been 3 days now since I last went.
Doctor Singh:	I see. I think an enema or a suppository will move things along! I'll ask the nurses to give you a little enema, that should work quite quickly. Walk around more to get some exercise.
Mr. Mane:	Yes, alright. I don't like feeling so full and I can't eat much.

Doctor Singh:	Mr. Smythe, how are you today?
Mr. Smythe:	Not bad doctor, but I am rather depressed and feel weak. I've had a bit of diarrhoea since the nurse gave me a couple of laxatives last night.
Doctor Singh:	That's no good but your bowel needs to be empty before you have the operation and I feel sure it will settle down in an hour or two. You can move around this morning – go outside and get some fresh air. This afternoon you will be given a bowel washout and then you will be quite empty for the operation.
Mr. Smythe:	Well, I might go for a walk, it will pass the time.
Doctor Singh:	Walk around as much as you can but don't go too far away!
Mr. Smythe:	Thank you, doctor.

Doctor Singh: Hello, Mr. Redding. How are you, this fine morning? You're going home this morning, aren't you?

Mr. Redding: Yes, that's right, but my back is really worrying me. I woke up with a really bad backache.

Dr. Singh: I'm sorry to hear that. I'll ask the physiotherapist to see you before you go. You must do some back exercises regularly and as often as you can. You could start swimming a couple of times a week as well. Gentle 'freestyle' will strengthen those weak back and abdominal muscles.

Mr. Redding: Yes, I like swimming, so I'll do that. Thank you doctor. When do I have to see you again?

Dr. Singh: I'd like to see you in 4 weeks – Nurse will make an appointment for you. If you have any problems in the meantime you can ring me on this number...

Doctor Singh: And here's Mrs. Clancy! How are you today?

Mrs Clancy: Good morning, doctor. I'm doing very well now thank you. Nurse helps me with the insulin injections and I'm going to try to do it myself today.

Doctor Singh: Excellent! Did the dietician come to see you?

Mrs. Clancy: Yes, she did. She came yesterday and I've enjoyed the food I've been given so far!

Doctor Singh: That's good. Try to eat everything that you get on the tray and let the nursing staff know if you don't finish. It's important to know how many calories you have in each meal. I'd like you to do a bit more exercise too.

Mrs. Clancy: I want to go to an aerobics class with a friend when I go home – there are classes twice a week.

Doctor Singh: That sounds like the perfect solution! I'll see you again tomorrow and depending on the results of your blood tests, you should be able to go home before the weekend.

Doctor Singh: Good morning, Mrs Steele. The operation went very well and I see that the intravenous is giving you enough to eat!

Mrs Steele: Yes, I'm not hungry at all ... my 'tummy' feels rather uncomfortable. I feel like I want to pass water again but I've just used a bedpan.

Doctor Singh: Let me see ... yes, your bladder is quite distended. Can I see Mrs Steele's 'fluid balance chart', Nurse, please? Thank you. Yes, I thought so ... I think you could pass a catheter, start her on sips of clear fluid. If she tolerates oral fluids then we'll talk about taking out the IV ...... Mrs. Steele, I've just asked nurse to put a tube into your bladder to take away the urine that is making you feel uncomfortable. You can suck on some ice or have sips of water now, and when you are drinking enough we can take out the intravenous.

Mrs Steele: I'd like that, thank you. Will the tube hurt?

Doctor Singh: No, it isn't very pleasant but you will feel much better when your bladder is empty. The tube can come out straight away and you can pass water normally after that. It will be easier for you to go to the bathroom without the intravenous but I want you to use a bedpan so that nurse can see how much urine you are passing.

Mrs Steele: Thank you, doctor.

🎧 Listening *Listen again and using the dialogues, complete the table. Against the name of each patient, write his or her problem and the decisions that were made.*

✎ *What are the problems and what will be done?*

PATIENT	PROBLEM(S)	TREATMENT
e.g. Mr. White	*He's got high blood cholesterol levels*	*He has to start a low cholesterol diet.* *Nurse is ringing the dietician to make appointment.*
Mr. Mane		
Mr. Smythe		
Mr. Redding		
Mrs. Clancy		
Mrs. Steele		

✎ *Now complete the sentences, using the appropriate modal verbs one or more times. Note that all modal verbs are followed by another verb in the infinitive.*

should   can   have to/has to   must   needs to   may/might   will

1. Mr. White .... start a low-cholesterol diet.
2. He .... have more blood tests in a few days.
3. Mr. Mane .... have his bowels open.
4. He .... walk around more to get some exercise.
5. Mr. Smyth .... have a bowel washout.
6. Mr. Redding .... go swimming.
7. He .... do his back exercises regularly.
8. Mrs. Clancy .... give herself insulin injections.
9. She .... do more exercise and .... have a diabetic diet.
10. The nurses .... catheterise Mrs. Steele.

11. The intravenous line .... be removed when she is tolerating fluids.
12. A fluid balance chart .... be filled-in accurately.
13. The amount of urine in a Catheter drainage bag .... be recorded on the fluid balance chart by the person who empties it.
14. The nursing staff .... ask a reliable patient, to keep a record of the fluids he drinks.
15. A patient keeping his own records .... understand how much fluid glasses and cups hold.
16. All records .... be written clearly.

☺ *Now, take turns in making each of the above sentences into questions: e.g.*

Does Mr White have to start a low-cholesterol diet?

Will he have more blood tests in a few days

Yes, he does.

Give 'short answers' to your partner's questions. Can you think of rules for short answer questions?

Yes, he will.

FEEDING PATIENTS

When a patient needs to be fed, it is because he cannot do this for himself. Eating must be an enjoyable experience and not 'rushed' or interrupted. Food should be easily digested and satisfy the patient's needs.

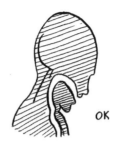

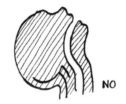

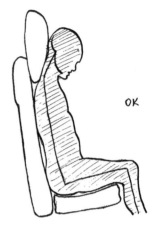

Preparation

- Wash your hands before starting.
- Make sure patients have been to the toilet or had a bed–pan before meals are served.
- Position the patient so that food will travel from the mouth to the oesophagus and not be inhaled causing *choking* or inhalation into the trachea.
- Put a serviette, table napkin or 'bib' under the patient's chin and over his chest to collect any spills.
- Place the tray near the patient so he can see what is on it. Have the tray at the correct, comfortable height for the person doing the feeding.
- If the patient is on a 'special diet' check the chart for any changes and check if there are any medications to be given with food. Also check that the food served corresponds with the doctor's orders.
- If the patient wears dentures (false teeth), check that they in place and are well–fitting!

ABBREVIATIONS USED FOR MEDICATION
a.c. = before food
p.c. = after food

Feeding

Ask the patient what he would like to eat first and describe what you are giving him.

- Cut food into bite–size pieces and place spoonfuls into his mouth, waiting until he has chewed and swallowed before proceeding.
- Some patients prefer to have drinks with their meal and this often helps chewing and swallowing too.
- When giving drinks, use a feeding cup or place the glass firmly on the patient's bottom lip before tilting the glass. Give small mouthfuls at a time.

After the meal

Remove the tray and the serviette or table napkin.

- Clean the patient's teeth or give him mouth care.
- Re–position the patient.
- Remember to fill in the patient's Fluid Balance Chart.

ENTERAL NUTRITION

When a patient needs nutritional supplementation and is unable to take food orally, enteral nutrition may be delivered via.

1. Naso-gastric tube (NG).
2. Naso-enteric tube (naso-duodenal or naso-jejunal).
3. Percutaneous endoscopic gastrostomy tube (PEG).

Indications for enteral nutrition

1. Unconscious patients.
2. Patients who have had head or neck surgery.
3. Patients with physical impairments:
   – CVA (stroke) patients (brain haemorrhage or cerebral vascular occlusion);
   – Patients with fractured maxilla or mandible (jaw);
   – Patients with obstructive lesions of the oesophagus or pharynx.
4. Hyper-metabolic states:
   – Burns victims;
   – Sepsis;
   – Multiple injuries.

Contraindications include

– The ability to eat or drink orally.
– Bowel obstruction.
– Severe mal–absorption.
– Recent small bowel or gastric surgery.
– Intractable vomiting.

Nursing Care

Guidelines must be strictly followed and for further advice contact a dietician or an ICU (Intensive Care Unit) Consultant. Close nursing supervision of all patients supported enterally is of utmost importance.
Confirmation of NG tube position is essential prior to NG feeding. Aspiration of 'gastric contents' or insufflation of air are useful but not always reliable tests. Radiological confirmation of tube position is advisable, especially in comatose or sedated patients.

Patient Monitoring:

1. NG TUBE (ONLY): The residual gastric volume should be assessed daily. NASO-ENTERIC TUBES: Do not aspirate, this may block the tube–flush 4 hourly with 10 ml. Normal Saline.
2. Mouth, skin and nasal care.
3. It is essential that a Fluid Balance Chart be maintained – a daily blood glucose test is advisable.
4. Bowel function. As enteral feeding can change bowel function, all bowel excretions must be recorded.
5. Tube Care: Flush (rinse) 20–50 ml. of water through the tube after feeding, or as directed, to prevent blocking.

Drug Administration through Naso–gastric/Enteric and Gastrostomy tubes

<u>Follow hospital guidelines.</u>
When using an enteral tube for drug administration, the following precautions must be observed:

1. Rinse (flush) the tube with 30–50 ml. of water *BEFORE* and *AFTER* administering any drugs.
2. Don't give non–liquid drugs via a narrow tube.
3. Crush tablets and mix with a little water before syringing through the enteral tube. The pharmacist may be able to suggest liquid medications as an alternative.
4. *NEVER* add medications to the food container or delivery set. Always give them through the enteral feeding tube.
5. Record times of drug administration. If problems develop, the chart can be checked to see if the medication was the cause of the problem.

Blocked feeding tubes

Narrow or 'fine–bore' tubes block more commonly. They can be irrigated (rinsed/flushed) with 15–20 ml. of water or Coca–Cola using a syringe. If this fails, the tube will need to be replaced.

☺ *With a partner, make a list of 'do's' and 'don'ts' for:*

(a) *feeding a conscious patient orally and*
(b) *feeding an unconscious patient enterally*

INTRAVENOUS FEEDING

Patients are given fluids intravenously to maintain normal body functions when it is not possible for them to drink normally and also for a wide variety of other conditions, to correct specific fluid and electrolyte imbalances and also to replace fluids lost in emergency situations.

The most common fluids used are **Normal Saline** *(0.9% sodium chloride),* **Dextrose 5%** *(glucose 5%) and a mixture of these two (usually* **4% glucose and .05% normal saline** *– known as 'four percent and a fifth'). Small amounts of potassium chloride can be added to these fluids to replace this electrolyte which is lost when a patient suffers severe vomiting and diarrhoea. When it is necessary to increase the volume of the plasma with an electrolyte solution equal to that of blood,* **Ringer's lactate solution** *is used. This contains the same concentrations of sodium, calcium, chloride and lactate as the blood. Another solution used is* **25% Serum Albumin,** *which contains five times the normal concentration of the plasma protein albumin and because it is a 'hypotonic' solution it draws fluid from the interstitial spaces between cells back into the circulation.*

Intravenous fluids are administered through a sterile, plastic 'giving set' (made up of tubing, a regulator and needle) A sterile (no–touch technique) procedure is used to insert the needle with the attached tubing into the patient's vein. The prescribed fluid is hung from an IV stand and connected to the tubing and needle. The needle is strapped into position and immobilised to prevent the needle puncturing the vein.

Liquid medication, such as antibiotics, analgesic and anaesthetic drugs can be given into the side–arm of the tubing ensuring that the surface of the side–arm has been disinfected to prevent the introduction of infective organisms. Care must also be taken not to introduce air-bubbles into the vein.

☺ **Discuss the words in blue in the text and add them to your expression and word lists.**

PREPARATION OF FOOD AND RECIPES

Household Appliances and Cooking Utensils

| casserole dish (ovenproof) |
| saucepan |
| pressure cooker |
| wok & chopsticks |
| bowl |
| food processor |
| blender |
| frying pan |
| kettle whistle |
| handle |
| lid |
| spout |

☺ *With your partner, label the pictures using the words in the box. Which of these is an electrical appliance, which do you use in the oven and which do you use on the gas or an electric hot–plate on top of the stove?*

✎ *Now draw the following items.*

a jug   a wooden spoon   a spatula   a whisk   beaters

a vegetable peeler   a lemon squeezer   scissors   a sharp vegetable knife

a strainer (also called a sieve [siv] *or a colander)   a garlic press   a baking tray and cake tin*

☺ *The verbs listed on the right are used for preparing and cooking food. What items above are used and what food goes with them? Can you mime the actions?*

✎ *Make some sentences using your new vocabulary.*

e.g. To fry *potatoes, fish or onions* you use a *frying pan* and *a little oil.*

....
....
....
....
....
....
....
....

| fry |
| crush |
| pour |
| boil |
| roll |
| cut |
| mix |
| beat |
| peel |
| drain |
| slice |
| squeeze |
| bake |
| roast |
| chop |

RECICES

Spinach and Salmon Roulade

This delicate dish can be eaten hot or cold and can be served as a light meal with salad (or sun-dried tomatoes) or as an entrée.

Nutritional information per serve
Protein 20 g.
Fat 6 g.
Carbohydrate 6 g.
Dietary fibre 3 g.
Sodium 285 mg.

It contains: *Vitamin A, Riboflavin (B2), Vitamin C, Calcium, Potassium, Niacin (B3), iron and Folic Acid.*

There are 665 kJ (155 calories) per serve.

INGREDIENTS:
500 g. spinach
50 g. flour
60 g. (2 Tablespoons) skim milk powder
50 g. chopped spring onions
3 eggs – separated
30 g. (1 Tablespoon) wheat-germ
100 g. sliced mushrooms
250 g. cottage cheese or ricotta
220 g. canned red salmon (drain the liquid and discard)
30 g. fresh lemon thyme (herb) and finely grated lemon rind
freshly ground black pepper

1. Place a sheet of baking paper on an oven tray. Preheat oven to 180°C.
2. Cook the chopped spinach by steaming or in the microwave, then purée it in a food procassor.
3. Add the flour, milk powder, spring onions and the egg yolks.
4. Beat the egg whites until they are firm and gently stir them into the spinach mixture.
5. Spread the mixture onto the prepared tray and sprinkle with wheat-germ.
6. Bake for 20 minutes.
7. While the roulade is baking, place mushrooms in a non-stick pan and cook for 3–4 minutes.
8. Beat together the cheese, salmon, thyme, lemon rind, pepper and mushrooms.
9. Turn the roulade out of the tin onto another piece of baking paper.
10. Gently spread the filling over the roulade and roll it up using the paper to help.

Leave to stand for 5 minutes and serve warm, or wrap in the paper and refrigerate to serve cold.

Hummous

This is a middle–eastern dish and popular all over the world as a savoury spread to put on bread or crackers.

It can be used as a 'dip' at parties and fresh vegetables, such as carrots, zucchini, capsicums and cucumber can be cut into straws to dip into this delicious paste.

INGREDIENTS: Chick peas (Ceci) – 1 can or 200 g. of peas that have been soaked and cooked.
60 g. Tahin (sesame seed paste, available from health food shops)
1-2 cloves of crushed garlic (more if desired)
the juice of half a lemon
60 g. Olive oil

1. Drain the chick peas, keeping about half a cup of the liquid.
2. Place all the ingredients together in an electric blender or food processor.
3. Add salt and pepper if desired and blend the ingredients to a smooth, creamy purée. Add the extra liquid from the can slowly, as necessary to get a soft consistency.
4. Arrange on a bed of lettuce and serve with bread, crackers or freshly cut vegetables.

GRAMMAR NOTES

-ing CLAUSES as CONJUNCTIONS

The -ing form used as a conjunction incorporates the idea of an active form of the verb and is therefore interchangeable.

food containing *calcium/iron* [fuːd kənˈteiniŋ-kælsiəm-aiən] (v. conjunction) = *Food which has calcium/iron etc. in it*

A *clause* is part of a sentence. Some sentences have two clauses: *Feeling hungry*, she bought a sandwich. In this sentence, 'she bought a sandwich' is the main clause and 'Feeling hungry' is the -ing clause.

The -ing form can be used (i) when two things happen at the same time or following 'while' or 'when' – the main clause usually comes first, (ii) when one action happens before another action – using Having (done) for the first action, and (iii) to explain something or say why someone did something – the -ing clause usually comes first.

(i) She was sitting up in bed reading a magazine. (= she was sitting and she was reading)
Her daughter broke her arm playing tennis.

(ii) Taking the keys out of his pocket, he unlocked the cupboard.
Having finished the handover, they went home.

(iii) Feeling ill, she went to bed. (= because she felt ill).
Being unemployed, he couldn't pay the phone bill. (= because he is unemployed).

EXPRESSION and WORD LIST

NOUNS

cereal [siəriəl] (*n.*) One of the various types of grass that produce grains that can be eaten or are used to make flour or bread.

chemical [kemikl] (*n.* + *adj.*) A substance obtained by or used in a chemical process.

choice [tʃɔɪs] (*n.*) If there is a choice of things, there are several of them and you can choose the one you want.

colourings [kʌləˈriŋz] (*n.*) Substances that are used to give a particular colour to food.

coma [kəʊˈmə] (*n.*) A deep unconscious state, usually lasting a long time and caused by serious illness or injury.

compost [kɒmˈpɒst] (*n.*) A mixture of decayed plants and food waste (organic material) that can be added to soil to help plants grow.

dehydration [diˈhaiˈdreiʃən] (*n. uncountable*) The loss of too much water from the body.

diet [daiət] (*n.*) **1.** The food that is eaten and drunk regularly. *e.g. How can I improve my diet?* **2.** If a doctor puts so. on a diet, he or she makes them eat a special type or range of foods in order to improve their health.

fat [fæt] (*n. uncountable*) **1.** Fat is the white or yellow, loose connective (adipose) tissue or extra flesh that animals and humans have under their skin, which is used to store energy and to help keep them warm. **2.** Fat is a solid or liquid substance contained in foods such as meat, cheese and butter, and used in cooking, which forms an energy store in your body.

fruit [fru:t] (*n.*) The plural of the noun can be either fruit or fruits, but it is usually fruit. Fruit is something that grows on a tree or bush and which contains seeds or a stone covered by edible flesh.

grain [grein] (*n.*) **1.** A grain of wheat, rice, or other cereal crop is a single seed from it. **2.** Grain is a cereal crop, especially wheat or corn that has been harvested and is used for food or in trade.

guidelines [gaidˈlainz] (*n.*) Guidelines are pieces of advice that an organization or person issues, intended to help you do sth.

hydration – fluid intake [haiˈdreiʃən fluːəd inˈteik] (*n. uncountable*) The absorption of water – the amount of fluids drunk or given.

intake [inteik] (*n.*) Your intake of a particular kind of food, drink, or air, is the amount that you eat or drink or breathe in.

market research [ma:kət ri:sɜ:tʃ] (*n.*) Market Research is the activity of collecting and studying information about what people want, need and buy.

meals [mi:əlz] (*n.*) Meals are the food you eat at breakfast, lunchtime and in the evening.

mouth care [maʊθ keə] (*n.*) Mouth care is the attention to oral hygiene – cleaning the teeth and keeping the mouth (the entire oral cavity) free of debris which can cause a build-up of bacteria and lead to sordes [sɔ:diz] (mouth sores and ulcers).

naso–gastric tube [neizəʊ gæstrik tjuːb] (*n.*) A naso-gastric tube is a sterilised cylindrical tube used to provide nourishment directly into the stomach, or to empty the stomach of its contents. It is passed through the nose into the stomach.

nourishment [nʌriʃmənt] (*n.*) If something provides a person, animal or plant with nourishment, it provides them with the food that is necessary for life, growth and good health.

pasta dishes [pa:stə] or [pæstə diʃəz] (*n.*) Recipes or food prepared using pasta, spaghetti, macaroni, sheets of lasagne pasta etc. are referred to as pasta dishes.

preservative [prəˈzɜ:vətiv] (*n.*) A substance that stops food from decaying (or 'going off!'). *e.g. Some people have adverse reactions to preservatives and colourings in food.*

ready–to–eat / pre–packaged meals [redi tu:(w)i:t pri:ˈpækidʒd mi:əlz] (*adj.* + *n.*) Food for an entire meal that is prepared in large quantities and sold – needs only to be re-heated or eaten from the container.

seeds [si:dz] (*n.*) The small, hard part of a plant from which another plant can grow.

suction [sʌkʃən] (*n. uncountable* + *adj.*) The process of removing air or fluid from something by drawing it out into another space. Gastric suction is used to empty the stomach.

supply of (calcium) [səˈplai] (*n.*) A supply of sth. is an amount of it which so. has or which is available for them to use.

vegetables [vedʒ'təbəlz] (*n.*) Vegetables are plants which you can cook and eat.

vitamins [vitəminz] or [vaitəminz] (*n.*) Natural substances found in food that are essential to health and growth of humans and animals. *e.g. Broccoli is rich in vitamins and cereals are enriched with vitamins.*

NOUNS WITH DEFINING ADJECTIVES

an adequate intake [ən ædəkwət'in'teik] (*adj. + n.*) The taking in or ingestion of enough (fluid or individual food substances) to supply the needs of the body. *e.g. An adequate intake of water and nutrients can be ensured by using intravenous infusions.*

enteral feeding [entərəl fi:diŋ] (*adj. + n.*) Giving nourishment artificially through a tube directly into the stomach, duodenum or jejunum, bypassing the mouth and oesophagus.

fresh fruit [freʃ fru:t] (*adj. + n.*) Fruit that has been picked recently (not preserved, processed or stored for a long period of time.)

gastric tube [gæstrik'tju:b] (*adj. + n.*) A sterilized cylindrical hollow pipe made of soft material (rubber or plastic) with one open end and a closed end with holes in it which is passed through the nose into the stomach using a medical procedure. The open end can be attached to a syringe or an infusion of liquid.

a good supply of (calcium) [ə'gʊd'sʌplai] (*adj. + n.*) A good supply of a substance is an adequate or more than adequate amount.

mouth care [maʊθ keə] (*adj. + n.*) Oral hygiene – cleaning the teeth, gums, tongue and palates to prevent sores developing.

a well-balanced diet [ə wel bælənst daiət] (*adj. + n.*) Food that is eaten regularly and contains all the necessary nutrients that the body needs to stay healthy.

ADJECTIVES

adequate [ædə'kwət] (*adj.*) If something is adequate, there is enough of it or it is good enough to be used or accepted.

cooked [kʊkt] (*adj.*) Food that is cooked, has been heated to prepare it to be eaten.

fresh [freʃ] (*adj.*) Something that is fresh has been produced, done, made, or experienced recently.

frozen [frəʊzən] (*adj.*) Frozen food has been preserved by being kept at a very low temperature.

fussy [fʌsi] (*adj.*) Concerned or worried about usually unimportant details- difficult to please. *e.g. A fussy eater will only eat food that he likes, or which has only been prepared in the way he likes it.*

genetically modified (GM) [dʒə'netikli mɒdə'faid] (*adj.*) Refers to food in which the information in its genes has been changed in some way.

intractable [in'træktəbəl] (*adj.*) A problem that is intractable is very hard to deal with i.e. difficult to solve.

obese [əbi:s] (*adj.*) A medical term to describe people who are so fat that they are unhealthy.

pre–packaged [pri: pækədʒd] (*adj.*) Food that is processed and packed before you buy it.

raw [rɔ:] (*adj.*) Raw food is food that is eaten uncooked, that has not yet been cooked, or that has not been cooked enough.

ready–to–eat [redi tu:(w)i:t] (*adj.*) Food that is ready to eat is pre-cooked or processed. *e.g. 'take-away' food.*

roasted [rəʊstid] (*adj.*) Food which is roasted is baked dry in an oven or over an open fire with oil or fat.

steamed [sti:md] (*adj.*) If food is steamed, it is cooked using steam instead of water.

unconscious/comatose [ʌn'kɒnʃəs kəʊ'mətəʊz] (*adj.*) In a sleep-like state due to injury or illness, not able to use the senses.

visible [vizəbl] (*adj.*) That can be seen.

wholegrain [həʊl'grein] (*adj.*) Made with, or containing whole grains.

wholemeal [həʊl'miəl] (*adj.*) Referring to bread or flour made using whole grains (of wheat) including the husk (the outer covering).

VERBS, AND VERBS AND NOUNS THAT GO TOGETHER

to be <u>allergic to</u> something [ə'lɜːdʒik] (v. + adj.) If you are allergic to sth., or have an allergic reaction to sth., you become ill or get a rash when you eat it, smell it, or touch it. *e.g. I like cats but I'm allergic to them.*

to be <u>interviewed by</u> [intə'vjuːd] (v. + adj.) A formal meeting where questions are asked to make an assessment. *e.g. She was interviewed by a dietician about her dietary habits.*

to be <u>stored in</u> (the liver) [stɔːd] (v.+ n.) When sth. is stored, it is kept in a particular place until it is needed.

to chew (masticate) [tʃuː] [mæstikeit] (v.) When you chew food, you use your teeth to break it up in your mouth so that it becomes easier to swallow.

to choose or to make a choice [tʃuːz tə meikə'tʃɔis] (v. + n.) To decide which thing you want from the number available.

to follow (guidelines) [fɒləʊ] (v.) If you follow something (rules, signs, etc.) you use these to show you which direction to go. To accept the advice or instructions given (in the guidelines) and to do what is expressed in these rules or suggestions.

to irrigate / rinse [irigeit – rins] (v.) Wash (the inside of a tube) with water only.

to plan a diet [plæn ə daiət] (v.+ n.) To make detailed list of foods and quantities of food which can be eaten by a person who needs to change his eating habits.

to preserve something [prə'zɜːv] to make sure that something is kept in optimal condition. *e.g. Sugar, salt, smoking and drying are some methods used to preserve food.*

to provide <u>for somebody / somebody with</u> (vitamins/nourishment) [tə prəvaid vaitəmənz-nʌriʃmənt] (v. + n.) To give somebody the necessary (vitamins/nourishment) needed to live. *e.g. A balanced diet should provide all the necessary vitamins.*

to spot the difference *between* things [spɒt θə difrəns] (v.) If you spot someone or something, you notice them, find things that are not the same by comparing them for a short period of time.

to suck [sʌk] (v.) To take liquid or air into the mouth by using the muscles of the lips and cheeks. *e.g. She wasn't able to suck on the straw, so I gave her the drink using a spoon.*

to swallow [swɒləʊ] (v.) When you swallow sth., you cause it to go from your mouth down into your stomach.

BIBLIOGRAPHY

Anatomy – Charlotte A. Johnston (ASR 1993)

Bournemouth Hospital (UK) Nursing Care Core Plans

Dictionary of Science and Technology – (Chambers 1999)

English for Academic Purposes Series – Medicine – David V. James – (Cassell 1989)

English in Medicine – Eric Glendinning & Beverly Holmstrom (Cambridge University Press 1991)

GCSE Study Guide Human Biology – Morton Jenkins (Letts Educational 1997)

Human Anatomy Colouring Book – Margaret Matt, Joe Ziemian (Dover 1982)

Medical Dictionary – The British Medical Association (DK 2002)

Learner's Dictionary – Collins Cobuild (HarperCollins 1996)

Medical–Surgical Nursing – Luckmann and Sorensen (W.B. Saunders 1974)

Medical Terminology – Andrew R. Hutton (2nd Edition 1999 – Churchill Livingstone)

Medicine – Tony O'Brien + Nursing Science – Rosalie Kerr/Jennifer Smith (Nucleus Series, Longman 1990)

Northern Hospital – Melbourne, Australia – Nursing Care Core Plans

Nursing – Ann Faulkner (2nd Edition 1996 – Chapman & Hall)

Occupational Therapy – Perspectives and Processes – Rosemary Hagedorn – (Churchill Livingstone 1995)

Rosemary Stanton's Healthy Cooking – (Golden Circle – Murdoch 1998)

The Human Body in Health and Disease – Memmler, Cohen and Wood (Lippincott 1996)

The New Oxford Advanced Learner's Dictionary (Oxford 2002)

The Usborne Illustrated Dictionary of Science (Usborne Publishing Ltd. 2001)

ACKNOWLEDGEMENTS

The author wishes to thank the many people whose contributions and constructive suggestions were used to bring this book to fruition. Very special thanks to Claudio Bez for his time and effort in producing the numerous illustrations which enliven the book, Werner Bauhofer for his endless patience during recording and cutting sessions to produce the accompanying CD and to the editors and production staff at McGraw-Hill in Milan.

The author warmly acknowledges the encouragement and support of family, friends, colleagues and well-wishers, without whose contributions this work would not have been possible. To those who so kindly supplied their voices for the CD I am extremely grateful : Claudia, Silvano, Peter and David Dorigotti, Anna Marchant, Mary Adams, Werner and Magdalena, Ulli Oberrauch, Mary Deganello, Fabio Fabbian, Gerard Vitti, Sandra and Glenda Campisi and Nassir Hussein.

APPENDICES

1

LISTENING EXERCISES

UNIT 1

1 – An introduction to a nursing career

Nurse Educator: Today I want to talk to you about your chosen profession. I have loved every minute of my nursing career and I'm sure you will all be caring, dedicated people. You will find the contact with many different types of people rewarding and satisfying because
Nursing is a profession which involves caring and sharing with people from all walks of life.

Care and empathy are illustrated, by each one of us, through communication and actions. A good basic education and professional nursing training are tools for an exciting, interesting and rewarding career.

I can understand why you want to know the reason for English being included in the syllabus when you have so many other new subjects and practical applications to consider.

English can widen your horizons tremendously, help to deepen your scientific knowledge and create many other work–related opportunities. The purpose of this book is to give all those people working in health care systems enough useful English language to read professional literature and to do research and to communicate successfully in English in their everyday lives. Basic grammar exercises, reading practice and dialogues use relevant vocabulary – and there are exercises to help you increase your knowledge of medical terminology too. *Good luck in your studies and have fun learning English – practise at every opportunity!*

2 – Phonetics

Phonetics are an important part of English because your pronunciation needs to be understood for effective communication. Medical terms especially may be written the same in your language but the English pronunciation is often very different. Listen carefully to these frequently used words, to hear the unstressed syllable that contains 'schwa', and check your answers:

doctor – patient – urgent – manager (*did you hear 'schwa' twice?*) – technician – computer – important – cleaner – America (*the first and last vowel sounds are both 'schwa'*) – recovery – practise (*you're right, there is no 'schwa' in the word practise*) – other – experience – foreign (*the word foreign means from another country but something that is foreign to you, is unknown*) – pharmacy

Did you answer correctly? Check the spelling from the list in your book. The next group of words are:

manual – profession – health – communicate – disadvantage – instruction – work.

3a – Countries and Nationalities

Good morning Rosie. Hello Annie! It's nice to meet you... welcome to the best and busiest ward in the hospital! There are four new nurses starting here this week – you're the first! Most of our staff are from different countries. I'm English – I was born in York – Rosie is Australian and Pat is Irish! Dr. Singh is Indian, Mr. James was born in Germany, and where do you come from? ....Oh, South Africa, really! ... It's beautiful there! Where exactly in South Africa?
Practice introducing yourself and your partner to other members in the class.

3b – Exercise

Now listen to the recording and write the correct word used for the nationality of people from that country. Is this word the same one used for the name of the language spoken in that country?

I come from England, or I can say – I'm from England – so, my nationality is English or I'm English (and I speak English!) Dr. Singh comes from India. He's from India He's Indian (from Delhi) Sister Rosie comes from Australia – she's from Australia – so – she's Australian (from Melbourne). *We all speak English at work!*

Correct your answers and check your spelling with the teacher.

Albania – Albanian; Argentina – Argentine; China – Chinese; England – English; France – French; Germany – German; Greece – Greek; Holland or The Netherlands – Dutch; Ireland – Irish; Italy – Italian; Japan – Japanese; Korea – Korean; Portugal – Portuguese; Scotland – Scottish; Spain – Spanish; Switzerland – Swiss; The United States – American; Turkey – Turkish; Wales – Welsh.

Can you name some more Eastern European and South American countries and their nationalities and do you know what language(s) they speak?

4a – At the hospital

Dr. Singh: Good afternoon Mr. James. May I introduce you to Professor Bertolli from Italy?

Prof. Bertolli: How do you do?

Mr. James: How do you do? Welcome to this beautiful country. It's a pleasure to meet you. I'm looking forward to working with you.

Prof. Bertolli: And you. I know you do a lot of research here and I would really like to *meet the staff in the genetics laboratory and also assist you in your work whenever possible…*

4b – In a bar

John: Hello Rosie! Do you know Steve? He's Irish and works in Intensive Care.

Rosie: No, I don't. Hello Steve, it's nice to meet you.

Steve: And you, Rosie. Where are you working Rosie?

Rosie: I'm in Surgical A1 – we're very busy at present but probably not as busy as Intensive Care. Four new nurses are starting this week and I have to show them around the hospital and teach them some procedures. Where are you working now John?

John: I'm in Orthopaedics – it's very interesting and the ward is full at the moment… I'm on night shift this week and it's getting late, so I'll say goodbye and see you tomorrow evening… Look after Rosie, Steve!

4c – In the ward

Sandra: Good morning Rosie. This is Mrs Green who was admitted last night. Mrs Green, this is Rosie, my Australian colleague, and she is going to get you ready for your operation.

Rosie: Good morning Mrs Green. I'm Rosie Kemp and I will be looking after you this morning.

Mrs Green: Hello nurse. Thank you. Do you know if doctor will see me before I have the operation?

Rosie: Yes, he's coming very soon. He's talking to another patient at the moment. Now, first I'd like to take your blood pressure and then you can change into a hospital gown. You mustn't eat or drink anything at all this morning, and your pre-med (the little injection that makes you sleepy) is due at eleven o'clock, *so first I'll take your blood pressure and then you can read for a little while. Pull up the sleeve of your nightgown…*

5 - Can/Can't

1. I *can* use a computer, but I *can't* programme them.
2. He *can't* do this exercise so *can* you help him?
3. When the children *can* swim very well, I want to take them to the seaside.
4. If he *can't* come to the party, I'll have to ask someone else.
5. The new patient *can't* walk unaided – we *can* put him in a wheelchair to go to X/Ray.
6. *Can* you read this? No, I *can't*, the writing's too small.
7. *Can* you open the door a little bit? I like watching the people in the corridor.
8. Jane *can* speak German but her brother *can't*.
9. The doctor's really busy at the moment, but he *can* see you in about 45 minutes. *Can* you wait here? You *can* have a cup of tea from the machine, if you like.
10. Where *can* Steven find some information about that? He looked for a book in the library, but *couldn't* find anything.

6 - In the ward

John: Good evening young lady! I'm looking after you again tonight. Are you feeling a bit better? You don't look very happy!

Cathy: Oh, hello John. Yes, I'm a little better, but my leg still hurts a lot.

John: This tablet is to help the pain and then I'm sure you'll sleep.

Cathy: Thank you. Can I move my leg off the pillow? I want to lie on my side.

John: I can help you turn over on your side, but your leg has to stay on the pillow, O.K.? Your leg will hurt more without it. Hold on to me and I'll help you turn. There you are. Lift up your leg and I'll move the pillow, that's better. Are you comfortable, now?

Cathy: That's much better, thank you – now I can sleep!

John: Good then. I'm going to check on the other patients now, but you can call me if you need anything – just ring the bell!

7 - Exercise

1. The new baby's got a very pretty *face*, large blue eyes, a sweet little nose and a cute mouth. She's gorgeous!
2. Anna's got such a long *neck*, *her* head seems a long way from *her* shoulders – She looks like a top model!
3. Mr. Gladstone has the injections in the gluteus maximus muscle – in *his buttocks* – you have to alternate sides!
4. My son has very big *feet* and has trouble finding comfortable shoes, he prefers to wear trainers or gym shoes.
5. Mrs. Mills has rheumatoid arthritis in *her hands*, she can't do up the buttons on her dressing gown. Can you help her?
6. A pulse or heart beat can be felt on a patient's *wrist*, over the carotid artery and over the temporal artery in front of the ear.
7. Physiotherapists encourage people to have good posture and to keep *their backs* straight whenever possible, most people suffer from back-ache, and nurses more than others.
8. We all have 4 *fingers* on each hand and 1 *thumb* but the digits on the feet are *toes* and we number them from the big toe to the little toe!
9. A footprint in the sand shows the *sole of the foot* including the *toes* and the *heel*. If someone has 'flat feet' you can see the 'fallen arches' in the footprint!
10. A newborn baby's *umbilicus* (or navel) doesn't form until the remaining umbilical cord atrophies or dies, and falls off. This doesn't happen for a couple of weeks and it is better to keep the area clean and dry.

8a - In the ward

Sister Joanna: Hello again Cathy, Mrs Manson. This is Nurse Margaret, she is helping me today and would like to stay while I ask you a few questions – is that all right?

Mrs Manson:	Good morning nurse. Yes of course – <u>you don't mind, do you</u> Cathy?
Cathy:	No, of course not. Hello nurse Margaret. Are you new here?
Nurse Margaret:	Yes, I'm still doing my nursing training – <u>You can call me Maggie, everyone else does</u>!
Sister Joanna:	So, now we have a few things to write down here. First, <u>I'd like to check</u> that I have your full name and address: Is this all correct Mrs Manson? (*Sister shows the admission chart to Mrs Manson*)
Mrs Manson:	Yes, that's fine. Perhaps I should write my husband's work telephone number too.
Sister Joanna:	That's a good idea, thank you. Now, <u>I'll take</u> Cathy's blood pressure and temperature. <u>Let's</u> put the thermometer under your arm ...that's it. Now give me your other arm and I'll wrap this cuff around it to take your blood pressure. Don't talk while I'm taking it, I won't be able to hear you! It might feel tight, but it won't hurt and I'll be quick! ...That's fine. Do you know how much you weigh, and how tall you are Cathy?
Cathy:	Not really – about 46 kilograms, I think. Mum says I've grown recently!
Sister Joanna:	Doctor will want to know exactly, so Maggie will take you to the scales and we can see how much you weigh and measure your height at the same time. Thank you Maggie ... see you shortly ... (*Maggie takes Cathy out of the room*). Mrs Manson, does Cathy wear glasses, or contact lenses?
Mrs Manson:	No, her eyesight's very goo She's a healthy girl and rar gets sick. She has never had an operation before, so she's a bit nervous about it.
Sister Joanna:	The anaesthetist will come round and talk to her soon, he's an excellent doctor and very good with young people. She won't be nervous for long! ... Here they are!

8b (*Maggie and Cathy come back into the room*)

Sister Joanna:	Thank you Maggie ... I'll write those here ... OK. (*She writes Cathy's weight and height on the chart*) Did you have breakfast this morning, Cathy?
Cathy:	No, I haven't eaten anything since last night. I'm not really hungry though.
Sister Joanna:	Do you eat well, Cathy? Can you eat everything?
Cathy:	Yes, ask Mum! *I eat like a horse!* I love rice and vegetables and chocolate, and ice-cream. I don't like tropical fruit very much – paw-paws and mangoes, but I love pineapple! I think *I'm allergic to* nuts.
Sister Joanna:	Oh! That's important. What happens when you eat them? What sort of reaction do you have?
Cathy:	My *skin gets itchy* and sometimes my eyes *get all puffy*.
Sister Joanna:	That's no good! I'll write down that you have this reaction to nuts. Tomorrow we can look at the diet cards and choose something nice for you (without nuts!) – I'm sure you'll be hungry by then. You

mustn't have anything to eat or drink until we tell you – and that means no chewing gum or sweets either! (*Your tummy has to be quite empty* when you have an anaesthetic.) Do you have any valuables – jewellery or money, that you would like me to put in the safe until after the operation?

Cathy: Yes, I have this necklace and my purse is in the drawer ... oh, and there's my watch too.

Sister Joanna: OK. I'll put them away now, and when I come back, I'll bring *a hospital gown* for you *to put on.* You will have *to get undressed* and change into a rather inelegant hospital gown! First, because I'm taking your precious things away, I'll get you to sign this form ... Here, that's right. I can see you have a Walkman too, maybe that should be put away ...mm..., we'll take that later. That's all for now. The doctor will call in very soon and I'll be back in about an hour or so. If you need anything, *this is the call bell – press this button and a nurse will come.* You can use that bathroom – make yourselves comfortable.

Cathy Thank you. Do you need anything Mum?

Mrs Manson: No, love. Thank you Sister ... and Maggie. We will just chat until the doctor comes....

9 – Time expressions

1. This patient can go home in three days.
2. This patient has been in a coma for six months.
3. Her baby is due in five weeks.
4. His appointment in Outpatients' is in ten days time.
5. This patient has had a high temperature for about a week, we don't know why at the moment.
6. The IV is to run continuously for 6 hours, then check for new orders.
7. The Gastric feeds are two-hourly (on even hours) and the tube must be aspirated every 4 hours.
8. The new patient has to be turned every 2 hours – and needs to have pressure area care.
9. Patients usually fast for at least six hours before having an operation – they cannot eat or drink anything.
10. Baby Marks, I think his name is Joseph, is two–months old – he was admitted here three days ago.

10 – Handover

Rosie: At Handover the night staff tell us about the patients and report any changes in their condition or any changes in doctor's orders. We have to record all the observations, treatment, IV's, drainage tubes or indwelling catheters (IDCs) and naturally, whether they are pre-operative or post–operative patients.

Annie: Yes, I see.

Rosie: All of this is recorded on the patient's history and care plan and with practice you will know what is important and relevant.

Annie: I hope so!

Rosie: As soon as the handover is finished, we do a Round of the patients, this is often called a Sight check. We just say hello to all of the patients in our care and check IV's, wound drainage tubes and urinary catheter tubes. Before 8 o'clock we do the 'general obs' which include: temperature, pulse, respirations and blood pressure – and give out any medications that are due. We have to check that patients who are going to theatre (the pre-operative patients) are ready: check that they are fasting and that the area for surgery has been shaved and is free from hair (if necessary). If any of the ladies are wearing nail polish, it has to be taken off from both the fingernails and the toenails because the anaesthetist will want to check the natural colour of the finger–tips and toes.

Annie: Oh, I didn't know that.

Rosie: There really is a lot to remember for patients going to theatre. It's also very important to ask if the patient has any false teeth, contact lenses or other prostheses that should be kept safety in the ward and recorded on the patient's chart.

Annie: Yes, of course.

Rosie: The breakfasts arrive at about 8 and some patients need help or have to be fed because they are unable to feed themselves. You could feed dear old Mrs Simpson this morning, she is almost totally blind but she is a real sweetheart!

Annie: Yes, thank you – I'd like to do that.

Rosie: At about half past 9, we do the Doctors' Rounds and the staff try to have a 15 minute break when possible. We have to organise our breaks so that there are enough trained staff in the ward at all times.

Annie: That's good! There seems to be so much happening all the time!

Rosie: Yes, it is always busy here. At 10 it's back to the paperwork! Try to do your 'nursing notes' and updates whenever you have a spare moment – you can always add to them during the day. The patients' midday meals arrive around 12. Check that patients are prepared to eat – and remember that for diabetics, you have to check their BSL's (their blood sugar levels) – and give insulin if

necessary, or other medications that should be taken with food. We don't have any diabetics here at the moment but it's important to remember the BSL's especially pre and post op. When we come back from lunch we re-check all our patients' charts and notes. The Hand–over to the evening staff is at 2. When you are in charge of the ward and have the keys, make sure that the evening staff take them – it's a real nuisance to be half-way home and feel them rattling in your pocket! Well, that's about it Annie and it's time we got started, you can stay with me today... We'll start in Room 4 and you can help Mrs Simpson with her breakfast ...

11a – Public health

Why is it necessary to have health campaigns?

1. – Campaigns are used to *discourage or prevent* the general public *from smoking and to ensure they are well–informed.*
   – Yes, young people often refuse to listen to their parents and usually want to do the same things their friends do.

2. – You can *make it easier for* your friends *to talk* to you by being a 'good listener'.
   – My friend has *tried to talk* and listen to her husband – he's at work every evening till very late:

3. She can't *stop or prevent* her husband *from working* long hours, but she is *encouraging* him *to do* more exercise at the weekends.

Public health education isn't easy but …

4. Nurses can *help* patients *to be* as independent as possible, *allowing* them *to build up* their self-confidence *and*

5. To *save* people *from having* heart attacks, doctors often *discourage* them *from smoking* and *encourage* them *to participate* in a more

active lifestyle and advise them to change their dietary habits.

6. You can't *force* people *to change*, so sometimes it is necessary to *allow* them *to make* their own decisions.

11b – Smoking

In most countries cigarette packets are now labelled with warnings, but these don't seem to discourage people from smoking. Addiction is a hard habit to break. Do young people start smoking to impress their friends? Are they copying someone they admire? Do they know what they are doing to their bodies? Perhaps lung cancer, throat cancer, stomach cancer, emphysema, chronic bronchitis, asthma and other respiratory problems are only words without significance, until the problems start.

12 – Pain

Doctor: "Nurse told me you didn't get much sleep last night. You had a lot of pain, so tell me *where does it hurt?*"

Patient: "I don't know really, doctor ... quite a lot here and my legs seemed to be aching all night"

Doctor: *"Have you got any pain in your chest?"*

Patient: No, not really – I just can't make myself comfortable. I don't like being in bed all the time.

Doctor: "When you breathe deeply, *is it painful anywhere?*"

Patient: "Yes, a little in my chest but here, *in the back of my leg, it's very sore.*

Doctor: "I see, mmm, *let me look at your wound* I'll just take the dressing off first. That's fine – it's a little inflamed, but that's quite normal. It's O.K. Don't touch it before nurse puts another dressing over it. I'd like to see you moving around a bit more – and I'll order a couple of

blood tests. Maybe we'll have a look at your legs with an ultrasound scan and it would be a good idea to have a chest X/Ray too. I'll give you something stronger for the pain and that should help you to sleep better tonight...

UNIT 2

13 – Julie and Mark at home

Julie: Hello, Love! *Did you have a good day* at school?

Mark: Yes, very good really. Most of the students *got good marks* in the maths test ... and guess what? We're invited to a holiday break-up dinner in the mountains *the weekend after next*.

Julie: Oh no! ... but I'm afraid *we won't be able to go* to the dinner. Mr. Burns' rooms rang today and they told me you can have the operation on Wednesday afternoon but you *have to go into hospital* on Monday morning at 8.30.

Mark: Oh, next week – that's a pity! Bad timing I suppose but *the sooner this is over the better*. I wonder what it will be like? I'll tell the staff tomorrow to take our names off the list. I'll have to ask someone to do my lessons next week. There are a couple of relief teachers available, I think. I understood the operation would be in 2 weeks – never mind.

Julie: It'll be fine, I'm sure. You should ring your parents and your sisters to let them know that *you have a definite date* for the operation. What do you think you need to take with you?

Mark: Not much really. I'd like to take a couple of books to read and probably two *or three pairs of pyjamas*, slippers, dressing gown and toiletries – I can't think of anything else. I'll take my CD player and a few disks too. The music has a calming effect.

Julie: Yes, OK. Don't forget to take the *MRI scan and the results of the blood tests*.

Mark: I'll put those in a bag now and I'll pack at the weekend. Will the operation be in the afternoon?

Julie: I don't really know, Mr. Burns' secretary didn't tell me, but I can ring tomorrow and ask her. I'll stay all day but I'm sure you'll have lots of beautiful nurses to tell you what to do and to *keep you company!*

Mark: I hadn't thought of that – but I'll probably be feeling so rotten *I won't notice!*

Julie: They'll look after you very well I'm sure. You probably won't be able to get out of bed for a couple of days and I'll come in as often as possible so don't worry. Let's go and *have a bite to eat…*

14 – Mark arrives at the hospital

Sister Pat: This is your room Mark – number 612. You will be on your own for a couple of days so you can choose the bed near the window or this one near the bathroom. …Hello Mary, this is Mark Andrews and his wife Julie.

Mary: Good morning Mr and Mrs Andrews. Can I get you a bottle of water and a glass?

Sister Pat: Thank you Mary, but Mark is having more tests today and can't have anything to eat or drink until later… Mary is a wonderful help and will help us to look after you Mark.

Mark: Thank you. I'd like to have the bed near the window if that's all right.

Sister Pat: Yes, of course. I'll leave you to change into your pyjamas and hop into bed – and then I'll come back in a few minutes to ask you a few questions. You can put your clothes in the cupboard on the left, but it isn't very big, so it's probably a good idea to take the suitcase home with you, Mrs Andrews… Mark, you can put the things you need in the cupboard near the bed.

Mark: Yes, thank you. Jules will take the case with her when she goes – you've got the car love, so that's no problem, is it? Can my wife stay here this morning, Sister?

Sister Pat: Yes, that's fine. I'll come back to speak to you both very soon… This is the handset, if you need anything just call. This button is the buzzer, and this one is to cancel your call (the light over the door turns off). This one is for the overhead light… OK?

15 – Changing bed sheets

Pat: First Annie, ask Mark if he has finished, if he shaved and if he was able to wash his private parts, legs and feet.

Annie: Did you shave, Mark? Oh, yes! I can see that you have – I'll take this little bowl away. Now, did you wash your legs and feet?

Mark: Yes, pretty well I think. I can move fairly easily this morning.

Pat: Good, Annie. Explain that you would like to wash his back and that he needs to turn onto his side.

Annie: Put your arm over to hold onto the edge of the bed and I'll help you onto your side, that's fine! Move your bottom over a bit more. That's good – are you comfortable? I'm going to wash your back and give you a little massage … Now, I'll just dry your back … OK … You can put this arm into your pyjama jacket and we'll put it on properly when you're sitting up. That's it.

Pat: While he is lying on his side and when you have finished washing his back, roll the soiled sheet up length-ways along Mark's back, take the clean bottom sheet and tuck the top and bottom corners neatly under the mattress, rolling the other half lengthways next to the soiled sheets. Here is the clean sheet ... *that's fine – nice neat corners!* Pull back the mackintosh towards you and take a 'draw sheet' or 'half-sheet' and place it over the plastic sheet, tucking the end of both sheets under the mattress. (Some hospitals use a kylie which is a disposable '2 in 1' waterproof sheet)

Annie: That's right, isn't it?

Pat: Yes, good. Next, help Mark to turn back to the other side, rolling over the pile of bed linen in the middle of the bed. Make sure he is comfortable lying on the other side and holding the side of the mattress if he needs to. His clean pyjamas are in the bedside locker, we'll dress him together...

Annie: I'll hold you, like this, Mark – now roll back towards me. That's fine. Hold onto this side of the bed now while I finish the other side. These soiled sheets go here in the linen bag and I've finished this side so you can lie on your back now Mark. Now, put that arm in here – this is the other sleeve. Right! Now we can put your trousers on ... first leg ... OK ... second leg ... lift up ... that's fine! and Pat will help me sit you up for breakfast.

Pat: Get a fresh top sheet off the trolley. That's it. We'll sit Mark up for breakfast, put on the top sheet and tuck it in at the bottom (mitred corners again) and then the blanket and the quilt.

Mark: Thank you ladies! I feel much better now – almost human!

Pat: You can take the trolley, Tony, we've finished in this room...

16 – Pronunciation Exercise: Minimal Pairs

Exercise 1

(a)	(day)	die	wide
(b)	walk	short	(work)
(c)	(sit)	seat	sheet
(d)	halve	(have)	part
(e)	(look)	lock	drop
(f)	cleans	please	(pins)
(g)	good	book	(food)

Exercise 2

She can *walk* when she goes home
Seat his relatives in the day room.
He can have *halve* his medication.
Lock the drug cupboard.
The title of the essay is *"To Die – In Peace"*.

UNIT 3

17 – Body systems

1. The Skeletal system consists of bones, cartilage, and ligaments. The two main divisions of this system are the axial skeleton and the appendicular skeleton. The various joints (or articulations) are also included.

2. The Muscular System is made up of 3 types of muscle: skeletal muscle and the tendons, cardiac and smooth muscles. Skeletal muscle is voluntary muscle and both cardiac and smooth muscles are involuntary muscle.

3. The Circulatory System is made up of the main organ, the heart and all the blood vessels which include the arteries, the veins and the capillaries.

4. The Respiratory system consists of the lungs and the air passages. The air passages (starting from the outside) include the nasal passages, the uvula and the pharynx (which is made up of the naso–pharynx, the oro–pharynx and the laryngo–pharynx), the larynx, the trachea, the two bronchi and the

left and right lungs, which consist of the bronchioles and the alveoli or air sacs, where the exchange of gases takes place.

5. The Nervous System is our body's communication network. The two major divisions of this system are the Central Nervous System (the CNS) and the Peripheral Nervous System (the PNS). The brain, brain stem and the spinal cord (which is actually continuous with brain but occupies a canal within the vertebral column) are the parts which make up the CNS. The nerves consist of the basic structural and functional component of the nervous system called "neurons" or nerve cells, and their fibres, which may be either "dendrites" or "axons". Neurons are divided into two major types: either "sensory" or "afferent" and "motor" or "efferent". Neurons communicate by means of electrical charges and chemical reactions called nerve impulses.

6. The Digestive System is made up of the mouth (including the tongue and the palate), the epiglottis or uvula, the pharynx, the oesophagus, the stomach, and the intestines (often referred to as the "bowel"). Parts of this system are sometimes referred to as 'the gut'. The Accessory organs of digestion are the teeth, the salivary glands, the liver, the gallbladder, and the pancreas.

7. The Excretory System (or the Urinary System) is composed of two kidneys, which lie behind the peritoneum and on either side of the vertebral column, extending from the twelfth thoracic vertebra (T12) down to the level of the third lumbar vertebra (L3). Each kidney is drained by a ureter which is a tube extending from the hilum of the kidney to the urinary bladder. The bladder is an elastic reservoir for urine and it can hold up to 600 millilitres of fluid. The single opening from the base of the bladder is the urethra and it extends to the external orifice, a distance of about 20 cm in a male and about 3 cm in the female.

8. The Reproductive System. Males and Females both have "gonads" that produce sex hormones and reproductive cells. Each structure in the system has a special function and all must function properly for reproduction to take place. The structures in the Male are the testes and their associated ducts, the seminal vesicles, the Prostate gland, and the Penis. In the Female, the gonads are the ovaries from where the ova travel down the Fallopian tubes or oviducts, into the uterus. If an ovum is not fertilised it exits the body through the vagina and vaginal orifice. The breasts are included as primary organs of the female reproductive system.

9. The Endocrine System consists of ductless Glands throughout the body: The Pituitary gland (also known as the Hypophysis) and the Pineal gland in the brain, the Thyroid and Parathyroid glands, the Thymus, the Adrenal glands, the Pancreas, and the gonads, the Ovaries and Testes are all parts of this system.

10. The Lymphatic System consists of lymph vessels and their valves and the lymph nodes, of which the tonsils and adenoids are well-known examples. Because the Lymphatic System is closely associated with the cardiovascular system and follows approximately the same course through the body, resembling the veins in structure, this system is frequently studied under the heading of the Circulatory System.

11. The Integumentary System is best known as "Skin" but is actually a most important system consisting of the epidermis, dermis, sebaceous glands (the oil–producing glands), and the sudoriferous or (sweat–producing) glands – as well as the hair follicles and the nails. It is the most visible system of the body. The skin has many functions and acts as a receptor for the special senses of 'touch' and 'pain' through its vast network of nerve endings. It is an amazing structure which can re–new itself, it can change in size (dramatically during pregnancy) and also with a loss or gain in weight. It plays a part in sexual attraction and can provide personal identification with the use of fingerprints.

18 – Exercise

To label diagram two, write down the following directions checking the names of the different regions in the box in your book.

To locate the different abdominal organs more accurately, it is helpful to divide the abdomen into nine anatomic regions. Two imaginary transverse planes and two saggital or 'longitudinal' planes make these divisions. Firstly, the three medial divisions are: the Epigastric Region (under the xiphoid sternum), the Umbilical Region (around the umbilicus) and the Hypogastric, (Pelvic or Supra–Pubic) Region. The upper, lateral regions are the Left and Right Hypochondriac Regions. The lateral divisions on either side of the Umbilical Regions are called the Left and Right Lateral (or Lumbar) Regions. The lower lateral divisions are the Left and Right Iliac (or Inguinal) regions.

19 – The skeletal system

1. The adult skeleton is made up of *206* individual bones.
2. Bones are a 'storehouse' for *calcium and phosphorous.*
3. What are the functions of the skeletal system? *To give the body its shape, to support the body and to protect all the delicate internal organs. The skeleton also provides places for the attachment of muscles and the bones, and act as levers to provide movement of skeletal muscles.*
4. List the 5 classifications of bone: *long bones* e.g. humerus, ulna, femur; *short bones* e.g. wrist & ankle bones; *flat bones* e.g. ribs, sternum, scapulae; *irregular bones* e.g. vertebrae, face bones; *sesamoid bones* are small bones which form in tendons, such as the patella.
5. A long bone is divided into the shaft or *diaphysis* and the two ends which are called the *ephyphyses* – the proximal epiphysis and the distal epiphysis.
6. The two main types of bone tissue are *hard (or compact)* bone and *cancellous (or spongy)* bone.

7. The two main divisions of the skeleton are the *axial skeleton,* (the skull, the bony thorax and the vertebral column), and the *appendicular skeleton* (which includes the shoulder girdle: the clavicle and scapula and the bones of the arms, and the pelvic girdle or pelvis and the bones of the legs).
8. The bones of the thorax include the *12 pairs of ribs,* the *12 thoracic vertebrae* and the *sternum.*
9. *In the foetus* the transformation of cartilage into bone begins *at the centre of the diaphysis,* but later, *secondary bone–forming centres develop across the ends (or epiphyses).* The long bones continue to grow at these centres throughout childhood and until about 20 years of age. The bone–forming regions eventually harden and can be seen as a thin line on X/Rays.
10. The two bones of the vertebral column that are made up of fused vertebrae, are the *sacrum* and the *coccyx.*

20 – Joints

Picture (a) shows *the elbow joint,* where the humerus meets the radius and ulna. This joint is *fully moveable* but only allows movement in one direction – it is capable of abduction (movement towards the body) and adduction (or movement away from the body – like a *hinge* on a door that allows opening and closing. It is a *synovial joint,* protected by a synovial capsule of connective tissue, and the bones are protected by a smooth layer of articular cartilage. So, although most people refer to their elbow, it is called: *a synovial joint (a freely–moveable joint or diarthrosis) or a hinge–joint* which describes the type of movement.

Picture (b) shows the *symphysis pubis* which connects the two anterior sides of the hip bones of the pelvis. It consists entirely of cartilage and softens during pregnancy, enlarging the pelvic cavity and allowing room for the foetus to grow. This type of joint can be called a *cartilaginous joint, a slightly moveable joint* or in medical circles, it is called *an amphiarthrosis.*

Picture (c) is the *knee* joint. It is also a *synovial joint*. It is basically also a *hinge* joint but has some properties of a *gliding* joint too. Can you write the medical term for a freely-moving synovial joint?

Picture (d) shows a rather different type of joint. There is no movement at this joint, that is, it is *immoveable*, (except in the foetus before the "*suture line*" hardens and becomes fibrous) but because it is the joining, or meeting, of two or more bones together, it is called a *fibrous* joint. The cranial bones of the skull are the best example of *immovable, fibrous joints*, called *Synarthroses* by the medical profession.

21 – Idiomatic Expressions

1. I thought she was very lazy until yesterday – she'd finished everything when I arrived – it was a real *eye–opener*!
2. My friend decided to study art, she said she *couldn't stomach* nursing or medicine!
3. Can you *give me a hand* to turn Mr. Biggs and attend to his pressure areas?
4. He got *cold feet* about going to the doctor, saying that it really wasn't necessary.
5. I may be *sticking my neck out*, I know it's taking a risk but I really have to do it.
6. Take each day as it comes, you are making good progress. You *can take heart* in these results!
7. That was an unnecessary thing to say, he was most offended. You are always *putting your foot in your mouth*!
8. Martin lied about his qualifications and will lose his job – he just *doesn't use his head*.
9. When the boss discovered the lie and called him to the office, he accused Martin of *pulling the wool over his eyes*!
10. When I have a problem, I think about it, work out a solution then *keep my fingers crossed*!
11. When Lisa heard that her friend was nauseated nearly every morning and guessed that she was pregnant, she had *hit the nail on the head*!

12. Michael's son had an accident when driving the family car home from a party. Michael *lost his head* when he found out that his son had been drinking.
13. Annette *paid lip service* to the group's holiday plans but later decided to have a different holiday with her boyfriend.
14. After making this decision, everyone in the group *gave her the cold shoulder*, they didn't speak to her for months.
15. I don't know if my friends can *put me up* when I go to London, so I'll just *play it by ear*. I can probably find a cheap 'bed and breakfast' if they don't have enough room.

UNIT 4

22 –The healthy diet pyramid

A well–balanced diet is simple – nothing is forbidden but some foods need a higher profile than others. Because it is the total intake that matters it is important to eat healthily most of the time with only an occasional indulgence. If you continue to eat 'junk food' or regularly eat things that are not 'healthy', your body will react badly.

For more than 10 years, this pyramid has given people an idea about 'good food' to include in their daily diets.

A new pyramid that has evolved, includes plant oils such as olive oil, canola, soy, corn, sunflower and peanut oils in the base of the pyramid and recommends that these be used at most meals. These vegetable or plant oils, as well as fish actually raise HDL levels and reduce LDL cholesterol levels, decreasing the ration of LDL or "bad cholesterol" to HDL or "good cholesterol". The message now is that not all fats are bad and not all carbohydrates are good. Studies have shown that people who eat a lot of mono-saturated and poly–unsaturated fat tend to have lower rates of heart disease. By including fish in the base of the pyramid and taking out white bread and white rice, the pyramid is much more acceptable and includes good sources of protein.

Fruit and vegetables should be eaten in abundance and more than 5 different types per day are recommended. Grains, wholemeal breads, wholegrain cereals, fruit, vegetables, nuts and legumes are important sources of energy – giving carbohydrate – and everything in this group, except seafood, is a good source of dietary fibre.

The 'new' pyramid still includes chicken, turkey and eggs in the middle section, although milk products – also called dairy products – including yoghurt and cheese, are slightly closer to the top – that is, they do not need to be included every day and if they are, then a maximum of only 2 servings. These are all important sources of protein, vitamins and minerals and except for dairy products, they are good sources of iron and zinc. Dairy products are a most important source of calcium but it is much healthier to take a calcium supplement than to overload on dairy products. Low–fat products are now available and it is worthwhile to substitute full-fat products with skim milk (milk with the fat taken out) and low fat cheese and yoghurt.

The two smaller sections at the top of the 'new' pyramid now include red meat and butter and processed and prepared food which contains excessive amounts of sugar, animal fat and salt. Naturally, sweets, white pasta, white rice, white bread and potatoes are now in the 'eat least' group! None of these are foods are necessary for a healthy diet as all the nutrients necessary are supplied naturally in the food in the bottom half of the pyramid and are now in the 'eat least' group.

23 – The digestive system

The primary organs of digestion are the mouth, the tongue and palates – hard and soft (the roof of the mouth), the pharynx, the oesophagus, the stomach and the large and the small intestines Food is ingested, chewed and softened in the mouth and then swallowed. The muscular soft palate and the attached uvula move upwards closing the entrance to the nasal cavities and trachea and food passes into the oesophagus.

The oesophagus is shown at the top of picture 4 and passes through the muscular diaphragm that separates the thoracic cavity from the abdominal cavity.

Peristalsis starts in the oesophagus and continues in the stomach and in the intestines. The stomach is a bag-like organ with muscular rings at the openings called *sphincters*

The stomach is also shown in picture 4 and picture 2 shows the sphincters and the duodenum.

Food enters the stomach from the oesophagus through the *lower oesophageal sphincter* (or the *cardiac sphincter*) and leaves the stomach to pass into the small intestine through the *pyloric sphincter*. The first part of the small intestine is the *duodenum*, and both the *pancreatic duct and the bile duct have openings into the duodenum.*

Have you labelled all of picture 2? Now, looking at picture 4 again label the parts of the small intestine – also known as the small bowel, and the parts of the large intestine (or large bowel).

The duodenum measures about 25 cm and the following *jejunum* is about 2 and a half metres long. With the lower section, the *ileum*, the small intestine measures over 6 metres! The large intestine is larger in diameter than the small intestine, but smaller in length, about one and a half metres long. The large intestine consists of the *caecum* the *colon* and the *rectum*.

The appendix is the small appendage on the lower posterior portion of the caecum. The part of the large intestine on the left in picture 4, is called the ascending colon; the transverse colon; joins the ascending and the descending colon and the lower portion of the descending colon is the rectum. Behind the fundus of the stomach in pictures 3 and 4, you can see the spleen (situated below the diaphragm and on the left side of our bodies.) The spleen is not part of the digestive system but is in close contact with the organs of digestion.

Now look at picture 6 and label the parts of the large intestine.

Picture 1 shows the lower portion of the large bowel, starting with the <u>descending colon</u>, <u>the rectum</u> and <u>rectal valves</u> and the muscular sphincter of <u>the anus</u>.

You can label the liver and <u>the gallbladder</u> on diagram 4, <u>the pancreas</u> on diagrams 3 and 5, and the gallbladder again on diagrams 5. You can also label <u>the common bile duct</u> and <u>the cystic duct</u> (from the pancreas) on diagram 5.

The liver is the largest gland in the body. It is a vital organ with many important functions. It secretes *bile* (that is important in the digestion of fats), stores glucose, forms blood plasma proteins (albumin, globulin and clotting factors), it synthesises *urea* (a waste product of protein metabolism), destroys old red blood cells, stores some vitamins and iron and removes or 'de-toxifies' poisonous substances such as drugs or alcohol. The pancreas is both an endocrine and an exocrine gland. The pancreas produces *insulin* which controls carbohydrate metabolism.

24 – Exercise

1.

Dr Singh: Good morning, Mr White. How are you today?

Mr White: I feel much better thank you doctor.

Dr. Singh: I have the results of your blood tests and I'm afraid your cholesterol levels are much too high. You will have to go on a diet.

Mr. White: A diet? What sort of a diet? My weight never changes.

Dr. Singh: It's a special low fat diet – reducing the amount of saturated fats and cholesterol you eat. I will ask the dietician to talk to you and she will tell you what you should eat and what you should avoid. She can help you to plan your meals each day.

Ward Nurse: Would you like me to telephone the dietician, doctor?

Dr. Singh: Yes, please – try to get an appointment for this morning.

2.

Doctor Singh: Good morning, Mr Mane. How are you today?

Mr. Mane: Good morning, doctor. I feel a little better but I can't 'open my bowels' – I can't go to the toilet. It's been 3 days now since I last went!

Doctor Singh: I see. I think an enema or a suppository will move things along! I'll ask the nurse to give you a little enema, that should work quite quickly... Walk around more to get some exercise – and have a drink every couple of hours, it's important to increase your fluid intake too.

Mr. Mane: Yes, alright. I don't like feeling so full... and I can't eat much.

3.

Doctor Singh: Mr. Smythe, how are you today?

Mr. Smythe: Not bad doctor, but I'm rather depressed and feel weak. I've had a bit of diarrhoea since the nurse gave me a couple of laxatives last night.

Doctor Singh: That's no good but your bowel needs to be empty before you have the operation and I feel sure it will settle down in an hour or two. You can move around this morning – go outside and get some fresh air. This afternoon you will be given a bowel washout and then you will be quite empty for the operation.

Mr. Smythe: Well, I might go for a walk, it will pass the time.

Doctor Singh: Walk around as much as you can but don't go too far away!

Mr. Smythe: Thank you, doctor.

4.

Doctor Singh: Hello, Mr. Redding. How are you, this fine morning? You're going home this morning, aren't you?

Mr. Redding: Yes, that's right, but my back is really worrying me. I woke up with a really bad backache.

Dr. Singh: I'm sorry to hear that. I'll ask the physiotherapist to see you before you go. You must do some back exercises regularly and as often as you can. You could start swimming a couple of times a week as well. Gentle 'freestyle' will strengthen those weak back and abdominal muscles.

Mr. Redding: Yes, I like swimming, so I'll do that. Thank you doctor. When do I have to see you again?

Dr. Singh: I'd like to see you in 4 weeks – Nurse will make an appointment for you. If you have any problems in the meantime you can ring me on this number...

5.

Doctor Singh: And here's Mrs. Clancy! How are you today?

Mrs Clancy: Good morning, doctor. I'm doing very well now thank you. Nurse helps me with the insulin injections and I'm going to try to do it myself today.

Doctor Singh: Excellent! Did the dietician come to see you?

Mrs. Clancy: Yes, she did. She came yesterday and I've enjoyed the food I've been given so far!

Doctor Singh: That's good. Try to eat everything that you get on the tray and let the nursing staff know if you don't finish. It's important to know how many calories you have in each meal ... I'd like you to do a bit more exercise too.

Mrs. Clancy: I want to go to an aerobics class with a friend when I go home – there are classes twice a week.

Doctor Singh: That sounds like the perfect solution! I'll see you again tomorrow and depending on the results of your blood tests, you should be able to go home before the weekend.

6.

Doctor Singh: Good morning, Mrs Steele. The operation went very well and I see that the intravenous is giving you enough to eat!

Mrs Steele: Yes, I'm not hungry at all ... My 'tummy' feels rather uncomfortable. I feel like I want to pass water again but I've just used a bedpan.

Doctor Singh: Let me see ... yes, your bladder is quite distended.

Can I see Mrs Steele's 'fluid balance chart', Nurse, please? Thank you.

Yes, I thought so ... I think you could pass a catheter, start her on sips of clear fluid. If she tolerates oral fluids then we'll talk about taking out the IV ...

Mrs. Steele, I've just asked nurse to put a tube into your bladder to take away the urine that is making you feel uncomfortable. You can suck on some ice or have sips of water now, and when you are drinking enough we can take out the intravenous line.

Mrs Steele: I'd like that, thank you. Will the tube hurt?

Doctor Singh: No, it isn't very pleasant but you will feel much better when your bladder is empty. The tube can come out straight away and you can pass water normally after that. It will be easier for you to go to the bathroom without the intravenous... but I want you to use a bedpan so that nurse can see how much urine you are passing.

Mrs Steele: Thank you, doctor.

2

ANSWER KEY

UNIT 1

1B

p. 5

🖉

Dr. Singh is the Senior House Officer.
The Consultant's name is Mr. James.
Her name's Pat.

p. 6

1. ☺ [əbəʊt] [pɒkət] [pju:pəl] [eiprən] [sɜːkəs].
    🖉 about pocket pupil apron circus.
3./4. 🖉 America [əmerikə] manager [mænədʒə] cleaner [kli:nə] urgent [ɜ:dʒənt] patient [peiʃənt] important [impɔ:tənt] foreign [fɒrən] pharmacy [fa:məsi] recovery [rikʌvəri] other [ʌθə] practice [præktəs] computer [kəmpju:tə] doctor [dɒktə] technician [tekniʃən].
5. 🖉 manual, experience, profession, health, communicate, disadvantage, instruction, work.

p. 7

🖉

UN The United Nations; WHO The World Health Organisation; CDC The Centers for Disease Control (in the US); DOB Date of Birth; M/F Male or Female; M/W/D Married, Widowed or Divorced; Ca (×2) Calcium/Cancer; BP Blood Pressure; TPR Temperature, Pulse and Respiration; Hb Haemoglobin; XR or X/R X/Ray(s); IV Intravenous; IM Intramuscular; GA General Anaesthetic; LA Local Anaesthetic; EDD Expected Date of Delivery;

NAD Nil/Nothing Abnormal Detected; OT Occupational Therapy/Therapist; TLC Tender Loving Care; FBE Full Blood Examination; ASAP As Soon As Possible; VIP Very Important Person; NB Nota Bene!! Pay attention/This is important; e.g. exempli gratia!! For example; i.e. id est!! That is..; c̄ con = with; TLC Tender Loving Care; etc. etcetera; OK all right; RN Registered Nurse; BSc Bachelor of Science; PhD Philosophy Doctor.

Pt.	🖉 Patient ☺ 1,2
K	🖉 Potassium ☺ 1,2
gm	🖉 gram ☺ 1,2,4,5
ht & wt	🖉 height and weight ☺ 1,2
fl. oz.	🖉 fluid ounce (Imperial measure) ☺ 1,2,4,5
RBC	🖉 Red Blood Cells ☺ 1,2
MS	🖉 Multiple Sclerosis ☺ 1,3
AIDS	🖉 Acquired Immune Deficiency Syndrome ☺ 1,2,3,5
HIV	🖉 Human Immuno–deficiency Virus ☺ 1,2,3,5
SID(S)	🖉 Sudden Infant Death (Syndrome) ☺ 1,2
R.	🖉 Right (side) ☺ 1,2
L.	🖉 Left (side) ☺ 1,2
IQ	🖉 Intelligence Quotient (psychology) ☺ 1,2,5
OD	🖉 Overdose (of drugs) ☺ 1,2
ENT	🖉 Ears, Nose and Throat (otorhinolaryngology) ☺ 1,2
BBC	🖉 British Broadcasting Corporation ☺ 3, 6
A & E	🖉 Accident and Emergency ☺ 1,2
EDD	🖉 Expected Date of Delivery/ Due Date ☺ 1,2
TB	🖉 Tuberculosis ☺ 1,2,3
PMT/PM	🖉 Pre–Menstrual Tension/Syndrome ☺ 1,2
OT/OR	🖉 Operating Theatre/Operating Room ☺ 1,2

| RC | Roman Catholic ☺ 2,3,5 |

RC — Roman Catholic ☺ 2,3,5
H₂O — Water (2 atoms of Hydrogen, 1 Oxygen) ☺ 1,2,5
(n.) — noun ☺ 5
(adj.) — adjective ☺ 5
(v.) — verb ☺ 5
(adv.) — adverb ☺ 5
(coll.) — colloquial language ('dialect') ☺ 5
(irreg.) — irregular ☺ 1,2,5
(reg.) — regular ☺ 1,2,5
BC — Before Christ ☺ 3,5
AD — *Anno Domini* (years after Christ) ☺ 3,5

p. 8

Albanian; Argentine; Chinese; English; French; German; Greek; Dutch; Irish; Italian; Japanese; Korean; Portuguese; Scottish; Spanish; Swiss; American; Turkish; Welsh.

p. 9

1. German, Italian, French, Romansch;
2. Italian, French, Portuguese;
3. (a) Dutch/German/English/Flemish,
   (b) Greek,
   (c) Arabic/French,
   (d) Arabic (+/– Hebrew);
4. English, Italian, French.

p. 10

1C; 2A; 3B.

p. 11

Hello, Jan. Hi, Andrew. What a nice surprise to see you here.
Cheers! Cheers!

Goodnight everyone! Goodbye, see you tomorrow.
Can I get you another pillow or a cushion? Yes, that's very kind of you. Thank you.
Good morning, I'm Barbara Scott. Pleased to meet you, Barbara.
How do you do? How do you do?
Thank you so much. Not at all, don't mention it.
Have a good weekend. Same to you!
Excuse me! Yes. Can I help you?
Do you mind if I sit here? No, not at all, please do.
Could you please tell me where the outpatients' department is? Yes, of course. Come with me.

1. C

p. 12

1. nurse; 2. dietician; 3. technical assistant; 4. dentist; 5. speech therapist; 6. surgeon; 7. physiotherapist; 8. doctor; 9. anaesthetist; 10. radiographer; 11. podiatrist (US) = chiropodist (GB); 12. laboratory technician; 13. occupational therapist; 14. health inspector; 15. pharmacist.

pp. 12/13

a   A radiographer; 10 (vi);
b   A surgeon; 6 (xiii);
c   A laboratory technician; 12 (i);
d   A physiotherapist; 7 (xi);
e   An anaesthetist; 9 (iii);
f   A nurse; 1 (ii);
g   An occupational therapist; 13 (xii);
h   A doctor; 8 (x);
i   A dietician; 2 (vii);
j   A dentist; 4 (ix);
k   A speech therapist; 5 (v);
l   A podiatrist; 11 (viii);
m   A pharmacist; 15 (xv);
n   A health inspector; 14 (xiv);
o   A technical assistant; 3 (iv).

Job titles

A doctor has a medical degree from a university. / A specialist has done extra study to specialise in a particular area and has more than one degree.

A radiographer is a technician who understands radiation, takes the pictures and looks after the machinery. / A radiologist is a doctor who is a specialist in (the study/science of) radiology.

p. 14

bi-: **biology** – *the study or science of life;*
biologist – *a person who is specialised in the study of biology;*
biological *(adj)* – *pertaining to biology.*

ur-: **urine** – *liquid chemical waste from the human body;*
urology – *the study of the urinary system;*
urologist – *a person specialised in the study of urology.*

psych-: **psychiatry** –*study and treatment of mental illness;*
psychiatrist – *a specialist in psychiatry;*
psychology – *the study or science of the human mind;*
psychologist – *an expert in psychology;*
psychological *(adj)* – *pertaining to psychology.*

cardi-: **cardiology** – *the science or study of the heart and its function;*
cardiologist – *a specialist in cardiology;*
cardiography/cardiograph – *recording of the electrical impulses of the heart's action.*

onc-: **oncology** – *the science or study of cancer;*
oncologist – *a specialist in the study of cancer.*

1D

p. 16

1. Neurolog**ical**; 2. Cardi**ac**; 3. Gastr**ic**; 4. Cran**ial**; 5. Pharmacolog**ical**; 6. Urolog**ical**;

7. Psycholog**ical**; 8. Diabe**tic**; 9. Neonat**al**; 10. Medic**al**; 11. Centr**al**; 12. Physic**al**.

p. 17

1. with; 2. in; 3. on; 4. about; 5. for; 6. to ... at; 7. for; 8. on, under; 9. on; 10. in ... for.

☺

1. **To** the neonatal ward; 2. **To** the emergency department; 3. **To** the blood bank; 4. **In** the technical services department; 5. **Ring the** pharmacy (not ring to...); 6. **In** Dermatology or **in** the Outpatients' Clinic; 7. **To** the Intensive Care Unit / **to** the Coronary Care Unit; 8. I'd like to work **in** / My favourite ward is ... (no preposition); 9. (Individual answers); 10. **To** the Laboratory.

p. 18

The Staff cafeteria is on the lower ground floor, next to the kitchen.

The Radiology Department is also on the ground floor, near the A&E Department (Accident and Emergency).

The Postnatal Ward and the Neonatal Unit are on the 2nd floor near the Labour Ward.

The Children's Ward is on the 6th floor and so is the Orthopaedic Ward.

The Operating theatres are on the 5th floor, next to the Recovery Room.

p. 19

1. Emergency, Intensive Care, the Operating Theatres and Recovery Room, Outpatients' Department, Blood Donation Services (the blood bank), the Central Sterilizing Department, wards;

2. Kitchen, Outpatients';
3. Operating Theatre, wards;
4. Practice/Surgery/Clinic, Operating Theatre.
5. Children's, Geriatric, Medical, Neurological or the Psychiatric;
6. Consultant's, ward;
7. Outpatients', swimming pool;
8. *Different answers*;
9. Radiology;
10. Neonatal, Children's;
11. Medical or *Research*;
12. wards / Geriatric, Neurology, Children's, Rheumatology;
13. Pharmacy;
14. Laboratory, Central Sterilizing Department.

p. 20

1. to X/Ray / on; 2. with; 3. in the operating theatre; 4. Emergency Department; 5. to the pharmacy; 6. in / Surgical / into; 7. at / hospital / in the kitchen / in Administration; 8. in / on; 9. to the Post–natal; 10. in theatre (or operating theatre).

p. 21

1. Community Health Centres; 2. surgeon; 3. ward; 4. procedures; 5. Specimens; 6. discharge; 7. microscopic examination; 8. to help (the) pain; 9. donate blood; 10. take medications.

1E

p. 23

1. works / doesn't work; 2. does; 3. does / do; 4. do / wait; 5. operates; 6. do / know / I don't. 7. does / take; 8. do / have; 9. does / drive / he does.; 10. do / do; 11. do / go; 12. do / go / I/we

don't; 13. does / start; 14. does / come; 15. do / want / they do; 16. don't / finish.

(a) Yes I do / No, I don't; (b) Yes, he is / No, he isn't; (c) Yes, he does / No, he doesn't; (d) Yes, we are / No, we aren't; (e) Yes, we/they do / No, we/they don't; (f) Yes, you are / No, you aren't.

p. 24

1. can ... can't; 2. can't ... can; 3. can; 4. can't 5. can't ... can; 6. Can ... can't; 7. Can; 8. can ... can't; 9. can ... Can ... can; 10. can ... couldn't.

p. 25

John: Good evening young lady! I'm looking after you again tonight. Are you feeling a bit better? You don't look very happy! PICTURE 2.
Cathy: Oh, hello John. Yes, I'm a little better, but my leg still hurts a lot.
John: This tablet is to help the pain and then I'm sure you will sleep.
Cathy: Thank you. Can I move my leg off the pillow? I want to lie on my side.
John: I can help you turn now, but your leg stays on the pillow, O:K? There you are. That's better. Are you comfortable? PICTURE 3.
Cathy: That's much better, thank you – now I can sleep!
John: Goodnight then. I'm going to check the other patients now but don't hesitate to call me if you need anything. PICTURE 1.

p. 27

1. (1); 2. (3); 3. (2); 4. (2); 5. (1); 6. (1); 7. (3); 8.(2); 9. (1); 10. (1) ...who's buzzing (1); 11. (3); 12. (3); 13. (1).

p. 28

☺

What's her full name? *Anna Kennedy*; How old is she? *She's 19 (nearly 20)*; What is she/Anna doing now? *She's doing her nursing training.*; What is she doing next week? *She's going to (start) work at the hospital*; Where will she start?/Where is she going to work? *She's starting in the surgical ward.*; How does she feel? *She's a bit nervous.*; What is easy for her?/ What does she <u>find easy</u>? *Making beds (isn't difficult) is easy for her/She <u>finds making beds</u> easy.* Why does she feel/think she will be a good nurse? *She feels (or thinks) she will be a good nurse because she looked after her grandmother when she was ill and did a good job.*

🖉

1. will finish; 2. will learn; 3. have to pass; 4. isn't going to have; 5. I'll take; 6. She's going; 7. We're staying; 8.will have.

1F

p. 29

🖉

Starting with 'A' (an anterior view), then N (a posterior view).

A–3 face; a–8 neck (internal –throat); N–27 head; n–19 hair (uncountable noun); b–9 shoulder; c–5 chest (or Thoracic Region); o–18 axilla / armpit; p–21 back/spine/backbone; d–6 nipple(s); e–1 breasts; q–24 elbow; r–23 wrist (silent 'w') ≠ *'pulse'= heartbeat*; f–15 arm (specifically: the 'forearm'); s–26 fingers; t–17 buttocks/bottom (*'bum'/ 'behind'/ 'seat'!*); g–14 thumb u–28 calf v–29 hip (bone) – *pelvis or 'pelvic girdle'*; h–10–umbilicus/navel (*'tummy/belly button'!*); w–25 Heel (bone: calcaneous); x–20 ankle; i–12 palm (front of the hand); y–16 sole of the foot; j–4 pubes/pubic area/genitalia; k–2 knee; z–22 toes (*not fingers of the feet!*); l–7 leg; m–13 foot (*irregular plural – feet*).

p. 30

🖉

1. face; 2. neck, her, her; 3. his buttocks; 4. feet; 5. her hands/fingers; 6. his/her wrist; 7. their backs; 8. fingers, thumb; 9. sole of the foot, heel; 10. umbilicus.

p. 31

🖉

reliable; punctual; organised; healthy; fat; stupid; thin; vivacious; withdrawn; tidy; polite; slow; bad; intelligent; good.

Antonyms 1: fast/slow; punctual/late (unpunctual is usually used for a person); timid/vivacious; polluted/pure; fat/thin; stupid/intelligent; withdrawn/vivacious; bad/good.

Antonyms 2: reliable/unreliable; punctual/unpunctual; possible/impossible; organised/disorganised; polite/impolite; confortable/unconfortable; healthy/unhealthy; pure/impure.

p. 32

🖉

1. messy; 2. successful; 3. handsome; 4. generous; 5. annoyed; 6. new; 7. old; 8. on time; 9. polluted; 10. reliable; 11. healthy; 12. vivacious; 13. terrible.

'So' and 'Such': *(explanation only).*
'So' adds more emphasis to an adjective (used more in spoken English): *e.g. so messy; so intelligent; so tired; so long.*
'Such' also adds more emphasis but comes before an adjective + plural noun: *e.g. such small machines; such interesting books; such crazy ideas.*
'Such + a/an' is used before an adjective + singular noun: e.g. *such a little baby; such an ugly situation; such a fat lady.*

'**So many**' *and* '**so much**' are used to make expressions of quantity more emphatic.
'**So much**' + uncountable nouns e.g. *so much snow; so much money; so much wine*.
'**So many**' + countable (plural) nouns e.g. *so many animals; so many charts; so many patients*.

p. 33

☺ *Meanings of idioms*
1. She is a good gardener / has a lot of success growing plants;
2. very useful / very convenient;
3. rude / impolite (but in an amusing or an annoying way, it wasn't really the correct thing to do);
4. she is sensible (has good sense) and has good reasoning powers;
5. a situation that suddenly became very bad and had to be dealt with quickly;
6. a lot of 'froth' (white bubbles);
7. play without sheet music – by hearing the music and being able to reproduce it.
   To play <u>a situation</u> 'by ear' means to decide how to deal with the situation as it develops rather than by having a plan to follow;
8. ran away;
9. interfere, or get involved, take any risks;
10. from a particular place or area (the same area where I live);
11. to have a lot of something (debt) to deal with;
12. feel nervous or agitated;
13. he is sensitive about something that happened in the past and becomes easily offended if it is mentioned because he feels he was treated unfairly;
14. treat somebody in an unfriendly way or to ignore them;
15. much better than other people;
16. A person who often drops things (or is 'clumsy');
17. *or to put your foot in your mouth*, say or do something that upsets, embarrasses or offends somebody;
18. I wanted to travel more or move, or do something different;
19. push hard (with your elbow);
20. make more effort (used in physical work, especially cleaning or polishing).

p. 34

✏

take blood; have pain; have/recover from an operation; make a bed; give an injection; take a pulse; develop a disease; sustain an injury; do rounds; cut the umbilical cord; feel ill.

1G

p. 37

✏ *Fasteners*
1. press stud; 2. velcro; 3. drawstring; 4. zip; 5. button–hole (*on the right*); 6. toggle; 7. hook and eye; 8. a bow; 9. a safety pin; 10. buckle; 11. ribbon; 12 button.
All other items can be found on (or added to) page 36.

p. 38

🎧

Cathy's mother; Sister Joanna Cathy is in the (orthopaedic ward) at the hospital; She is in hospital; She is sitting on a chair beside the bed; On the Admission Chart; Mr Manson's contact number at work, Cathy's blood pressure, and information about her medical and physical history; Nurse Margaret is going to weigh Cathy and measure her height accurately on the ward scales.

p. 39

1a; 2e; 3f; 4g; 5k; 6h; 7j; 8d; 9i; 10b; 11l; 12c.

p. 40

🎧 *Check with tape script 8b for complete dialogue.*

211

1H

p. 41

Other words

appliance (countable noun) *a machine that is designed to do a particular thing in the house (food preparation, cleaning).*

device (countable noun) *an object or a piece of equipment designed to do a particular job (bomb, explode, ignite, power).*

instrument (countable noun) *a tool or device used for a particular (usually scientific or delicate) task.*

contraption (countable noun) *a strange – looking piece of equipment that you don't know the name of.*

gadget (countable noun) *A small tool or device that does something useful.*

tool (countable noun) *an instrument held in your hand and used for making things (a hammer, a screwdriver etc.).*

apparatus (uncountable noun) *the collection of tools or other pieces of equipment that are used for a particular activity.*

p. 42

1d; 2r; 3c; 4b; 5p; 6h; 7m; 8t; 9f; 10q; 11o, 12f; 13u; 14i; 15j; 16e; 17a; 18s; 19k; 20s; 21n; 22l; 23g.

p. 43

What is each thing used for?

A *skin marking pencil* is for marking areas usually before an operation. Varicose veins are marked because the veins 'collapse' (they are difficult to see) when the patient is anaesthetised.

A *wooden spatula* can be used as a tongue depressor or for applying creams or lubricant.

An *otoscope* is an instrument used for examining the ear and for seeing the tympanic membrane.

A *small bowl* can be plastic or metal, sterilised or not and can be used for holding antiseptics and other solutions or as a container for gauze swabs, cotton balls etc. They can also be disposable and made of fine plastic or cardboard.

Cotton wool balls are used for applying solutions or for removing nail polish.

A *stethoscope* is used for listening to heart sounds or a 'pulse' – the heart beat.

A *box of tissues* is used for many things: blowing your nose, wiping away tears, for wiping babies' bottoms!

A *torch* is used mainly for seeing in the dark! A smaller 'pencil' torch is used for doing neurological observations , for checking the reaction of the eyes to light stimulus and also for looking at the mouth and throat.

A *sphygmomanometer* is used for taking blood pressure.

Scissors. Different types of scissors and scissors of different sizes are used for cutting different things.

Forceps. Forceps are generally used for picking up something or holding things when using a 'no–touch' sterile technique.

Lubricant is used to make it easier to pass tubes, optic devices or a speculum into body orifices (openings).

Blades are used for cutting. Scalpel blades are packaged individually and attached to a *handle*.

A *Urinometer* is used for measuring the pH of urine.

A *percussion hammer* is used for testing reflexes.

An *ophthalmoscope* is an instrument with a concave mirror and a lens for examining the interior of the eye through the pupil.

A *tape measure* is used for measuring the girth of a patient (the measurement of the abdomen), for measuring swollen limbs, for measuring parts for prostheses.

A *vaginal speculum* is used for widening the vaginal passage for examination or biopsy of the cervix.

A *kidney dish* (cardboard) is used as a disposable vomit bowl or container to carry things, a metal kidney dish or bowl can be sterilised and used for instruments such as scissors and forceps when doing a sterile procedure.

A *paper towel* may be sterile or non–sterile and is multi–purpose, a cover, a towel, a sterile wrapping etc.

Sterile rubber gloves are used for doing any sterile procedure and by all the staff in the operating theatres.

A *thermometer* is used for measuring body temperature. This may be taken orally, in the axilla or in the rectum.

A *scalpel handle* is used to connect a sharp blade, forming a 'knife' for cutting delicate tissue.

1I

p. 46

1. A. She's going *home*;
   B. She's *at home*;
2. She's *at* the bus stop. She's *waiting for* the bus;
3. Mr Brown's *going to bed*;
4. He's *in bed*;
5. The patient is *going to the X/Ray Department* (to X/Ray);
6. A. The stethoscope is *on the bedside table* (on the locker);
   B. It's *under the locker*;
7. It's *on the patient's chest*/(It's *over the patient's heart*);
8. The visitor is *going up* (to the wards/*in the* lift);
9. He's *in* the lift;
10. The mop is *in* the bucket;
11. Jamie's *in* hospital. (A PATIENT);
12. His friend is *going into* the bar;
13. John and Judy are *coming out* of the bar;
14. The Children's ward is *on the sixth floor*.

p. 47

1. at/at; 2. in; 3. for; 4. by; 5. of; 6. to/from; 7. on/in/on; 8. with; 9. of/to/with; 10. for/in/on 11. in; 12. for/from/to; 13. on/for; 14. at/on/in; 15. at/on/on.

1J

p. 48

1. T; 2. F – *A roster is the timetable of hours worked by shift-workers*; 3. T; 4. F – *If you are 'on duty', you are rostered to work*; 5. F *2000 is the same as 8 p.m.*; 6. T; 7. F *English–speaking people usually use a.m. and p.m.*; 8. T; 9. T; 10. T.

0205 or 1405 or 5 past 2 a.m. or p.m.;
0320 or 1520 or 20 past 3 a.m. or p.m.;
0035 or 1235 or 25 to 1 a.m. or p.m.;
0810 or 2010 or 10 past 8 a.m. or p.m.;
0645 or 1845 or – to 7 a.m. or p.m.;
0540 or 1740 or 20 to 6 a.m. or p.m.;
0530 or 1730 or – past 5 a.m. or p.m.;
0115 or 1315 or – past 1 a.m. or p.m.;
0900 or 2100 or nine o'clock a.m. or p.m.;
1050 or 2250 or 10 to 11 a.m. or p.m.;
0755 or 1955 or 5 to 8 a.m. or p.m.;
2400 or 1200 or 12 midday or 12 midnight.

p. 49

Rosie goes to work by train. It takes an hour. She is on duty from half past 6 until half past 3. Steve goes to work by car and train. It takes an hour. He is on duty from half past 7 until half past 4.
Pat rides her bicycle to work. It takes half an hour. She is on duty from 2 p.m. until 11 p.m. Mr Singh drives to work. It takes 10 minutes. He is on duty from half past 7 until 6 o'clock. Mr James walks to work. It takes (him) half an hour. He starts at 8 and usually finishes at 2 p.m.

John and Judy ride a motorbike to work. It takes thirty–five minutes. John is on duty from 10 p.m. until 7 a.m.

p. 50

🖉

Two million, three hundred thousand; Six hundred and ninety–nine; Four thousand, six hundred and twenty–one; Twelve thousand and forty–two, One million (or one metre!); Nine <u>point</u> two, five percent; Ninety–eight; 'oh' (nought/zero) point 'oh', 'oh', three; Thirty–four point three, two, one; Eighty–seven; Two hundred and four; Nine hundred <u>and</u> two.

Fractions
a/one half; a/one quarter; one third; one sixth; three quarters; one eighth; three twentieths; eleven thirteenths; two third; nine tenths.

Powers and mathematical symbols
ten to the power of 3 *or* ten cubed; five to the power of 2 *or* five squared; ten to the power of minus six *or* one divided by one million;
a 'Euler' number squared; pi [pai] = *approximately* 3.141592...;
A (area of a circle) = πr^2 : equals π multiplied by r (the radius) squared;
C (circumference of a circle) = $2\pi r$: equals two (times or multiplied by) π (times or multiplied by) r;
V (volume) = $\frac{4}{3}\pi r^3$ (volume of a sphere) = four 'over' three pi [pai] r [a:(r)] squared = (4 divided by three) multiplied by π multiplied by r cubed.

☺
1. *What is three quarters of 4?* 3;
2. *What is half of 90?* 45;
3. *What is half of point 'oh' five?* 0.025;
4. *What is a quarter of two hundred?* 50;
5. *What is three quarters of one litre?* 750 mls. [milz] – millilitres;
6. *What is one tenth of five kilograms?* 500 gms. [græmz] – grams;
7. *How many cents are there in one dollar or one Euro?* 100;
8. *What is half of one?* 0.5;

9. *How many days are there in a fortnight?* 14;
10. *What does 'x' mean?* ('x' is – or stands for – any real number) any real number;
11. *What is thirty-three multiplied by eleven?* 363;
12. *What is ten to the power of 3?* 10×10×10 = 1,000;
13. *How many patients are there in the medical ward.....?*;
14. *How many floors are in the main part...? How many wards are there on each floor?*

p. 51

🖉 *Check with tape script 9.*

1K

p. 53

🖉

wakes up; gets up; has; gets; has breakfast; listens; leaves; locks; rides; arrives; starts; 8 o'clock; half past 5; has; cooks; seven o'clock; watches; reads; goes; goes; meets; go; listen.

p. 57

🖉

Paragraph headings: 1d; 2c; 3b; 4e; 5a.

Answer the questions
She decided that she wanted to be a nurse.
She applied at a university to do the Bachelor of Nursing Degree.
During their first year, the trainee nurses spent most of their time at lectures but were able to 'observe' various procedures in the hospital.
She wants to study Paediatric Oncology.

Time clauses
when I had finished high school; takes three years; During the first year; In the second year; In the final year; By the end of the third year; After graduating; The first year of working; This is the time (or at this time, in this period..);

stayed ... for 18 months before applying; since then; At the moment.

1L

p. 62

Irregular verbs
blow, break, dream, drink, eat, fall, draw; get, go, kneel, have, cut; write, stand up, put on, read, sew, shake, sweep, take off, run, wake up, sit down, sing, sleep.

p. 63

If you have problems learning this, I'll help you. (*offer*).

If you do that again, I'll kill you. (*threat*).

If it's sunny this afternoon, I'm going to take my mother for a drive. (*intention*).

If it looks as though it might rain, take an umbrella. (*imperative/order*).

If the fog gets thicker, the plane may/might not be able to land in Verona. (*speculation*).

If you break a mirror, you'll have 7 years bad luck (*superstition/prediction*).

If you are looking for Chris, you'll find him in the office. (*fact/future prediction*).

If you haven't seen the doctor yet, you'd better make an appointment – you should see him soon. (*advice*).

(If you don't) Tidy your bedroom (or) you'll be grounded for a week! (*imperative*).

p. 64

1. go, will have (*1st*);
2. Bring, come (*1st Imperative*);
3. change/are changed, will ring (*1st*);

4. will have to wait, is (*1st*);
5. don't read, will never pass (*1st*);
6. becomes, implants (*Zero*);
7. will have, finish (*1st*);
8. will call, needs (*1st*).

1. have made/are making, I'd love;
2. 'd/would have, did not/didn't spend;
3. ate, would not/wouldn't be;
4. were, would study;
5. would ... do, were;
6. would ... be able;
7. is/was, will/would;
8. will give, go out;
9. would change, knew;
10. Would ... feel, found.

1M

p. 66

☺

1. Hot liquid placed too near the edge of a table covered with a tablecloth (with a toddler in the house) – *burns*;
2. Eating too much food / Being obese – *diabetes, obesity, high blood pressure + stroke (CVA), thrombosis, heart attack*;
3. Driving too fast/carelessly – *death or serious injury, brain or head injury*;
4. Opening/Fixing an electrical appliance still connected to a power source – *electrocution, death or serious injury*;
5. Smoking when pregnant (and before conception) – *still born or underweight baby, lung* (and other) *cancer*;
6. Lying exposed to hot sun – sunbathing – *sunstroke, sunburn, skin cancer*;
7. Standing on inappropriate furniture to reach light fittings or high places – *fall or electrocution, brain or head injury*.

p. 67

Check with tape script 11 for complete sentences.

p. 68

🖉

YOUR SMOKING CAN HARM OTHERS: Tobacco smoke causes ...
SMOKING KILLS: In Australia, tobacco smoking causes ...
SMOKING IS ADDICTIVE: Nicotine, a drug ...

☺

1. Tar is condensed smoke and it contains many different chemicals which cause cancer. (These chemicals are carcinogens);
2. There are 0.8 milligrams of nicotine in each cigarette. (nought point eight milligrams = 8 tenths of a gram);
3. 'On average' refers to the usual or normal amount which may vary slightly (and is probably a little higher);
4. Expired air breathed out from animals and humans contain carbon monoxide and so do exhaust fumes from automobiles. Carbon monoxide is a poisonous gas formed when carbon burns partly but not completely;
5. Individual answer;
6. Dependency is the state of relying on somebody or something for something, especially when it is not necessary;
7. Addiction is the condition of being addicted or dependent on a harmful drug of some kind, and where the person is unable to stop taking it;
8. lung cancer, throat cancer, stomach cancer, emphysema , chronic bronchitis, asthma and other respiratory problems;
9. 10. ll. & 12. Individual answer.

p. 69

🖉

My mother is lonely. You should buy her a pet – a dog or a cat.

I think I'm getting the 'flu.(influenza). You should go home to bed.

John can't sleep. He shouldn't drink so much coffee.

I've got a bad toothache. You should go to the dentist.

She is very overweight. She should go on a diet.

Ruth isn't happy – her boyfriend's away on business. She should ring him to see what he's doing.

☺ Example answers: 'taking risks':
1. Hot drinks etc. should be put on the centre of a table, out of reach of children; Tablecloths shouldn't be used if there is a toddler in the house;
2. Nobody should eat too much (over–indulge). We shouldn't eat a 'high-calorie' diet;
3. Speed limits on the roads should (must be) observed; People shouldn't exceed the speed limit for any reason;
4. Appliances should be fixed by an expert; Electrical appliances shouldn't be repaired by someone who doesn't know what he's doing;
5. Women should be aware that smoking can harm their unborn baby; Women shouldn't smoke when they want to have a baby or during pregnancy;
6. People should protect their skin when out in the sun – they should wear a hat, use sunscreen and wear a shirt; People shouldn't lie in the sun for long periods without protecting themselves from the sun;
7. A ladder should be used to change light bulbs or when reaching high things in the home; People shouldn't stand on chairs instead of using a ladder.

1N

p. 70

☺

• ....probably only a few! • They usually stay at home in the care of family, their local GP or by seeking advice from a chemist. •.... genetic influences, living conditions and habits (such as smoking or drug abuse) and obesity (being overweight). •...An acute disease can be severe, possibly needing medical intervention but does not last for a long period of time. / A chronic disease may not be very severe but continues over a long period of time with continual medical care.

p. 71

1. the heart (belongs to the circulatory system);
2. the brain (belongs to the central nervous system–CNS);
3. the lungs (belong to the respiratory system);
4. the kidneys (belong to the urinary (or excretory system).

p. 72

Exercise 1. 1f; 2d; 3m; 4a; 5k; 6h; 7j; 8n; 9l; 10b; 11c; 12e; 13o; 14i; 15g.

Exercise 2. 1. rectangular; 2. pear–shaped; 3. semi–circular; 4. kidney/bean–shaped; 5. triangular; 6. a wedge–shaped; 7. crescent–shaped; 8. square; 9. spherical, circular; 10. dome–shaped; 11. oval, elliptical; 12. cubic; 13. conical; 14. rod–shaped, cylindrical, tubular; 15. spiral.

p. 73

Exercise 3. 1. crescent–shaped; 2. cubic; 3. cylindrical or tubular; 4. square; 5. spherical; 6. conical; 7. square; 8. bean–, kidney–; 9. pear–; 10. shapes; 11. berry– or like bunches of grapes; 12. The lungs are vaguely shaped like triangles or pyramids.

Exercise 4. *Bacilli* – **s** *Cocci* – **t** (streptococci) **q** (diplococci) **p** (staphylococci) *Spirilla* – **r**.

p. 75

1T; 2F – Enzymes *speed up* chemical reactions; 3T; 4F – Enzymes have different shapes depending on the *substances it combines with*; 5F – Temperature and pH changes *can change the enzyme and stop its action*; 6F – The first part of the name of the enzyme refers to the *substance or the type of action it is involved in*; 7T; 8F – *All chemical reactions in the body require enzymes as catalysts*; 9F. Enzymes *do not change* during chemical reactions; 10. T.

10

p. 78

Exercise 1. haematoma; erythema; urticaria; cyanosis; oedema.

Exercise 3. *example answers*: a. He is scratching. His skin is itchy. He's got/he has a rash or urticaria; b. He's got a swelling or an area of inflammation on his heel; c. His skin is yellow – he's jaundiced. He's got a pain in the area of his liver; d. He is crying and he's got a very big bruise on the top of his arm.

Exercise 4. *example answers*:
1. d. He was hit with a base–ball – he's got a huge(very big) bruise on his arm;
2. b. He's been running a marathon – he's got a swelling or an area of inflammation on his heel;
3. a. Look, he's scratching! He must be itchy. He's got a nasty rash;
4. c. He's got liver disease and he's very jaundiced.

☺
Exercise 5. 1. sign (may be a symptom); 2. symptom; 3. symptom (dehydration could be a sign); 4. symptom; 5. sign; 6. sign; 7. sign; 8. sign; 9. sign; 10. symptom.

p. 79

a. sciatica; b. viral infection/influenza; c. hay fever – allergic reaction; d. asthma; e. stress; f. appendicitis; g. indigestion – gastritis; h. hepatitis; i. lung cancer; j. an insect bite/sting; k. a middle ear infection.

p. 80

Example answers: 1. He may have a cold, the 'flu or an allergy; 2. She has probably got a sore throat or laryngitis [læ'rin'dʒaitis] (she has lost her voice); 3. He has a temperature (He's febrile); 4. He probably has chronic bronchitis; 5. He is overweight, sweating and feeling hot, he may be ill.

1P

p. 82

a. = a condition of low levels of sugar in the blood; b.= the formation of a new/permanent opening into the stomach; c. = inflammation of the appendix; d. = a condition of low oxygen; e. = referring to /pertaining to the head.

p. 84

a. = heart muscle; b. = the membrane that lines the inside of the heart; c. = inflammation of the liver; d. = difficulty in passing urine or painful passing of urine; f. = inside the skull.

1–5 given as examples; 6. An opening made (surgically) into the stomach; 7. Removal of a kidney; 8. Inflammation of the appendix; 9. Inflammation of the Pancreas; 10. Stones (or calculi) in the kidney (= kidney stones); 11. Inflammation of the Stomach; 12. Inflammation of the Liver.

1Q

p. 85

Check with tape script 12.

1. Pain – noun only – not usually used as a verb; 2.Wound – a noun / verb; 3. Sore – a noun and an adjective – never a verb; 4. Painful – only an adjective; 5. Wounded – adjective (passive verb – to be wounded); 6. Hurt – can occasionally be used as a noun, usually as an adjective or a verb; 7. Ache – noun + part of two-word nouns and as a verb; 8. Aching – an adjective and verb; 9. Injury – noun (verb – to injure sb. or sth.); 10. Injured – adjective.

p. 86

Many possibilities given but only one or two to be used in each sentence – where they make sense!

Example:
1. I *sometimes /often/ usually/ generally/ very often/ frequently/* can't *ever* walk upstairs without a lot of pain *when the weather is cold.*

p. 87

Where is it?	How bad is it?	Does it last long?
generalised	Dull severe burning	persistent
radiating	stabbing excruciating	nagging*
localised	nagging* sharp unbearable	intermittent
	gnawing slight intolerable	occasional

* N.B. 'nagging' can mean 'dull', 'continuous', 'persistent', or all three!

a. backache; b. earache; c. headache; d. toothache; e. stomach ache.

p. 88

(a) oedema/edema; (b) jaundiced; (c) persistent; (d) sore; (e) haematomas/hematomas; (f) shortness of breath / oedema; (g) wound; (h) injured; (i) inflamed; (j) unbearable; (k) losing;

(l) urticaria / rash / urticaria; (m) sign / symptom; (n) toothache.

p. 90

1 + 2 = Personal Hygiene

p. 92

indoors – *inside a building*; to feed somebody – *give a person something to eat and/or drink*; label – *put a name on something using a piece of paper*; due – *something is expected to happen at that time*; diagnose – *identify a disease or illness*; shift – *set working hours (can also mean to move something)*; outdoors – *out in the fresh air, not in a building*; attend – *to be present in a particular place e.g. a meeting*; facet – *a small part of something*; addiction – *being unable to stop taking harmful substances*; canteen – *a restaurant in a public workplace or university*; check – *make sure something is in order.*

1. by; 2. for/about; 3. as ... of; 4. on; 5. up ... to; 6. for/ after; 7. of; 8. by; 9. to/from; 10. in; 11. by; 12. on/off; 13. by; 14. for; 15. to; 16. on; 17. to; 18. of; 19. down; 20. off; 21. on/over; 22. to; 23. on; 24. up; 25 in; 26. on; 27. of; 28. to; 29. with.

1R

p. 94

from left to right:
for; for; since; for; forever (or for ever); for; since; since; for; for; since; for; since; for; for; since; since; since; for; since; since.

1. never; 2. ever; 3. This is the first time; 4. already; 5. yet; 6. just; 7. yet; 8. just; 9. already; 10. ever...ever.

p. 95

(1) have known; (2) have been; (3) has had; (4) has...worked; (5) has travelled; (6) has been; (7) has spoken; (8) has seen; (9) has been; (10) has...been; (11) has spent; (12) has lived; (13) has visited; (14) has sung; (15) has had; (16) has...sung; (17) has...made; (18) has done; (19) has worked; (20) has been.

• She has not (hasn't) been on television • She has travelled a lot • She has never been unemployed • She has sung (or 'has been singing') since she was 6.

UNIT 2

2A

p. 99

1. *'walks of life'* = profession or occupation; *'lifestyle'* = the way of life / mode of living;
2. *'skills'* = the ability to do things well, to have expertise; *'abilities'* = the capacity or power to do things;
3. *Example answer:* Patients lose their identity, have little social outlet, may over–react to situations, may not be able to practice their religion etc.;
4. *Example answer:* to repeat instructions and information as necessary, answer questions honestly to prevent anxiety, assess the patient's reactions correctly, be sympathetic and give encouragement to build trust and companionship, etc.;
5. *Individual answers;*

219

6. neonate; baby; toddler; pre–schooler; child; teenager; adolescent; young adult; middle–aged; elderly; old;

7. A teenager is *aged between thirteen and nineteen*; a toddler (just walking) is *aged between about 10 months old and 2 years old*; a person 'in their 40's' is *aged between 40 and 49 years old*;

8. *Individual answers*;

9. *'an active lifestyle'* – a way of life that includes a lot of movement, exercise and activity; 'a sedentary lifestyle' – a way of life that includes a lot of sitting and very little movement or exercise;

10. *Various combinations.*

2B

p. 100

Accepted abbreviations
BP = Blood Pressure; TPR = Temperature, Pulse and Respiration rates; Y = Yes; N = No; Pt. = Patient; RIB = Rest/Remain in Bed; PO = Per Orale (by/in the mouth – orally); O/A = On Admission; (H)PU = (Has) Passed Urine; NPU = Has Not Passed Urine; BO = Bowels Open (The patient has had a bowel action/defecated/passed faeces [fiːsiːz]); IV = Intravenous (by way of a vein) *'Phlebo' is not used in English except as a prefix, e.g. phlebitis*; IM = Intramuscular (into a muscle [mʌsəl]); NAD = Nil (nothing) Abnormal Detected; O/E = On Examination; C/O = Complaining Of.

p. 101

Normal adult observations: T: ranges from about 36–37; P: ranges from about 64–80; R: from about 16–20; BP: 100–130/60–80. (verbalisation: One hundred to one hundred and thirty over or on sixty to eighty).

nervous, anxious, frightened, depressed, tired, uncertain, worried, distressed, scared, terrified, sad

Nouns from the Adjectives:
happy – happiness
nervous – nervousness
surprised/surprising – surprise
excited – excitement
anxious – anxiety
frightened/afraid – fright
depressed – depression
tired – tiredness (lethargy)
bored – boredom
dirty – dirt
delighted/delightful – delight
lonely – loneliness
responsible – responsibility
uncertain – uncertainty
worried – worry
distressed – distress
scared – scare
terrified – terror
fearful – fear
sad – sadness

In order of severity – depending on the circumstances and the quantifiers of strength: uncertain, sad, worried, nervous, anxious, fearful, frightened, angry, scared, distressed, terrified.

p. 102

Check with tape script 13.

p. 103

1. Mary is the ward help (sometimes called a 'ward's maid'– she could also be a Nurse Assistant or a voluntary worker); 2. The room is unoccupied (there are no other patients in that room); 3. There are 2 beds – Mark chooses the bed near the window; 4. Julie is going to take his suitcase and probably his 'street clothes' home; 5. Yes, Mark is fasting before he has some laboratory or other tests and examinations (perhaps a colonoscopy or gastroscopy).

☺

Example Admission Procedure order: 1(e); 2(f); 3(h); 4(g); 5(c); 6(i); 7(d); 8(a); 9(b).

2C

p. 104

🖉

O/E = On Examination; ENT = Ears, Nose & Throat *(a very commonly used abbreviation – an ENT surgeon, for example)*; Pulse rate: 80 beats per minute; reg. = regular; BP = Blood Pressure; CNS = Central Nervous System; –ve. = negative; ? = possible/queried; 2/7 = in two days.

p. 105

🖉

Example questions: **1.** Can you tell me your full name? First name? Surname? Could you spell that please? **2.** Have you been in this hospital before? Did you come here from another ward or hospital? If the answer is 'yes' – When? Which ward? **3.** Can I take/ I'd like to take – your blood pressure/temperature etc. (to put on your chart) **4a.** How tall are you? Do you know how tall you are? I'd like to see how tall you are – I'll measure your height... **4b.** How much do you weigh? Do you know how much you weigh? I'd like to see how much you weigh. Can you stand on the scales please? I'd like to check your weight. **5.** Are you eating well/normally? Have you lost any weight recently? Are you trying to lose weight? Are you on a special diet (diabetic, low–cholesterol, vegetarian etc.)? **6.** Do you wear glasses? Do you wear glasses for reading/driving the car etc.? Do you wear contact lens? Do you have any problems with your eyes? **7.** Can you hear well? / Do you have any problems with your hearing? Do you wear a hearing aid/hearing aids? **8.** *Speech assessment done by interviewer.* **9.** Have you got / Do you have... any money or anything valuable that you would like to put in a safe place? (in a locked cupboard or the hospital safe). Could you please sign here to say that ...?

2D

p. 107

🖉

1. F – *Patients at risk have a low score on the Norton Scale*; 2. F – *Patients who are ambulant are not at risk (although elbows, shoulders and heels can often redden when in bed for a lengthy period)*; 3. T; 4. F – *The first sign of trouble is reddening of the skin. This appears prior to (before) any abrasion of the skin*; 5. F – *Fat people are at risk because they are generally less mobile*; 6. T; 7. T; 8. T.

2E

p. 108

🖉

1. *Linen* refers to all sheets, covers, towels, shirts, underwear and pillow and cushion covers;
   Linen on a bed: mattress cover, sheets, draw–sheets, blankets or eiderdowns, quilts, pillow and cushion covers (towels, flannel/face cloths);
   In a 'linen cupboard': mattress cover, sheets, draw–sheets, blankets or eiderdowns, quilts, pillow and cushion covers, (towels, flannel/face cloths, bath mats, patients' gowns etc.);
   On a 'linen trolley': sheets, draw–sheets, (quilts, pillow and cushion covers, towels, flannel/face cloths etc.);
2. *Clean linen* is stacked neatly at the back of the trolley. *Dirty linen* would be put into a bag made of material (to go to the laundry). The *rubbish bag* is the coloured bag (probably disposable plastic) used for paper scraps, dead flowers, food scraps, disposable cups, dishes etc. and newspapers, bottles, cans which are not recycled in other ways;
3. *Three different types of sheets:* 'bottom' sheet, 'top' sheet, draw–sheet;
4. A *pillow case* is a cover for a pillow (or cushion) that can be changed for hygienic reasons;

5. A *blanket* is used for warmth, can be made of cotton, wool or synthetic fibres, and is placed between the top sheet and the quilt. A *quilt* is a cover and may or may not provide a lot more extra warmth. It is usually a heavier fabric than the sheets. A *duvet* is a heavier quilt and may or not have a cover for a down or acrylic–filling. (A duvet=an eiderdown);

6. A bed can be prevented from moving *by locking it*. You can 'wheel a bed along' *by unlocking the wheels and pushing it*;

7. The *levers* are moved up or down and a handle is turned or wound (wind [waind] wound [waund] wound) to raise or lower one of the ends of the bed or to raise or lower the height of the whole bed;

8. Incontinent patients or patients with leaking/ open drainage wounds need to sit or lie on a waterproof sheet.

9. (a) a bowl of warm water, soap, a face cloth, one or two towels, toiletries and extra hot water for shaving 'gear' for male patients, clean pyjamas or nightgown (b) 1 or 2 long sheets, a draw sheet, pillow cases and possibly a clean quilt. (c) Cleaning equipment if the bed has not been cleaned since the previous admission. (A mattress protector, 2 long sheets, a mackintosh, a draw sheet, pillow cases, blanket(s) and a quilt.);

10. A patient with toilet privileges stays in bed, but may get up to go the toilet.

p. 109

🎧 *Individual Answers*.

p. 111

🖉

1. ...has been/had been taken; 2. ...had been feeling; 3. ...has been admitted; 4. Has...seen; 5. Has...been taking/taken; 6. ...has been taking; 7. Has...lost; 8. Have...been put; 9. ...has been taken; 10. ...had been eating; 11. ...have ...been

doing; 12. ...have ...been ...been waiting; 13. had been feeding ...had fallen; 14. ...has had.

2F

p. 112

🖉

1. table; 2. wheelchair; 3. shower; 4. sofa / couch; 5. drug trolley; 6. chair; 7. washbasin; 8. bed; 9. heater; 10. toilet; 11. bidet; 12. sterilizer; 13. telephone; 14. desk; 15. bedpan & urinal; 16. locker; 17. dangerous drugs; 18. switch; 19. magazine; 20. bath; 21. linen trolley; 22. television; 23. chart/history trolley; 24. cupboard.

p. 113

🖉 *Matching exercise*

1. A Day Room is provided *because* patients like to have somewhere to relax away from other patients;

2. Most rooms have bathrooms *because* a lot of patients wash independently;

3. The door–ways are wider than normal *so that* patients in wheelchairs can pass through;

4. The beds are arranged *so* staff can see the patients from the doorway;

5. Furniture and fittings are designed *so* they can be cleaned easily;

6. Telephones are available on each floor *because* patients need to be able to contact their families;

7. Visiting hours are usually restricted *but* close family members are sometimes allowed to come in at other times;

8. There is a locked cupboard in the Nurses' Station which is used for keeping valuables *and* there is also one for dangerous or addictive drugs;

9. Urinals are sometimes called 'bottles' *and* bedpans are sometimes called 'pots' or 'potties';

10. Clean linen is stored in a cupboard or on a trolley *but* dirty linen is put immediately into a bag.

p. 114

2. A dressing gown is (used) *for* wearing over pyjamas; 3. *Sterile* forceps are (used) *for* picking things up using a 'no–touch' technique; 4. A bedpan is (used) *for* collecting *urine and* faeces; 5. A crutch or walking stick is (used) *for* helping lame or unstable patients to walk; 6. A bra is (used) *for* supporting breasts; 7. A toothbrush is (used) *for* cleaning your teeth; 8. A razor is (used) *for* shaving (clearing an area of hair); 9. A urinometer is (used) *for* testing the 'specific gravity' (SG) of urine; 10. Scissors are (used) *for* cutting various materials; 11. A urinal is (used) *for* passing urine (micturating/urinating) *into* in bed – males only!; 12. A wheelchair is (used) *for* transporting patients who are unable to walk.

p. 118

Direct and Reported Speech:

knew; was feeling; had enjoyed; hadn't been feeling; had been; had been waiting; had been wanting.

2 and 3 to be checked by the teacher.

p. 119

2. She said she could help me. 3. They told her (that) they might go to Munich. 4. They asked me what they should do. 5. The mother told the teacher (that) she had to leave early that day. 6. He told his friend (that) that was a good video. 7. She told her boyfriend (that) she wanted to study that day. 8. My mother reminded me that is was Jackie's birthday the next day. 9. She said that she would meet me there. 10. She said (that) he had bought a new car. 11. His parents said that he was going to watch TV. 12. She told her husband that her appointment was at 8.30 the following morning. 13. They said (that) they had moved to the country a couple of years ago/before. 14. She said (that) she might sell her bicycle. 15. The boy told the teacher (that) he couldn't think of anything to write about.

2G

p. 120

Sample questions:
1. Is the patient fully informed? Does he/she know exactly what is happening?;
2. Are the relatives happy with the arrangements? Is the patient happy with the arrangements? Have the relatives' or carer's wishes been considered?;
3. Has the patient been given all the necessary information, prescriptions and pamphlets? Does the patient understand how to look after himself when he goes home?.

p. 122

Check answers with tape script 16.

UNIT 3

3B

p. 127

1. mitosis; 2. tissue; 3. myocardium; 4. the brain; 5. cartilage; 6. epithelium; 7. cell; 8. organ; 9. smooth–muscle; 10. function.

p. 128

1. Skeletal System; 2. Muscular System; 3. Circulatory System; 4. Respiratory System; 5. Nervous System; 6. Digestive System; 7. Urinary System; 8. Reproductive System; 9. Endocrine System; 10. Lymphatic System; 11. Skin (Integumentary System).

p. 129

🖉

1. ...is made up of *or* consists of...; 2. ...is composed of ...; 3. ...is made up of...; 4. ... make up ...; 5. ...consist of?; 6. ... consists of ...; 7. ... is composed of ... .

🖉

Verbs and Nouns: regulation; form; secretion; destroy; excretion; reproduce; defenCe!; cover; provision; store; dilation/dilatation; circulation; digest; removal; eliminate; filtration; produce; concePtion; line; development; protect; situation; function.

p. 130

🖉

Functions: 1 (b); 2 (j); 3 (e); 4 (a); 5 (k); 6 (g); 7 (d); 8 (f); 9 (c); 10 (i); 11(h).

p. 131

🖉

1. blood...oxygen; 2. kidneys...regulate; 3. kidneys...excrete; 4. liver; 5. liver; 6. heart; 7. ovaries...secrete...are produced; 8. secretes ...Pancreas; 9. form ...cartilage ...bone. 10. kidneys ...urinary system ...the excretory system; 11. ...are composed; 12. reproduce ...division; 13. covers ...is made up of ...lines; 14. are situated; 15. conception.

3C

p. 133

🖉

1. the Midline; 2. lateral; 3. medial; 4. distal; 5. proximal; 6. posterior / dorsal; 7. anterior / ventral; 8. superior / cranial; 9. inferior / caudal.

🖉

1. superior; 2. medial; 3. proximal; 4. anterior *(and inferior)*; 5. lateral; 6. posterior; 7. midline;

8. proximal; 9. distal *(and inferior to...)*; 10. superior *(talking about the brain or head, it is better not to use 'cranial')*; 11. superior *(and medial – the oesophagus runs along the midline)*.

🖉

the eye (from top to bottom) – (b), (c), (d), (a); *the heart* (on the left half of the diagram) – top (b) bottom (a).

p. 134

🖉

1. the Ventral Cavity; 2. the Thoracic Cavity; 3. the Cranial Cavity; 4. the Dorsal Cavity; 5. the Abdominal Cavity; 6. the Spinal Cavity.

🖉

1. Thoracic Cavity; 2. Diaphragm; 3. Spinal Cavity; 4. Dorsal Cavity; 5. Abdomino–pelvic Cavity;
6. *Example answers:*

The *stomach* lies inferior to (below) the diaphragm and superior to (above) the intestines.
The *liver* lies laterally and to the *right* of the stomach
The *appendix* is situated *at the lower end of* the ascending colon.
The *pancreas* (partially) behind (posterior) and under (inferior to) the stomach
The *transverse colon* lies *between* the ascending and the descending colon. It is inferior to the liver, the stomach, the duodenum, the pancreas and the spleen.
The *duodenum* (a c–shaped tube and part of the small intestine) is situated *between* the stomach and the small intestine.
The *ascending colon* is situated laterally on the *right* side of the abdominal cavity, *between* the transverse colon and the small intestine.
The *descending colon* is situated laterally on the *left* side of the abdominal cavity, between the transverse colon (superiorly) and the rectum (inferiorly).
The *gallbladder* is situated anteriorly to the liver and superior–laterally to the duodenum.

The Common Bile Duct leads from the gallbladder *to* the duodenum – the pancreatic duct also drains into the CBD.
The caecum is attached to the inferior (dorsal) part of the ascending colon.

p. 135

1. (i) RUQ; (ii) RLQ; (iii) LUQ; (iv) LLQ.

(v) The Epigastric Region; (vi) The Left Hypochondriac Region; (vii) The Right Hypochondriac Region; (viii) The umbilicus; (ix) The Umbilical Region; (xi) The Left Lateral Region; (x) The Right Lateral Region; (xii) The Right Inguinal or Iliac Region; (xiii) The Left Inguinal or Iliac Region; (xiv) The Pelvic / Pubic or Hypogastric Region.

3D

p. 138

1. 206 bones; 2. calcium (salts) & phosphorus; 3. to give shape, support, protection of internal organs, provision for the attachment of muscles, lever–action, storage of: fat, calcium, magnesium, phosphorous, potassium, sulphur and sodium and the formation of Red Blood Cells; 4. long, short, flat, irregular, sesamoid; 5. diaphysis, 2 epiphyses – the proximal epiphysis and the distal epiphysis; 6. cancellous (or spongy bone), hard (or dense bone), cartilage; 7. The Axial Skeleton and the Appendicular Skeleton; 8. ribs, Thoracic vertebrae, sternum; 9. in both ends of long bones, i.e. in the epiphyses; 10. The sacrum [sei'krəm] and the coccyx [kɒkśiks].

Matching: 1. yellow marrow; 2. skull; 3. cartilage; 4. lumbar; 5. periosteum; 6. red marrow; 7. diaphysis; 8. endosteum; 9. coccyx; 10. radius; 11. epiphysis; 12. patella; 13. inter–costal; 14. strong, fibrous – ligament.

3E

p. 139

🎧 *Check with tape script 20.*

p. 141

1. *Because* swelling *is caused by* an increase in fluid (lymph, white blood cells and / blood) into the tissues around the fracture / *Because* an increase in circulation to the part – and fluid, lymphocytes and possibly blood entering the tissues, *results in / causes/leads to* swelling;
2. Because pain *results from* pressure on nerve endings. (caused by extra fluid in the tissues) – Because the increasing pressure on nerve endings results in / causes/ leads to pain – Because pain results from/ is caused by increasing pressure on nerve endings;
3. *Because* heat *results from/ is caused by* an increase in circulation. – *Because* an increase in circulation to the part *results in / causes/ leads to* a sensation of heat. – *Because* a sensation of heat *results from/ is caused by* an increase in circulation;
4. *Because* the body tries to keep the part still, this *results in/causes/leads to* loss of function. – *Because* loss of function *results from/ is caused by* the body trying to keep the part still;
5. Not enough (insufficient) calcium in circulation, *results in/causes/leads to* osteoporosis [ɒstiəu'pərəusis]. (weak, fragile, brittle bones). – A deficiency in Calcium (and hormonal changes) *results in / causes/ leads to* fragile bones that break easily *because* fractures can *result from* fragile bones, Osteoporosis and a deficiency in Calcium;
6. *Because* fractures can be *caused by* the decrease in collagen (elastic fibres) that occurs with aging, and the decrease in the amount of calcium in circulation, which *results in/causes/leads to* osteoporosis. – *Because (there is often a deficiency of calcium and there are also*

hormonal changes) bones in the elderly do not absorb calcium easily and bone cells do not reproduce as efficiently, and this results in / causes/ leads to bones which are more likely to break. – *Because* fractures (can be) *caused by lack of bone density, the bones of old people are more likely to break;*

7. *Because* exercise *results in/causes/leads to* an increase in oxygen to the tissues and gives more mobility and strength to the muscles, it also increases the strength of bones and therefore decreases the risks of osteoporosis in older people! *(It also strengthens heart muscle and increases the oxygen supply to the brain)* – *Because* exercise increases the circulation and oxygen supply to both bones and muscles, strengthens bones and muscles, lowers cholesterol levels, improves agility and also improves feelings of physical and mental well–being, it is very important.

3F

p. 143

Example Answers: When exercising or lifting heavy items or even bending to pick something up off the floor, watch what you are doing (1) keep the vertebral column straight and balance yourself with a hand on your thigh if necessary; (2) keep the vertebral column straight and bend your knees; (3) ...don't use jerky movements and don't move too quickly; (4) + (5) keep the vertebral column straight and bend your knees.

3G

p. 146

1. Age; 2. Sex; 3. Heredity; 4. Living Conditions and Habits; 5. Occupation; 6. Physical Exposure; 7. Pre–existing Illness; 8. Psychogenic Influences.

p. 147

SKIN – <u>they</u>: The skin and the mucous membranes; <u>which</u>: mucous; <u>these</u>: any foreign impurities.

SECRETIONS – <u>them</u>: disease–causing organisms. ... most secretions contain chemicals that can destroy disease–causing organisms.

REFLEX ACTIONS – <u>them</u>: any micro–organisms. Sneezing and coughing and vomiting and diarrhoea expel any micro–organisms...

PHAGOCYTOSIS – <u>This process</u>: a process called phagocytosis; <u>these</u>: Natural Killer Cells (Nk Cells); <u>them</u>: cells with abnormal membranes, such as tumour cells or cells infected with a virus.

NATURAL KILLER CELLS (NK CELLS) – <u>These</u>: NK Cells; <u>them</u>: cells with abnormal membranes, such as tumour cells or cells infected with a virus.

INFLAMMATION AND FEVER – <u>this</u>: An inflammatory reaction; <u>these</u>: four classic symptoms

INTERFERON – <u>This</u>: Interferon; <u>It</u> : Interferon

IMMUNITY – <u>It</u>: Immunity.

p. 151

Idioms: 1(i); 2(c); 3(a); 4(f); 5(b); 6(g); 7(h); 8(d); 9(e); 10(l); 11(o); 12(m); 13(n); 14(j); 15(k).

🎧 *Check answers with tape script 21.*

p. 152

UNIT 4

4A

p. 154

🖉 *Questions 1–5 require individual answers.*

☺
6. A plum is fresh fruit, prunes are dried plums.
7. *Check with your teacher.*
8. 1. *grapes* are not classed as a berry fruit; 2. An *apple* is not a tropical fruit *or* A *banana* is crescent–shaped; 3. A *zucchini* (courgette) is green, not orange *or* a *tomato* is a fruit not a vegetable *or* *pumpkin* is rarely eaten raw; 4. A *passion fruit* is full of seeds/ it is a fruit not a vegetable; 5. An *orange* is usually orange and the others are usually yellow *or* a *pear* is not a citrus fruit; 6. A *calf* is a the name of a baby cow and not the name of the meat we eat (veal describes this kind of meat.); 7. A *crayfish* is a 'shellfish'; 8. These are all seafood, but only *octopus* is not a shellfish; 9. Salami, ham and bacon are processed foods made from pig meat, whereas *chicken* is not processed; 10. Flour, sugar and rice are carbohydrate foods (or manufactured from grain or plants), *butter* is an animal fat.

p. 155

☺
A *prescription*: an official piece of paper on which the doctor writes the type of medicine and the necessary dose, which is to be taken and which enables this medicine to be obtained from a chemist or a pharmacist. (verb: to prescribe [prə'skraib]).

A *receipt*: a piece of paper that shows that goods or services have been paid for.

A *recipe*: a set of instructions that tells you how to cook something and the items of food you need for it (the ingredients).

p. 156

🖉
The five main food groups are: 1. carbohydrates [ka:bəʊ'hai'dreits]; 2. proteins [prəʊ'ti:nz]; 3. fibre [faibə]; 4. vitamins [vaitə'minz] or [vitə'minz]; 5. minerals [minə'rəlz]; 6. fats [fæts].

🎧 *Check with tape script 22.*

4C

p. 159

Quantifiers

🖉 *Exercise 1*
(a) a book; (b) some air; (c) some rain; (d) an atom; (e) some sugar; (f) a molecule; (g) some information; (h) a five dollar note; (i) some snow; (j) an apple; (k) an exercise.

🖉 *Exercise 2*
(a) many – 9; (b) much – 3; (c) many – 8; (d) much – 7; (e) much – 5; (f) many – 6; (g) much – 1; (h) many – 4; (i) much – 2.

☺ *Exercise 3: (All possible answers given)*
1. There has been *a lot of, some, a little, no* rain this month;
2. The river is flooding, *too much, so much, a lot of* water is coming down from the mountains;
3. There is still *some, a lot of, a little* snow above 2000 metres;
4. You can't pick *any, many, a lot of, a few* apples until they are bigger;
5. How *much* meat can you eat?;
6. I would like *some, a little, a (bottle/can of), a lot of* Coca Cola please;
7. There *aren't any or there aren't many* or There are *some, a lot of or a few* violent programmes on TV;
8. I've got *no, some, a little, too much* free time this weekend;
9. Vegetarians don't eat *any* meat;
10. He doesn't know *any, many, some, a few of* the answers.

☺

Example Answers:	Picture A	Picture B
Orange juice	There's *some / quite a lot of*	There's *some / a little*
Grapefruit juice	There *isn't any*	There's *some / quite a lot of*
French bread	There's *some / plenty of*	There's *some / plenty of*
Beef Curry	There's *some / plenty of / quite a lot of*	There's *some / plenty of / quite a lot of*
Rice	There's *some / plenty of / quite a lot of*	There's *some /plenty of / quite a lot of*
Hamburgers	There are *some / plenty of / quite a lot of*	There are *some /plenty of / quite a lot of*
Pizza	There's *some / quite a lot of*	There *isn't any*
Steak	There's *some / quite a lot of*	There *isn't any*
Chips	There's *some / quite a lot of*	There *aren't any*
Sausage rolls	There *aren't any*	There are *some / quite a lot of*
Doughnuts	There are *some / quite a lot of*	There are *some / quite a lot of*
Cheesecake	There's *some / quite a lot of / plenty of*	There's *some / quite a lot of / plenty of*
Fruit Salad	There *isn't any*	There's *some / quite a lot of / plenty of*
Apple Cake	There's *some/ a little – a few pieces*	There *isn't much/ there's one piece*
Chocolate Cake	There *isn't any*	There's *some / lots of*
Crisps (Chips)	There's *some / plenty of / a lot of*	There's *some / plenty of / a lot of*
Cheese sandwiches	There are *some /quite a lot of / plenty of*	There *aren't any*
Chicken sandwiches	There are *some / a few*	There are *some / a few*
Cheese rolls	There *aren't any*	There are *some / quite a lot of*
Salad	There *isn't any*	There's *some / plenty of / quite a lot of*
Tomatoes	There are *some / a few*	There are *some / a few*
Hard-boiled eggs	There are *some / a few*	There *aren't many / there are only one or two*

p. 161

🖉

Michael:

What do I buy most? Well, I buy many meats *a lot of meat*, because I need a few energy *a little/ a lot of energy* to go to the gym and for leading a pretty busy life. It's easy to cook and I buy <u>any</u> *some / a few /a lot of* vegetables from the freezer at the supermarket, I don't buy <u>some</u> *any / many* fresh vegetables because I only have a little fridge. I buy <u>much</u> *a lot of / some / several* packets of ready–to–eat meals so I have time to do other things in the evenings. I have very <u>few</u> *little* time for cooking and I love pasta dishes and fresh fruit. I buy <u>several</u> *some / a little / quite a lot of* fruit at the market on my way home from work. I eat <u>too many</u> *too much / a lot of* bread too, but I usually buy wholemeal bread or the bread rolls with seeds and grains in it, so I think that's quite good for me really.

Karin:

I am quite a fussy shopper! I like to buy <u>much</u> *some / a lot of / a few* things at the health food shops and I buy 'free range' eggs and things like that. I don't buy <u>many</u> *much* chocolate or <u>much</u> *many* sweets but I love ice–cream! I'm allergic to <u>any</u> *some / a few / a lot of* chemicals and colourings in food, so I look at the labels and look at all the ingredients before I buy <u>something</u> *anything*. I like cooking for my friends and because <u>much</u> *a lot / a few / several* of them are vegetarian I eat <u>many</u> *a lot of* fresh fruit and vegetables too. They like fish so I buy fresh trout and cook it with too <u>many</u> *much* butter and lots of almonds – it's delicious but probably has far <u>too much</u> *too many* calories! I always have breakfast – I enjoy having yoghurt and fruit and a big cup of milk coffee while I watch the news before I go to work. I'm cooking <u>any</u> *some* chicken for supper tonight, with <u>much</u> *some / a lot of / a few* potatoes, some spinach and baby carrots – sounds good, doesn't it?

4E

p. 163

🖉 *To label the diagrams check with tape script 23.*

p. 165

☺

1. The teeth first break up food into smaller pieces. The actions are biting and chewing (and grinding);

2. The soft palate and the uvula move upwards to close the entrance to the trachea so that swallowing can take place. It is made of muscle tissue;
3. Peristalsis is the name given to the wave–like contractions;
4. When food arrives in the stomach, it is churned and mixed with Hydrochloric acid and Pepsin which turn the food into a semi–liquid substance;
5. Mucous membranes secrete 'mucous' (mucus – USA) which lubricate the passages and also add liquid to the food that passes through the digestive system;
6. *Individual answer*;
7. The small and the large intestine = The small and the large bowel;
8. The Pyloric sphincter closes while digestion takes place and opens to let the semi–liquid food (chyme) pass into the duodenum, the first part of the small intestine;
9. Pepsin – breaks down some proteins in the stomach. Ptyalin – starts the digestion of starches (carbohydrates) and is secreted by the salivary glands;
10. Bile is produced in the liver, stored in the galbladder and reaches the intestine by way of the cystic duct. Bile breaks down fats into fatty acids.

p. 166

🖉

absorbed; carried; removed; stored; are converted; is formed; are stored; are destroyed; are detoxified; synthesised; bile; breaks down.

p. 167

🖉

Appendectomy: Surgical removal of the appendix; *Gastroscopy*: An examination of the stomach using a type of endoscope inserted through the mouth; *Gastrotomy*: A surgical opening into the Stomach; *Hepatoma*: A type of liver cancer/growth/tumour; *Ileostomy*: An operation in which part of the small bowel is cut and an artificial opening called a 'stoma' is made onto the outside abdominal wall; A *laparotomy*: is an exploratory operation to make an opening through the abdominal wall; *Lobectomy:* An operation performed to cut out a lobe in the liver, lung or thyroid gland; *Oesophagitis* is Inflammation of the oesophagus; *Paralytic Ileus*: The intestine is paralysed. There is no peristalsis or normal movement in the bowel; *Peptic (Gastric ulcer/ation)*: An ulcer or many ulcers in the gastro–intestinal tract. The major cause of peptic ulcers is "helibacter pylori" bacterial infection; *Sigmoidoscope*: The endoscopic instrument inserted into the anus to examine the rectum and the sigmoid colon (used to perform a sigmoidoscopy); *Splenectomy*: Surgical removal of the Spleen; *Ulcerative Colitis*: Chronic inflammation and ulceration of the lining of the colon and rectum.

4F

p. 168

FULL	SOFT/LIGHT	FLUIDS ONLY	CLEAR FLUIDS ONLY
milk/cream/yoghurt eggs – raw/cooked	milk/cream/yoghurt eggs – raw/cooked	milk/cream/yoghurt eggs – raw (in drinks)	
meat/fish/poultry vegetables/fruit	meat(minced)/fish/poultry vegetables/fruit(cooked)	vegetables/fruit (juices only)	vegetable water only sugar
wholegrain bread refined white bread	refined white bread rice	sugar ice-cream	clear soups water
muesli, rice semolina, fruit juices porridge (rolled oats)	semolina porridge – finely ground sugar, biscuits	clear soup custard fruit juices	Cordial – clear fruit syrups (to be checked with physician)
sugar, banana, walnut cake, custard, mashed potato, ice-cream, biscuits clear soup, spaghetti with meat sauce, lettuce and tomatoes, butter/cheese	ice-cream clear soup custard, fruit juices mashed potato (purée) spaghetti + ground meat lettuce and tomatoes butter/mild cheese	butter	

p. 169

1. can; 2. can't / isn't allowed to / mustn't; 3. are ... allowed to; 4. mustn't; 5. can / is allowed to; 5. are not allowed to; 7. are not allowed, 8. can; 9. isn't allowed to; 10. can't.

1. (iii); 2. (iv); 3. (i); 4. (v); 5. (ii).

PATIENT	PROBLEM(s)	TREATMENT
e.g. Mr. White	*He's got high blood cholesterol levels*	He has to start a low–cholesterol diet. Nurse is ringing the dietician to make an appointment.
Mr. Mane	He is constipated , feels 'full' and isn't eating well	He will have an enema and has to do more exercise.
Mr. Smythe	He is depressed and weak. He has diarrhoea (following laxatives)	He is being prepared for surgery and will have a bowel washout later. He can walk around.
Mr. Redding	He has back ache and seems worried about going home	He will have physiotherapy before going home and should do the exercises regularly and go swimming. Nurse will make an appointment for Mr. Redding to see the doctor in outpatients' in 4/52. He can ring the doctor at any time if he has any problems.
Mrs. Clancy	is a diabetic and has to learn to give herself insulin and have a diabetic diet.	She still needs assistance with her insulin injections and diet and she will start a regular exercise regime.
Mrs. Steele	Has an intravenous infusion and is on 'nil orally'. She isn't hungry and her abdomen feels uncomfortable. She is not passing enough urine and has a distended bladder	She will have a catheter inserted to drain the urine from her bladder. She can start clear oral fluids and have the IV can come out (be removed) when she is drinking enough.

1. has to; 2. needs to; 3. can't / has to / should; 4. can ... is allowed to; 5. has to / must; 6. can / is allowed to; 7. must / has to; 8. can / is allowed to; 9. should / must ... has to; 10. have to / will; 11. can / will; 12. must; 13. has to / must; 14. can; 15. must / should / has to; 16. must / should / have to.

4H

p. 180

Household appliances
1. Frying pan; 2. Casserole dish; 3. wok and chopsticks; 4. blender; 5. food processor; 6. bowl; 7. kettle; 8. saucepan (and lid); 9. pressure cooker.

3

GLOSSARY

accessories [ək'sesə'riz] (*n. pl.*) Items or articles that you wear but are not essential clothing. *e.g. a belt, jewellery, a handbag.* 1-G/H

accident [æksidənt] (*n.*) **1.** An accident happens when a vehicle hits another vehicle, a person or an object. **2.** Something that happens by chance and is not deliberately intended. 1-E/F

accident victims [æksə'dənt vik'timz] (*n.*) A victim is someone who has been hurt or killed by something. An accident victim has been hurt [hɜːt] or killed [kild] as the result of an accident. 1-I-Q

addiction [ədikʃən] (*n.*) An addiction is the condition of taking harmful [haːm'fl] drugs and being unable to stop taking them. An addict is a person who is addicted to a harmful substance. 1-I-Q

adequate [ædə'kwət] (*adj.*) If something is adequate, there is enough of it or it is good enough to be used or accepted. 4

admissions [əd'miʃəns] (*n.*) Admissions are the new patients accepted into the hospital. 1-B/C/D

aid [eid] (*n. uncountable*) is money, equipment or services that are provided for people or countries who need it.

  an aid worker [eid wɜːkə] (*n.*) is a person, usually working for a charity organisation, who offers his services in other countries. 1-A

alignment [ə'lain'mənt] (*n. uncountable*) The alignment of something is its position in relation to something else or its correct position. 3

allergy [ælədʒi] (*n.*) A particular allergy causes a person to become ill or have a reaction to something that does not normally make people ill.

  allergic [ə'lɜːdʒik] (*adj.*) 1-G/H

alternative medicine [ɔːl'tɜːnə'tiv medsən] (*adj. + n.*) describes a different form of medicine, in contrast with traditional forms. 3

apparatus [æpə'reitəs] (*n. uncountable*) Apparatus is the equipment needed to do a particular job or activity and may include tools, machines and other instruments. 1-G/H

appetite [æpə'tait] (*n.*) The desire to eat. *e.g. The baby has a healthy appetite.* 1-G/H

appliance [əplai'əns] (*n.*) is a machine or device used at home, usually electrical. *e.g. a toaster and a washing machine are household appliances.* 1-G/H

to apply [əplai] **for a position** (*v. + prep. + n.*) To *apply for* a job or a position, or membership to an organisation, you ask for it by formally writing a letter of application. 1-I-Q

to attend to [əten'tuː] **a patient's personal hygiene** (*v. 'to inf.'+ n.*) If you attend to something, you deal with it. If you attend to a patient's personal hygiene, you help the patient to wash, clean his teeth, do his hair and shave. 1-I-Q

bacteria [bæk'tiəriə] (*n. pl.*) Micro-organisms, some of which cause disease. 3

basic information (about the patient) [beisik in'fɔːmeiʃən ə'baut] (*adj. + n. uncountable*) Basic information refers to the important or 'necessary to know' facts (about the patient). 1-I-Q

bathroom [baː'θ'ruːm] (*n.*) A room in a house that contains a bath or a shower, a washbasin and sometimes a toilet. 1-G/H

to be admitted [əd'mitid] (*v.*) To be formally permitted to stay in hospital for treatment. 1-E/F

to be allergic to something [ə'lɜːdʒik] (*v. + adj.*) If you are allergic to sth., or have an allergic reaction to sth., you become ill or get a rash when you eat it, smell it, or touch it. *e.g. I like cats but I'm allergic to them.* 4

to be discharged [dis'tʃaːdʒd] (*v.*) To be formally allowed to go home from hospital – appropriate documents and records are compiled in the patient's history. 1-E/F

to be 'due' [djuː] (*v. + adj.*) If something is due at a particular time, it is expected to happen or to arrive at that time. *e.g. When are the medications due? What time is the 'pre-med' due? When is your sister's baby due?* 1-I-Q

to be given a print–out [printaut] (*v. passive + n.*) If you are given a printout, you are presented with a piece of paper from the computer, giving information about (the patients). 1-I-Q

to be <u>interviewed by</u> [intəˈvjuːd] (*v. + adj.*) A formal meeting where questions are asked to make an assessment. *e.g. She was interviewed by a dietician about her dietary habits.* 4

to be <u>labelled with</u> something [leibəld wið] (*v. passive + prep. + n.*) If something is labelled, there is a piece of paper (or label) attached to it, giving information about it *e.g. All medications are labelled with directions for use and dosages. Cigarette packets are labelled with warnings.* 1-I-Q

to be 'on call' [ɒn kɔːl] (*v. + phrase*) If a doctor is on call, he/she is ready to go to work at any time if needed, especially for emergencies. 1-I-Q

to be 'on duty' [ɒn djuːti] (*v. + adj*) If someone is on duty, they are working. 1-I-Q

to be <u>rostered on</u> (morning shift) [rɒstid ɒn] (*v. passive + prep.*) If someone is rostered on then they are working at the time stated on a roster or timetable. 1-I-Q

to be <u>stored in</u> (the liver) [stɔːd] (*v. + n.*) When sth. is stored, it is kept in a particular place until it is needed. 4

to be transferred [trænsˈfɜːd] (*v. passive*) **(to another ward or hospital)** If a patient is transferred he is taken from the first place to a second place. 1-I-Q

bed–making [bed meikiŋ] (*n.*) The activity of arranging the sheets and covers neatly on a bed. 1-I-Q

behaviour [bəˈheivjə] (*n. uncountable*) The way that people or animals do things. **behave** (*v.*) [bəˈheiv]. 3

bomb [bɒm] (*n.*) A bomb is a device which explodes and damages a large area. 1-I-Q

bone [bəʊn] (*n*) The hard parts inside the human body that form the skeleton. 3

break down [breikˈdaʊn] (*v. + prep.*) To form smaller parts or particles. 3

canteen [kænˈtiːn] (*n.*) A canteen is a dining area in a factory, shop or college where meals are <u>served to</u> the people who work or study there. The staff canteen is the dining area for the hospital staff. 1-I-Q

care [keə] (*n. uncountable*) Looking after somebody or something and keep them in a good state or condition.

health care [heiθ keə] (*n. uncountable*) refers to all the areas related to medicine and the attention to individual well–being.

patient [peiʃʲənt] **care** (*n. uncountable*) refers to all areas involved – mental, physical and psychological – in looking after a patient. 1-A

career [kəˈriə] (*n.*) A career is the job or profession that someone does for a long period of their life.

a rewarding [riˈwɔːdiŋ] **career** is stimulating and brings job satisfaction and/or benefits. 1-A

cartilage [kaːtəˈlidʒ] (*n. uncountable*) Cartilage is a strong flexible substance in the human body, found especially at the ends of long bones and in joints. 3

cell [sel] (*n.*) A cell is the smallest part of a plant or animal that is able to function independently. 3

cereal [siəriəl] (*n.*) One of the various types of grass that produce grains that can be eaten or are used to make flour or bread. 4

to change [tʃeindʒ] **into a hospital gown** [gaʊn] (*v. + n.*) To remove personal day or night clothes and wear a gown (a cotton body cover) supplied by the hospital. 1-E/F

to chat [tʃæt] (*v.*) To talk in an informal and friendly way. 1-G/H

to check [tʃek] (*v.*) If you check something, you make sure that it is in good working order, or that it is correct and satisfactory. 1-I-Q

to check [tʃek] **urinary drainage** [juːrənˈri dreinidʒ] **tubes** [tjuːbz] **bags** (*v. + n.*) If you check drainage bags and tubes, you make sure they are draining freely, that there are no 'kinks' in tubes (that may block) and also check or measure the amount of urine in the bag. 1-I-Q

chemical [kemikl] (*n. + adj.*) A substance obtained by or used in a chemical process. 4

to chew (masticate) [tʃuː] [mæstikeit] (*v.*) When you chew food, you use your teeth to break it up in your mouth so that it becomes easier to swallow. 4

choice [tʃɔis] (*n.*) If there is a choice of things, there are several of them and you can choose the one you want. 4

to choose or to make a choice [tʃuːz meikəˈtʃɔis] (*v. + n.*) To decide which thing you want from the number available. 4

classification [klæsəˈfikˈeiʃən] (*n.*) A division or category so that things with similar characteristics are in the same group. 3

clinic [klinik] (*n.*) A clinic is a building where people go to receive medical advice or treatment. 1-A

clothes [kləʊðz] (*n. pl.*) Clothes are things that people wear, such as shirts, trousers, dresses etc. *e.g. I like casual clothes.*   1-G/H

colourings [kʌlərɪŋz] (*n.*) Substances that are used to give a particular colour to food.   4

coma [kəʊmə] (*n.*) A deep unconscious state, usually lasting a long time and caused by serious illness or injury.   4

Community Health Centres [kəmjuːnəti helθ sentəz] (*adj. + n.*) Buildings in the city and suburbs where medical services are available to the general public.   1-B/C/D

to complain about [kəmˈpleɪn] (*v. + adv.*) If you complain about something, you say that you are not satisfied with it. To complain of pain or to complain about a pain in a particular area is to say that the pain is worrying. 1-I-Q

complementary medicine [kɒmpləˈmentri medsən] (*adj. + n.*) Referring to different forms of medicine which can be used together and 'complement' [kɒmpləˈment] each other.   3

compost [kɒmˈpɒst] (*n.*) A mixture of decayed plants and food waste (organic material) that can be added to soil to help plants grow.   4

computer [kəmˈpjuːtə] **printout** [prɪntaʊt] (*n.*) A printout is a piece of paper on which information from a computer has been printed. *e.g. Staff are given a printout at handover.*   1-I-Q

Consultant [kənˈsʌltənt] (*n.*) An experienced doctor who specialises in one area of medicine.

Head/Chief Consultant [hed / tʃiːf kənˈsʌltənt] (*n.*) The experienced specialised doctor in charge of a particular ward or department.   1-B/C/D

contraption [kənˈtræpʃən] (*n.*) The word contraption can be used for any machine or device when it looks unusual and you don't know what it is used for.   1-G/H

cooked [kʊkt] (*adj.*) Food that is cooked, has been heated to prepare it to be eaten.   4

cramp [kræmp] (*n.*) A sudden, strong pain caused by a muscle suddenly contracting.   3

to cut down [kʌ(t)daʊn] **(the number)** (*v. + n.*) To reduce the number or amount of something. *e.g. Cutting down on the total amount of fats in the diet, may help reduce cholesterol levels.*   1-I-Q

defence [dəˈfens] (*n.*) ('*defense*' in American English) Defence is action that is taken to protect against attack.   3

dehydration [diˈhaiˈdreiʃən] (*n. uncountable*) The loss of too much water from the body.   4

deposits [dəˈpɒzəts] (*n. pl.*) These are substances that have been left somewhere as the result of a chemical process.   3

depression [dəˈpreʃən] **1** (*n. uncountable*) A mental state of sadness and not being able to enjoy anything. **2** (*n.*) A depression in a surface is an area which is lower than the parts surrounding it.   3

development [diˈveləpˈmənt] (*n.*) Development is the gradual growth or formation of something. e.g. *Midwifery students study the development of the embryo.*   1-I-Q

device [dəˈvais] (*n.*) A device is something that was invented for a specific purpose. *e.g. an electronic device.*   1-G/H

to diagnose [daiəgˈnəʊz] (*v.*) (*Often used in the passive form*) If an illness or disease is diagnosed then it is identified. *e.g. These people are diagnosed as being weather sensitive.*   1-I-Q

diet [daiət] (*n.*) **1.** The food that is eaten and drunk regularly. *e.g. How can I improve my diet?* **2.** If a doctor puts so. on a diet, he or she makes them eat a special type or range of foods in order to improve their health.   4

a well–balanced diet [ə wel bælənst daiət] (*adj. + n.*) Food that is eaten regularly and contains all the necessary nutrients that the body needs to stay healthy.   4

discharges [disˈtʃaːdʒəz] (*n.*) Discharges are those patients who are permitted to go home or are being transferred to another hospital.   1-B/C/D

disease [diˈziːz] (*n.*) An illness that affects the health of a person, animal or plant. 1-E/F; 3

to do shift [ʃift] **work** (*v. + n.*) *or* **to work on (night shift)** If a group of people work **shifts**, they work for a set period before being replaced by another group of workers, so that there is always a group working. 1-I-Q

to do the rounds [raʊndz] (*v. + n.*) To visit patients individually one by one. *e.g. Ward staff do regular rounds of all the patients and doctors do a daily round with the full medical team.* 1-E/F

to donate blood [dəʊˈneit blʌd] (*v. + n.*) To have blood taken to give freely to another person.   1-B/C/D

drain [drein] (*n.*) A drain is a type of pipe or tube that takes away liquids, causing it to flow somewhere else. **drain** (*v.*) If you drain something, you dry it by causing water (or liquid) to drain out of it.   3

drawer [drɔːə] (*n.*) A drawer is part of a desk, chest or box–shaped piece of furniture to put things in. To open the drawer you pull it out towards yourself.   1-G/H

empathy [empəθi] (*n. uncountable*) The ability to share another person's feelings and emotions as if they were yours.   1-A

empty [em'ti] (*adj.*) Something that is empty, has nothing in it. *e.g. an empty bag, an empty room, an empty box.*   1-G/H

enteral feeding [entərəl fiːdiŋ] (*adj. + n.*) Giving nourishment artificially through a tube directly into the stomach, duodenum or jejunum, bypassing the mouth and oesophagus.   4

environment [enˈvairənˈmənt] (*n.*) **1** Someone's environment is all the circumstances, people, things and events around them that influence their life. **2** Your environment consists of the particular surroundings in which you live or exist. **3** The environment (*n. uncountable*) is the natural world of land, sea, plants and animals.   1-A; 3

exchange [eksˈtʃeindʒ] (*n.*) A passing from one area to another in different directions at the same time. *e.g. gaseous exchange.*   3

explosion [eksˈpləʊʒən] (*n.*) An explosion is a sudden, violent burst of energy (possibly caused by a bomb).   1-I-Q

eyesight [aiˈsait] (*n.*) The ability to see. *e.g. I have good eyesight, I don't need to wear glasses.* 1-G/H

facets [fæsəts] (*n.*) A facet of something is a single part or aspect of it. There are many facets of nursing to choose from: public health, children's nursing, medical or surgical nursing and all the specialised areas.   1-I-Q

fastener [faːsəˈnə] (*n.*) Something such as a clasp, button, zip or small hook that fastens sth. especially clothing.   1-G/H

fat [fæt] (*n. uncountable*) **1.** Fat is the white or yellow, loose connective (adipose) tissue or extra flesh that animals and humans have under their skin, which is used to store energy and to help keep them warm. **2.** Fat is a solid or liquid substance contained in foods such as meat, cheese and butter, and used in cooking, which forms an energy store in your body.   4

fatigue [fəˈtiːg] (*n. uncountable*) A feeling of extreme physical or mental tiredness.   3

to feed [fiːd] **a baby or a patient** (*v. + n.*) When you feed a patient, you give them something to eat and/or drink. *e.g. A baby can be breastfed or bottle-fed and an older baby is fed more solid food.*   1-I-Q

fibrous [faiˈbrəs] (*adj.*) Referring to a substance that contains a lot of fibres, or looks as if it does.   3

to follow (guidelines) [fɒləʊ] (*v.*) If you follow something (rules, signs, etc.) you use these to show you which direction to go. To accept the advice or instructions given (in the guidelines) and to do what is expressed in these rules or suggestions.   4

foramen [fəˈreimən] (*n.*) A natural opening in a bone or other body structure. **foramina** (*n. pl.*) [fəˈræminə].   3

framework [freimˈwɜːk] (*n.*) A framework is a structure that forms support or frame for something.   3

fresh [freʃ] (*adj.*) Something that is fresh has been produced, done, made, or experienced recently.   4

  fresh fruit [freʃ fruːt] (*adj. + n.*) Fruit that has been picked recently (not preserved, processed or stored for a long period of time.)   4

frozen [frəʊzən] (*adj.*) Frozen food has been preserved by being kept at a very low temperature.   4

fruit [fruːt] (*n.*) The plural of the noun can be either fruit or fruits, but it is usually fruit. Fruit is something that grows on a tree or bush and which contains seeds or a stone covered by edible flesh.   4

function [fʌŋkˈʃən] (*n.*) The function of something is the useful thing it does or is intended to do.   3

fussy [fʌsi] (*adj.*) Concerned or worried about usually unimportant details- difficult to please. *e.g. A fussy eater will only eat food that he likes, or which has only been prepared in the way he likes it.*   4

gadget [gædʒət] (*n.*) A small machine or device that does something useful. *e.g. a corkscrew, a potato peeler etc.*   1-G/H

gamete [gæmˈiːt] (*n.*) A sex cell, which is either the sperm of the male or the ovum (egg) of the female.   3

gastric tube [gæstrikˈtjuːb] (*adj. + n.*) A sterilized cylindrical hollow pipe made of soft material (rubber or plastic) with one open end and a closed end with holes in it which is passed through the nose into the stomach using a medical procedure. The open end can be attached to a syringe or an infusion of liquid.   4

genetically modified (GM) [dʒəˈnetikli mɒdəˈfaid] (*adj.*) Refers to food in which the information in its genes has been changed in some way.   4

to get undressed [get ʌnd'drest] (v.) Take off the clothes that you are wearing.   1-G/H

to give an injection [in'dʒekʃən] (or a 'pre-med') (v. + n.) The use of a syringe and needle to introduce medication into the body – (into a muscle: **intramuscular** [intrə'mʌskju:lə]; into a vein: **intravenous** [intrə'vi:nəs]; under the skin: **hypodermic** ['haipəu'dɜ:mik]).   1-E/F

to give sound [saund] **advice** [əd'vais] (v. + adj. + n.) If you give a person sound advice, what you tell them to do in a given situation is correct and appropriate.   1-I-Q

to give up [givʌp] **(smoking)** (v. + n.) When you give up doing something you stop doing it.   1-I-Q

to go on a diet [daiət] (v. + n.) When you go on a diet, you start eating different food – usually with a reason: to lose weight, to reduce the amount of sugar or fats in your body etc.   1-I-Q

grain [grein] (n.) **1.** A grain of wheat, rice, or other cereal crop is a single seed from it. **2.** Grain is a cereal crop, especially wheat or corn that has been harvested and is used for food or in trade.   4

groove [gru:v] (n.) A deep line cut into the surface of something.   3

guidelines [gaid'lainz] (n.) Guidelines are pieces of advice that an organization or person issues, intended to help you do sth.   4

gym [dʒim] (n.) **1.** A club, building or large room, usually containing special equipment for people to do physical exercise. **2.** The activity of doing physical exercise in a gym.   1-G/H

haematopoiesis [hem'æt'əu'pɔ'i:sis] (n. uncountable) (or **haemapoiesis, haematogenesis, haematosis**) The differentiation process by which new blood cells are made.   3

handover [hænd əuvə] (n.) The handover of something is when control of that thing is given from one group to another, that is, at the time of 'handover' the responsibility for the patients' well-being is passed from the staff on night shift to the staff on morning shift.   1-I-Q

to hang clothes [hæŋ kləuðz] (v. + n.) To put clothes on a hook, coat–hanger or clothes–line. (The clothes are attached in a high place without touching the ground.)   1-E/F

to have a heart attack [hævə ha:t 'ətæk] (v. + n.) / **a myocardial infarction.** To have severe pain or collapse due to the sudden death of part of the heart muscle because of a blockage in the blood supply to the heart.   1-E/F

to have an infection [in'fekʃən] (v. + n.) When you have an infection, there is a disease-causing micro-organism present in your body – in the bladder [blædə] = in the urinary bladder.   1-I-Q

to have an operation [hæv ən 'ɒpə'reiʃən] (v. + n.) To undergo major or minor surgical intervention.   1-E/F

to have moles (on your skin) [məulz] (v. + n.) To have black spots of pigmentation (a naevus) on the skin.   1-E/F

health [helθ] (n. uncountable) is the condition of the human body and the extent to which it is free from illness or can resist illness.   1-A

height [hait] (n.) The height of a person or a thing is their size or length from the bottom to the top.   1-G/H

to help/relieve the pain [help/rili:v pein] (v. + n.) To alleviate or reduce any discomfort.   1-B/C/D

hormone [hɔ:'məun] (n.) A chemical substance which occurs naturally in the human body and stimulates other organs.   3

horse [hɔ:s] (n.) A large animal that people can ride.   1-G/H

hungry [hʌŋ'gri] (adj.) When you are hungry you want some food because you haven't eaten for a long time.   1-G/H

hydration – fluid intake [hai'dreiʃən flu:əd in'teik] (n. uncountable) The absorption of water – the amount of fluids drunk or given.   4

hygiene [hai'dʒi:n] (n.) The practice of keeping yourself and your surroundings clean in order to prevent disease.   1-I-Q

illness [il'nəs] (n.) A perception of not being in good health, not well. The word 'illness' is also used to mean a disease or disorder. Illness is the opposite of good health.

minor illnesses [mainə ilnəsəz] (adj. + n.) Minor illnesses are disorders that are not serious or complicated.

seasonal [si:zənəl] **illnesses** (adj. + n.) Illnesses that are seasonal appear more in one season than another.   1-I-Q

imaginary [im'ædʒ'inri] (adj.) Referring to something that exists in your mind but not in real life.   3

indoors [ind:ɔ:z] (adv) If something happens indoors, it happens inside a building.   1-I-Q

injury [indʒəri] (n.) An injury is physical damage to the body as a result of an accident or fighting   1-E/F

instrument [in'strəmənt] (*n.*) **1.** A tool or device used to do a specific scientific task or for measuring speed, altitude, pressure, density etc. **2.** A musical instrument such as a guitar, piano or violin. 1-G/H

intake [inteik] (*n.*) Your **intake of** a particular kind of food, drink or air is the amount that you eat, drink, or breathe in. Breathing [bri:ðiŋ] involves a regular intake of (oxygen) [reg'ju:lə inteik əv ɒksidʒən]. 1-I-Q; 4

  an adequate intake [ən ædəkwət'in'teik] (*adj.* + *n.*) The taking in or ingestion of enough (fluid or individual food substances) to supply the needs of the body. *e.g. An adequate intake of water and nutrients can be ensured by using intravenous infusions.* 4

Intensive Care [in'tensiv keə] (*n. or adj.*) The specialised unit or department where extremely ill patients can be cared for individually and monitored on a 'one-to-one' basis by specially trained staff. 1-B/C/D

intractable [in'træktəbəl] (*adj.*) A problem that is intractable is very hard to deal with i.e. difficult to solve. 4

intravenous line (or drip) [intrə'vi:nəs lain or drip] (*adj.* + *n.*) An intravenous line or drip refers to the bag, tubing and needle, used to give food or medications continuously into the veins of sick people. Make sure that no air bubbles enter the intravenous line. 1-I-Q

to irrigate/rinse [irigeit – rins] (*v.*) Wash (the inside of a tube) with water only. 4

itchy [i'tʃi] (*adj.*) An unpleasant feeling on your skin that makes you scratch. 1-G/H

jewellery [dʒu:əlri] (*n.*) Various ornaments that people wear. *e.g. bracelets, brooches necklaces and rings.* 1-G/H

joint [dʒɔint] (*n.*) A place where two main parts come together. In the body, it is where two bones meet and move together. 3

lecturer [lek'tʃə'rə] (*n.*) A teacher at a university or college.

  visiting lecturers (adj. + n.) Teachers who come from other universities or colleges on a temporary basis. 1-A

to lie (on your side, on your back etc.) (*v.*) To be in a horizontal position (on your back etc), not sitting or standing. 1-E/F

ligament [ligə'mənt] (*n.*) A band of tough [tʌf], fibrous, partly elastic tissue – important components of joints. 3

locker [lɒkə] (*n.*) A small metal or wooden cupboard (usually with a lock and key) where you can keep personal belongings. 1-G/H

to lower [ləu(w)ə] (*v.*) (**blood pressure** [blʌd preʃə], **cholesterol** [kəl'estə'rɒl]) To lower something is to reduce it. 1-I-Q

machine [mə'ʃi:n] (*n.*) A piece of equipment which does a particular type of work and which usually uses electricity or power from an engine. 1-G/H

to make a bed [meik ə 'bed] (*v.* + *n.*) To tidy or change the bed-clothes so that the bed can be slept in. 1-E/F

market research [ma:kət ri:sɜ:tʃ] (*n.*) Market Research is the activity of collecting and studying information about what people want, need and buy. 4

material [mə'ti:riəl] (*n.*) **1.** a solid substance, **2.** a type of cloth or **3.** things you need for a particular activity. 1-G/H

meals [mi:əlz] (*n.*) Meals are the food you eat at breakfast, lunchtime and in the evening. 4

to measure [me'ʒə] (*v.*) You measure a quantity that can be expressed in numbers. *e.g. The length of a baby or the height of a person, using a ruler or tape measure.* 1-G/H

measurement [meʒə 'mənt] (*n.*) The result, usually expressed in numbers, that you obtain by measuring something. 1-G/H

  measurements are considered **within normal limits** 2

meiosis [mei'əusis] (*n. uncountable*) The type of cell division that occurs in the ovaries and testes during the reproduction of gametes. 3

microscopic examination [maik'rəu'skɒpik eks'æmineiʃən] (*adj.* + *n.*) The analysis of a specimen under a microscope to analyse or identify it. 1-B/C/D

mitosis [mai'təusis] (*n. uncountable*) The type of cell division in which the chromosomes within the nucleus of the cell are exactly duplicated into each of two daughter cells. 3

mouth care [mauθ keə] (*n.*) Mouth care is the attention to oral hygiene – cleaning the teeth and keeping the mouth (the entire oral cavity) free of debris which can cause a build–up of bacteria and lead to sordes [sɔ:diz] (mouth sores and ulcers). 4

muscle [mʌsəl] (*n.*) A structure composed of bundles of specialized cells capable of contraction and relaxation to create movement. 3

naso–gastric tube [neizəu gæstrik tju:b] (*n.*) A naso–gastric tube is a sterilised cylindrical tube used to provide nourishment directly into the stomach, or to empty the stomach of its contents. It is passed through the nose into the stomach. 4

nourishment [nʌrɪʃmənt] (*n.*) If something provides a person, animal or plant with nourishment, it provides them with the food that is necessary for life, growth and good health. 4

obese [əbi:s] (*adj.*) A medical term to describe people who are so fat that they are unhealthy. 4

offspring [ɒfˈsprɪŋ](*n. uncountable*) Human and animals' young (babies/children) can be referred to as their offspring. 3

ongoing [ɒnˈgəʊɪŋ] (*adj.*) An ongoing situation has been happening for quite a long time and seems likely to continue for some time in the future. *e.g. The ongoing treatment seems to be successful.* 1-I-Q

operation [ɒpəˈreɪʃən] (*n.*) Cutting open the human body under anaesthetic by a surgeon, in order to repair, replace or remove a damaged or diseased part. 1-G/H

opportunity [ɒpəˈtjuːnəti] (*n.*) An opportunity is a situation in which it is possible for you to do something that you want to do.

> **work related opportunities** (*adj. + n.*) Different situations or areas where you can work in your chosen field. 1-A

organ [ɔːˈgən] (*n.*) A collection of various tissues integrated into a distinct structural unit to perform specific functions. 3

outdoors [aʊtˈdɔːz] (*adv.*) If something happens outdoors, it happens out in the fresh air, not in a building. 1-I-Q

overweight [əʊvəˈweɪt] (*adj.*) Weighing more than the normal weight for height. (Body Mass Index). 1-I-Q

pasta dishes [paːstə] or [pæstə dɪʃəz] (*n.*) Recipes or food prepared using pasta, spaghetti, macaroni, sheets of lasagne pasta etc. are referred to as pasta dishes. 4

pathology [pəθˈɒləˈdʒi] (*n. uncountable*) The study of disease – its causes, mechanisms and effects on the body. 3

personal hygiene [pɜːsənəl haɪˈdʒiːn] (*adj. + n.*) To look after your personal hygiene you keep yourself clean, especially to prevent the spread of disease. 1-I-Q

personnel [pɜːsəˈnel] (*n.pl.*) The people who work for an organisation (or the armed forces). 1-A

physiology [fɪziˈɒlədʒi] (*n. uncountable*) The study of body functions, including physical and chemical processes of cells, tissues, organs and systems, and their various interactions. 3

to plan a diet [plæn ə daɪət] (*v.+ n.*) To make detailed list of foods and quantities of food which can be eaten by a person who needs to change his eating habits. 4

posture [pɒsˈtʃə] (*n.*) The relative position of parts of the body at rest or during movement. Good posture consists of balancing the body weight around the body's centre of gravity in the lower spine and pelvis. Maintaining good posture helps prevent neck and back pain. 3

pre–packaged [priː pækədʒd] (*adj.*) Food that is processed and packed before you buy it. 4

to prescribe/order treatment/medications [prəˈskreɪb/ɔːdə medəˈkeɪʃənz] (*v. + n.*) When a doctor prescribes or orders something, he tells you what to do or what to take. 1-B/C/D

prescription [prəˈskrɪpʃən] (*n.*) An official piece of paper on which a doctor writes the types of medicine you should have and which allows you to buy it from a pharmacy or chemist's. 1-B/C/D

preservative [prəˈzɜːvətiv] (*n.*) A substance that stops food from decaying (or 'going off!'). *e.g. Some people have adverse reactions to preservatives and colourings in food.* 4

to preserve something [prəˈzɜːv] (*v.*) To make sure that something is kept in optimal condition. *e.g. Sugar, salt, smoking and drying are some methods used to preserve food.* 4

procedures [prəˈsiːdjəz] (*n.*) The usual or correct way of doing something. *e.g. the procedure for setting up an intravenous line.* 1-B/C/D

professional [prəˈfeʃəˈnl] (*n.*) A Professional is a person who has a job that requires advanced education or training. 1-A

to protect [prəˈtekt] (*v.*) To prevent someone or something from being harmed or damaged. 3

protection [prəˈtekˈʃən] (*n. uncountable*) If something gives or offers protection, it prevents people or things from being harmed or damaged. 3

to provide for somebody / somebody with (vitamins/nourishment) [tə prəˈvaɪd vaɪtəmənz-nʌrɪʃmənt] (*v. + n.*) To give somebody the necessary (vitamins/nourishment) needed to live. *e.g. A balanced diet should provide all the necessary vitamins.* 4

purse [pɜːs] (*n.*) A small bag, usually for coins but may refer to a woman's handbag. 1-G/H

to <u>put</u> a dressing <u>on/over</u> the wound [wu:nd] (*v.* + *n.*) A dressing is a (sterile) cover used to prevent infective organisms entering an open wound or operation site. *e.g. The nurse put a sterile dressing over the suture line when the surgeon had finished operating.* (Also: **to change a dressing**: to remove a soiled dressing and replace it). 1-I-Q

rarely [reə'li] (*adv.*) If something rarely happens, it doesn't happen very often. *e.g. I rarely wear a hat.* 1-G/H

rate [reit] (*n.*) The rate, is the speed or the amount of time it takes for something to happen. 1-A

raw [rɔ:] (*adj.*) Raw food is food that is eaten uncooked, that has not yet been cooked, or that has not been cooked enough. 4

reaction to sth. [ri:'ækʃən] (*n.*) An unpleasant affect or illness, possibly caused by chemicals or food substances. 1-G/H

ready–to–eat [redi tu:(w)i:t] (*adj.*) Food that is ready to eat is pre-cooked or processed. *e.g. 'take-away' food.* 4

ready–to–eat / pre–packaged meals [redi tu:(w)i:t pri:'pækidʒd mi:əlz] (*adj.* + *n.*) Food for an entire meal that is prepared in large quantities and sold – needs only to be re-heated or eaten from the container. 4

to recover [rikʌvə] (*v.*) to return to good health following an illness or injury. 1-E/F

recovery [ri'kʌvri] (*n. uncountable*) If a sick person makes a recovery, he or she gets well (returns to good health). 1-A

relationship [rə'leiʃən'ʃip] (*n.*) The way in which two people, groups or countries behave towards each other. 1-A

to review (a situation) [riv'ju:] (*v.* + *n.*) If you review a situation, you consider it carefully to see what is wrong with it or how it could be changed. *e.g. The day after changing the treatment, the doctor reviewed his condition.* 1-I-Q

rheumatoid arthritis [ru:mə'tɔid ˈa:θ'raitis] (*n.*) a long–lasting disease that causes joints (articulations) and muscles to become stiff, swollen and painful. 1-E/F

risk [risk] (*n.*) If something is a risk, it is likely to cause harm. Also (n. phrase): If someone is at risk, they are put in a situation where something unpleasant might happen to them. 1-I-Q; 2

roasted [rəustid] (*adj.*) Food which is roasted is baked dry in an oven or over an open fire with oil or fat. 4

scales [skeilz] (*n. pl.*) A piece of equipment used for weighing things or people. 1-G/H

to see a doctor (*v.* + *n.*) To go to a doctor for a visit or to have the doctor come and speak to a patient. 1-E/F

seeds [si:dz] (*n.*) The small, hard part of a plant from which another plant can grow. 4

senior house officer [si:njə haus ɒfəsə] An experienced doctor on the staff of a particular ward or department. 1-B/C/D

to shave [ʃeiv] (*v.*) To remove hair from the body, using a razor or shaver.

    a close [kləus] **shave** (*coll. phrase*) A close shave is an event that was almost an accident or disaster but was luckily avoided. 1-G/H

shift [ʃift] (*n.*) You work **a shift**, when it is necessary to have groups of people always working and you work for a set number of hours and are then replaced by another group of people. 1-I-Q

    to be *on* night shift Shifts are the irregular hours worked by staff on a rotating roster.

    morning/afternoon or evening/night shift refers to the hours worked at that time on a regular basis. 1-B/C/D

shrapnel [ʃræp'nəl] (*n. uncountable*) Shrapnel consists of small pieces of metal which are scattered after a bomb or shell explodes. 1-I-Q

sick [sik] (*adj.*) Ill, not well. Sick usually means physically ill but it can be used to mean mentally ill. 1-G/H

skill [skil] (*n.*) A skill is a type of work or activity which requires special training and knowledge. 1-A

specimen [spesəmən] (*n.*) A small amount (or sample) of tissue, blood, urine etc. taken for analysis. 1-B/C/D

to spot the difference *between* things [spɒt ðə difrəns] (*v.*) If you spot someone or something, you notice them, find things that are not the same by comparing them for a short period of time. 4

staff [sta:f] (*n.pl.*) The staff of an organisation are the people who work for it.

    hospital staff/personnel (*n. pl.*) are the people who work for that hospital. 1-A

staff nurse [sta:f nɜ:s] (*n.*) A staff nurse is a hospital nurse who is trained and has a rank just below that of a sister or charge nurse. 1-B/C/D

239

stage [steidʒ] (*n.*) A stage of an activity, process or period is one part of it. Children express their feelings differently, depending on their age and stage of development, that is on the **developmental** [diveləpˈməntl] (*adj.*) **stage** of the individual. 1-I-Q

steamed [stiːmd] (*adj.*) If food is steamed, it is cooked using steam instead of water. 4

stomach [stʌmək] (*n.*) The main digestive organ of the human body where food is mixed to a liquid before passing into the intestines. 1-G/H

strenuous [strenˈjuːəs] (*adj.*) Refers to an activity or action which involves a lot of energy or effort. 3

structure [strʌkˈtʃə] (*n.*) The way in which something is made, built or organized. 3

to suck [sʌk] (*v.*) To take liquid or air into the mouth by using the muscles of the lips and cheeks. *e.g. She wasn't able to suck on the straw, so I gave her the drink using a spoon.* 4

suction [sʌkʃən] (*n. uncountable + adj.*) The process of removing air or fluid from something by drawing it out into another space. Gastric suction is used to empty the stomach. 4

supervision [suːpəˈviʒən] (*n.*) is the supervising of an activity, person or place. That is, a knowledgeable person watches to make sure that the activity is done correctly or that other people are behaving correctly. *e.g. Newly trained staff and trainees need supervision by the permanent, experienced staff.* 1-I-Q

supply of (calcium) [səˈplai] (*n.*) A supply of sth. is an amount of it which so. has or which is available for them to use. 4

  a good supply of (calcium) [əˈgʊdˈsʌplai] (*adj. + n.*) A good supply of a substance is an adequate or more than adequate amount. 4

support (*n.*) [səˈpɔːt] The provision of something to help a person or thing stand alone.
support (*v.*) [səˈpɔːt] To provide what a person or thing needs to stand alone. 3

surgeon [sɜːdʒən] (*n.*) A doctor who is specially trained **to *perform surgery* i.e. to *do an operation***. 1-B/C/D

surgery [ˈsɜːdʒəri] (*n.*) Medical treatment that involves cutting open the body and often removing or replacing parts. 1-A

survival (*n. uncountable*) [səˈvaivəl] Managing to live and not die following difficult circumstances. 3

to swallow [swɒləu] (*v.*) When you swallow sth., you cause it to go from your mouth down into your stomach. 4

swollen [swəʊlən] (*adj.*) When swollen, part of the body becomes larger and rounder than normal, usually as the result of injury or disease. 1-E/F

syllabus [siləˈbəs] (*n.*) The subjects studied in a particular course.

  nursing syllabus The subjects included in the nursing degree (university) course. 1-A

system [sistəm] (*n.*) The body's organs and other parts that are grouped together to perform a particular function. 3

to take a dressing off [teikə dresiŋ ˈɒf] (*v. + n.*) To remove and discard the cover over a wound or IV site. 1-I-Q

to take a pulse [pʌls] (*v. + n.*) To measure [meʒə] heartbeats [haːtˈbiːts]: the rhythmic beating of the heart pumping blood around the body, felt manually at the wrist [rist], over the temporal bone [temprəlˈbəun], the carotid artery [kəˈrɒtidˈaːtri] in the neck or over the femoral artery [ˈfemrəlˈaːtri] in the groin [grɔin] (inguinal [iŋˈgwənəl] area). 1-E/F

to take a risk [teik əˈrisk] (*v. + n.*) If you take a risk you choose to act in a bold way, possibly with unpleasant or undesirable results. 1-I-Q

to take blood pressure [teik ˈblʌd ˈpreʃə] (*v. + n.*) To measure the systolic and diastolic pressure of the blood circulating in the body, using a machine called a sphygmomanometer [ˈsfigməuˈmænɒmətə]. 1-E/F

to take drugs, tablets or medication [teik drʌgz, tæblətz medəˈkeiʃən] (*v. + n.*) To inject or ingest these substances (regularly). 1-B/C/D

tall [tɔːl] (*adj.*) Someone or something that is tall, has a greater height than normal or average. 1-G/H

to teach procedures [tiːtʃ prəˈsiːdjəz] (*v. + n.*) To show or teach someone the usual and correct way or method of doing something. 1-B/C/D

tendon [tenˈdən] (*n.*) A strong, flexible, fibrous cord that joins muscle to bone or muscle to muscle but is inelastic. 3

to test a specimen [test əˈspesəmən] (*v. + n.*) To analyse or examine a sample of body tissue to identify it or make a diagnosis. 1-B/C/D

tissue [tiˈʃuː] (*n.*) A collection of cells specialized to perform a particular function. 3

to treat [triːt] (*v.*) When a doctor or nurse treats a patient, they try to make them well again. *e.g. To treat minor illnesses at home, the patient is not seriously ill and can stay at home and be cared for by his family.* 1-I-Q

toiletries [tɔilətˈriz] (*n. pl*) Toiletries are things you use when washing or taking care of your body. 1-G/H

tools [tu:lz] (*n.*) A tool is any hand-held instrument or simple piece of equipment you need to do your job properly.

the tools of your trade are the skills or abilities, instruments or equipment you need to be able to do your job properly.　　1-A

trainee [treiˈniː] (*n.*) A trainee is someone who is employed at a junior level in a particular job in order to learn the skills needed for that job.　　1-E/F

training [treiniŋ] (*n. uncountable*) Training is learning the skills for a particular profession or activity.

nursing training (*n. + n.*) is the course you do while learning the skills and theory to become a professional nurse.　　1-A

umbilical cord [ˈʌmbilikəl ˈkɔːd] (*n.*) The tube [tjuːb] connecting an unborn baby to its mother, through which it receives oxygen [ɒksidʒən] and nourishment [nʌriʃˈmənt].　　1-E/F

unconscious/comatose [ʌnˈkɒnʃəs kəʊˈmətəʊz] (*adj.*) In a sleep-like state due to injury or illness, not able to use the senses.　　4

unique [juːˈniːk] (*adj.*) The only one of its kind.　　3

to update [ʌpˈdeit] (**nursing care plans**) (*v. + n.*) To add the most recent information.　　1-I-Q

valuables [vælˈjubəlz] (*n. pl*) Small objects you own that are usually worth a lot of money. *e.g. mobile phone, jewellery etc.*　　1-G/H

vegetables [vedʒˈtəbəlz] (*n.*) Vegetables are plants which you can cook and eat.　　4

virus [vaiˈrəs] (*n.*) The smallest known type of infectious agent. It is debatable whether viruses are truly living organisms or just collections of molecules capable of self-replicating under specific conditions. Outside living cells, viruses are inert.　　3

visible [vizəbl] (*adj.*) That can be seen.　　4

visiting hours [vizəˈtiŋ aʊəz] (*n.*) The times when friends or relatives are permitted to come into the hospital to visit patients.　　1-E/F

vitamins [vitəminz] or [vaitəminz] (*n.*) Natural substances found in food that are essential to health and growth of humans and animals. *e.g. Broccoli is rich in vitamins and cereals are enriched with vitamins.*　　4

ward [wɔːd] (*n.*) A room in a hospital which has beds for many people. A **surgical ward** [sɜːdʒikl wɔːd] (*n.*) is the department or rooms in a hospital for patients who will have or have had surgical operations.　　1-B/C/D

ward charge nurse [wɔːd ˈtʃɑːdʒ ˈnɜːs] (*n.*) A senior nurse who is in charge and has the responsibility of a ward or department.　　1-B/C/D

warning [wɔːniŋ] (*n.*) A warning is something that is communicated, said or written, to tell people of a possible problem or danger.　　1-I-Q

weight [weit] (*n.*) The weight of a person or thing is how heavy they are, measured in grams, ounces, kilos, pounds, tons or tonnes.　　1-G/H

to weigh (so. or sth.) [wei] (*v.*) To measure how heavy something is.　　1-G/H

wholegrain [həʊlˈgrein] (*adj.*) Made with, or containing whole grains.　　4

wholemeal [həʊlˈmiəl] (*adj.*) Referring to bread or flour made using whole grains (of wheat) including the husk (the outer covering).　　4

workers [wɜːkəz] (*n. pl.*) Particular people who do the kind of work mentioned.　　1-A

workplace [wɜːkˈpleis] (*n.*) or **work place** This is the place where you work.　　1-I-Q

to wrap [ræp] (*v.*) To fold something around a thing to cover or protect it. *e.g. You wrap a gift, you 'wrap up' to keep warm and you can wrap the cuff of a sphygmomanometer (a blood–pressure measuring device) around a person's arm.*　　1-G/H

WEIGHTS AND MEASURES

Length

METRIC		
1 kilometre (km)	= 1000 metres	= 0.6214 miles
1 metre (m)	= 100 centimetres	= 1.094 yards
1 centimetre (cm)	= 10 millimetres	= 0.394 inches
NON–METRIC		
1 mile	= 1760 yards	= 1.609 kilometres
1 yard (yd)	= 3 feet	= 0.914 metres
1 foot (ft)	= 12 inches	= 30.48 centimetres
1 inch (in)		= 25.4 millimetres

Area

METRIC		
1 square kilometre (km²)	= 100 hectares	= 0.386 square miles
1 hectare (ha)	= 100 ares	= 2.471 acres
1 are (a)	= 100 square metres	= 119.6 square yards
1 square metre (m²)		= 1.196 square yards
NON–METRIC		
1 square mile	= 640 acres	= 2.59 square kilometres
1 acre	= 4840 square yards	= 0.405 hectares
1 square yard	= 9 square feet	= 0.836 square metres
1 square foot	= 144 square inches	= 929.30 square centimetres
1 square inch		= 6.452 square centimetres

Weight

METRIC		
1 tonne	= 1000 kilograms	= 19.688 hundredweight
1 kilogram (kg)	= 1000 grams	= 2.205 pounds
1 gram (g)	= 1000 milligrams	
NON–METRIC		
1 ton	= 20 hundredweight	= 1.016 tonnes
1 hundredweight (cwt)	= 8 stone	= 50.8 kilograms
1 stone (st)	= 14 pounds	= 6.356 kilograms
1 pound (lb)	= 16 ounces	= 454 grams
1 ounce (oz)		= 28.35 grams

Capacity

METRIC		
1 decalitre (dal)	= 10 litres	= 2.2 gallons (2.63 US gallons)
1 litre (l)	= 100 centilitres	= 1.76 pints (2.1 US pints)
1 centilitre (cl)	= 10 millilitres	= 0.018 pints (0.021 US pints)
NON–METRIC		
1 gallon (gal)	= 4 quarts	= 4.546 litres
1 quart (qt)	= 2 pints	= 1.136 litres
1 pint (pt)	= 20 fluid ounces	= 56.8 centilitres
1 fluid ounce (fl oz)		= 28.4 millilitres

Note that American non–metric measurements are different from British measurements. One US pint is equivalent to 0.833 UK pints, and contains 16 US fluid ounces.

PERIODIC TABLE OF THE ELEMENTS

Periodic Table of the Elements

1a	2a	3b	4b	5b	6b	7b	8			1b	2b	3a	4a	5a	6a	7a	0
H 1																	He 2
Li 3	Be 4											B 5	C 6	N 7	O 8	F 9	Ne 10
Na 11	Mg 12											Al 13	Si 14	P 15	S 16	Cl 17	Ar 18
K 19	Ca 20	Sc 21	Ti 22	V 23	Cr 24	Mn 25	Fe 26	Co 27	Ni 28	Cu 29	Zn 30	Ga 31	Ge 32	As 33	Se 34	Br 35	Kr 36
Rb 37	Sr 38	Y 39	Zr 40	Nb 41	Mo 42	Tc 43	Ru 44	Rh 45	Pd 46	Ag 47	Cd 48	In 49	Sn 50	Sb 51	Te 52	I 53	Xe 54
Cs 55	Ba 56	La 57	Hf 72	Ta 73	W 74	Re 75	Os 76	Ir 77	Pt 78	Au 79	Hg 80	Tl 81	Pb 82	Bi 83	Po 84	At 85	Rn 86
Fr 87	Ra 88	Ac 89	Rf 104	Ha 105	?? 106												

Lanthanide Series	Ce 58	Pr 59	Nd 60	Pm 61	Sm 62	Eu 63	Gd 64	Tb 65	Dy 66	Ho 67	Er 68	Tm 69	Yb 70	Lu 71
Actinide Series	Th 90	Pa 91	U 92	Np 93	Pu 94	Am 95	Cm 96	Bk 97	Cf 98	Es 99	Fm 100	Md 101	No 102	Lr 103

Elements Listed by Atomic Number

Atomic Number	Name	Symbol
1	Hydrogen	H
2	Helium	He
3	Lithium	Li
4	Beryllium	Be
5	Boron	B
6	Carbon	C
7	Nitrogen	N
8	Oxygen	O
9	Fluorine	F
10	Neon	Ne
11	Sodium	Na
12	Magnesium	Mg
13	Aluminum	Al
14	Silicon	Si
15	Phosphorus	P
16	Sulfur	S
17	Chlorine	Cl
18	Argon	Ar
19	Potassium	K
20	Calcium	Ca
21	Scandium	Sc
22	Titanium	Ti
23	Vanadium	V
24	Chromium	Cr
25	Manganese	Mn
26	Iron	Fe
27	Cobalt	Co
28	Nickel	Ni
29	Copper	Cu
30	Zinc	Zn
31	Gallium	Ga
32	Germanium	Ge
33	Arsenic	As
34	Selenium	Se
35	Bromine	Br
36	Krypton	Kr
37	Rubidium	Rb
38	Strontium	Sr
39	Yttrium	Y
40	Zirconium	Zr
41	Niobium	Nb
42	Molybdenum	Mo
43	Technetium	Tc
44	Ruthenium	Ru
45	Rhodium	Rh

Atomic Number	Name	Symbol
46	Palladium	Pd
47	Silver	Ag
48	Cadmium	Cd
49	Indium	In
50	Tin	Sn
51	Antimony	Sb
52	Tellurium	Te
53	Iodine	I
54	Xenon	Xe
55	Cesium	Cs
56	Barium	Ba
57	Lanthanum	La
58	Cerium	Ce
59	Praseodymium	Pr
60	Neodymium	Nd
61	Promethium	Pm
62	Samarium	Sm
63	Europium	Eu
64	Gadolinium	Gd
65	Terbium	Tb
66	Dysprosium	Dy
67	Holmium	Ho
68	Erbium	Er
69	Thulium	Tm
70	Ytterbium	Yb
71	Lutetium	Lu
72	Hafnium	Hf
73	Tantalum	Ta
74	Wolfram	W
75	Rhenium	Re
76	Osmium	Os
77	Iridium	Ir
78	Platinum	Pt
79	Gold	Au
80	Mercury	Hg
81	Thallium	Tl
82	Lead	Pb
83	Bismuth	Bi
84	Polonium	Po
85	Astatine	At
86	Radon	Rn
87	Francium	Fr
88	Radium	Ra
89	Actinium	Ac
90	Thorium	Th

Atomic Number	Name	Symbol
91	Protactinium	Pa
92	Uranium	U
93	Neptunium	Np
94	Plutonium	Pu
95	Americium	Am
96	Curium	Cm
97	Berkelium	Bk
98	Californium	Cf
99	Einsteinium	Es
100	Fermium	Fm
101	Mendelevium	Md
102	Nobelium	No
103	Lawrencium	Lr
104	??	Rf
105	??	Ha

6

ENGLISH ALPHABET

A B C D E F G H I J K L M N O P Q R S T U V W X Y Z
a b c d e f g h i j k l m n o p q r s t u v w x y z

THE VOWELS

Practise saying the vowels: a [ei]   e [i:]   i [ai]   o [əʊ]   u [ju:]

THE PRONUNCIATION OF LETTERS OF THE ALPHABET

For pronunciation it is important to group the 26 letters of the alphabet according to the main vowel sound. *Now read and practise the pronunciation of all the letters of the alphabet:*

[ei] a h j k   [i:] b c d e g p t v   [e] f l m n s x z   [ai] i y
[əʊ] o   [u:] q u w   [a:] r

ENGLISH PHONETIC SYMBOLS

VOWELS

1. [i:] as in see [si:]
2. [i]   as in miss [mis]
3. [e]   as in ten [ten]
4. [ae] as in cap [kaep]
5. [a:] as in bath [ba:θ]
6. [ɒ]   as in hospital [hɒspətəl]
7. [ɔ:] as in morning [mɔ:niŋ]
8. [ʊ]   as in book [bʊk]
9. [u:] as in you [ju:]
10. [ʌ] as in under [ʌndə]
11. [ɜ:] as in turn [tɜ:n]
12. [ə] as in better [betə]

Note that <u>long</u> vowel sounds are followed by a colon ':'

[a:]   [i:]   [u:]   [ɔ:]   and   [ɜ:]

DIPHTHONGS
(2 vowel sounds together)

13. [ei] as in pain [pein]
14. [ai] as in my [mai]
15. [aʊ] as in how [haʊ]
16. [ɔi] as in boy [bɔi]
17. [ɪə] as in hear [hɪə]
18. [eə] as in care [keə]
19. [ʊə] as in pure [pjʊə]
20. [əʊ] as in go [gəʊ]

CONSONANTS

21. [p] as in patient [peiʃənt]
22. [b] as in bottle [bɒtl]
23. [t] as in take [teik]
24. [d] as in drug [drʌg]
25. [k] as in cardiac [ka:diˈaek]
26. [g] as in go [gəʊ]
27. [f] as in four [fɔ:]
28. [v] as in venous [vi:nəs]
29. [s] as in serum [si:rəm]
30. [z] as in size [saiz]
31. [l] as in live [liv]
32. [m] as in milk [milk]
33. [n] as in no [nəʊ]
34. [h] as in hurt [hɜ:t]
35. [r] as in run [rʌn]
36. [j] as in yes [jes]
37. [w] as in window [winˈdəʊ]
38. [θ] as in thank you [θaeŋkˈju:]
39. [ð] as in the [ðə]
40. [ʃ] as in sheet [ʃi:t]
41. [ʒ] as in television [teləˈviʒən]
42. [tʃ] as in child [tʃaild]
43. [dʒ] as in geriatric [dʒeriˈaetrik]
44. [ŋ] as in ring [riŋ]

N.B. In longer words [ˈ] marks the start of a stressed syllable.

7

IRREGULAR VERBS

Infinitive	Past Simple	Past Participle
be	was/were	been
bear	bore	borne *
beat	beat	beaten
become	became	become
begin	began	begun
bend	bent	bent
bind	bound	bound
bite	bit	bitten
bleed	bled	bled
blow	blew	blown
break	broke	broken
breed	bred	bred
bring	brought	brought
build	built	built
burn	burnt	burnt
buy	bought	bought
catch	caught	caught
choose	chose	chosen
come	came	come
cost	cost	cost
creep	crept	crept
cut	cut	cut
deal	dealt	dealt
dig	dug	dug
do	did	done

Infinitive	Past Simple	Past Participle
draw	drew	drawn
dream	dreamt	dreamt
drink	drank	drunk
drive	drove	driven
eat	ate	eaten
fall	fell	fallen
feed	fed	fed
feel	felt	felt
fight	fought	fought
find	found	found
fly	flew	flown
forget	forgot	forgotten
forgive	forgave	forgiven
forbid	forbade	forbidden
freeze	froze	frozen
get	got	got
give	gave	given
go	went	gone/been**
grind	ground	ground
grow	grew	grown
hang	hung/hanged	hung
have	had	had
hear	heard	heard
hide	hid	hidden
hit	hit	hit

* The verb bear (p.p. borne) in the sense of 'give birth to' is formal e.g. she's borne him 4 children. Modern usage: she's had 4 children. The p.p. is not used in the passive in this sense – the past participle born is used in the passive e.g. she was born in 1995.

** Gone refers to movement away from a place – e.g. he's gone home (he isn't here).

** Been is used as the past participle of both 'be' and 'go' e.g. I've never been in hospital. They've been to the cinema. 'They've been to the cinema' = They went to the cinema and have returned.

Infinitive	Past Simple	Past Participle
hold	held	held
hurt	hurt	hurt
keep	kept	kept
kneel [niːəl]	knelt [nelt]	knelt [nelt]
know [nəʊ]	knew [njuː]	known [nəʊn]
lay	laid	laid
lead	led	led
lean	leant	leant
leave	left	left
lend	lent	lent
let	let	let
lie	lay	lain
light	lit	lit
lose	lost	lost
make	made	made
mean	meant [ment]	meant [ment]
meet	met	met
pay	paid	paid
put	put	put
read [riːd]	read [red]	read [red]
ride	rode	ridden
ring	rang	rung
rise	rose	risen
run	ran	run
say [sei]	said [sed]	said [sed]
seek	sought	sought
sell	sold	sold
see	saw	seen
send	sent	sent
set	set	set
sew	sewed	sewn
shake	shook	shaken
shear	sheared/shore	shorn
shine	shone	shone

Infinitive	Past Simple	Past Participle
shoot	shot	shot
show	showed	shown
shut	shut	shut
sing	sang	sung
sink	sank	sunk
sit	sat	sat
sleep	slept	slept
slide	slid	slid
smell	smelt	smelt
sow	sowed	sown/sowed
speak	spoke	spoken
spell	spelt	spelt
spend	spent	spent
spread	spread	spread
spring	sprang	sprung
stand	stood	stood
steal	stole	stolen
stick	stuck	stuck
strike	struck	struck
swear	swore	sworn
sweep	swept	swept
swim	swam	swum
take	took	taken
teach	taught [tɔːt]	taught [tɔːt]
tear	tore	torn
tell	told	told
think	thought [θɔːt]	thought [θɔːt]
throw	threw [θruː]	thrown
understand	understood	understood
wake	woke	woken
wear	wore	worn
win	won	won
write	wrote	written